# CARPENTRY AND LIGHT CONSTRUCTION

**Fifth Edition**

**Ronald C. Smith**

*Structures Department,
Southern Alberta Institute
of Technology (deceased)*

**Ted L. Honkala**

*Architectural and Civil Engineering Technologies Department,
Southern Alberta Institute
of Technology*

REGENTS/PRENTICE HALL
*Englewood Cliffs, NJ 07632*

**Library of Congress Cataloging-in-Publication Data**

Smith, Ronald C.
    Carpentry and light construction / Ronald C. Smith, Ted L.
Honkala.—5th ed.
        p.   cm.
    Rev. ed. of: Principles and practices of light construction. 4th
ed. c1986.
    Includes index.
    ISBN (invalid) 0–13–096579–0
    1. Building.  2. Carpentry.  I. Honkala, T. L.   II. Smith, Ronald
C. Principles and practices of light construction.   III: Title.
    TH145.S577  1994
690—dc20
                                                    92–46551
                                                    CIP

Acquisitions editor: Ed Francis
Editorial/production supervision: Inkwell Publishing Services
Prepress buyer: Ilene Levy-Sanford
Manufacturing buyer: Edward O'Dougherty
Cover photo: Paul Barton/The Stock Market

 © 1994, 1986, 1980, 1970, 1963 by Regents/Prentice-Hall, Inc.
A Simon & Schuster Company
Englewood Cliffs, New Jersey 07632

Printed in the United States of America
10  9  8  7  6  5  4  3  2  1


ISBN 0-13-096579-0

Prentice-Hall International (UK) Limited, *London*
Prentice-Hall of Australia Pty. Limited, *Sydney*
Prentice-Hall Canada Inc., *Toronto*
Prentice-Hall Hispanoamericana, S.A., *Mexico*
Prentice-Hall of India Private Limited, *New Delhi*
Prentice-Hall of Japan, Inc., *Tokyo*
Simon & Schuster Asia Pte. Ltd., *Singapore*
Editora Prentice-Hall do Brasil, Ltda., *Rio de Janeiro*

# CONTENTS

# 4

## THE FOUNDATION  *69*

# 5

## THE FLOOR FRAME  *123*

# 6

## THE WALL FRAME  *145*

# 7

## THE CEILING AND ROOF FRAME 175

# 8

## STAIR BUILDING 223

# 9

## EXTERIOR FINISHING 243

# PREFACE

The demand for new buildings, large and small, continues to be heard throughout the world. Increases in population, a continuing rise in the standard of living in many areas, urban renewal and rural development plans all contribute to the demand.

New ideas and theories of construction are continually being introduced into the building industry. Improved labor-saving methods and techniques of building are being developed. Prefabrication, for example, has been introduced into every facet of construction. New methods and materials are being incorporated into a variety of building products, such as particle board, finger jointing, and vinyl. The advent of plastics to the building industry has been making large inroads into traditional wood product areas, such as windows, siding, fascia, soffits, and many interior trim finishes. In recent years, the concern with energy conservation has brought forth an increased demand for energy-efficient buildings.

This book has been written with the hope that it will assist in developing competence in both contemporary and innovative building arts for the practitioner and novice builder. While the main thrust of the book has been in the residential construction area, some procedures and materials commonly used in light commercial have also been included.

That purpose is achieved in three ways. First, every effort has been made to give an accurate, up-to-date account of conventional methods used in light construction. Second, some of the new ideas in design and construction that have been put into practice are described. Third, the book aims to help the student in the construction field realize the importance of construction planning.

I want to acknowledge my debt and to express my gratitude to all those with whom I have worked through the years, especially my previous co-author Ron Smith, and to others who have so generously contributed illustrations and other materials. Without their help and cooperation, this book would not have been possible.

*Ted L. Honkala*

# 1

# TOOLS

Tools are an essential part of the woodworking trades, and, until recently, carpenters, cabinetmakers, millworkers, and others who are involved in the craft of shaping wood have relied on hand tools to do the job. Now many of these tools have been adapted to use electric power, which makes their operation faster and easier, while others use compressed air to provide the power.

Over the years tools have been improved in many ways. They have been made lighter, stronger, and of better material. Special tools have been developed to do specific jobs, while others have been redesigned to perform a number of operations.

Probably in no other trade may the workman be called upon to perform so many different operations in the course of his or her day's work as in the woodworking trades. Therefore he/she must have at his/her disposal and be familiar with a wide variety of tools, each with a specific use. It is the purpose of this chapter to describe and explain the use of the common tools—*hand, electric,* and *pneumatic*—which are available for use in modern light construction.

## HAND TOOLS

Hand tools may be divided into the following groups, based on the type of work done with them:

1. Assembling tools
2. Boring tools
3. Cutting tools
4. Holding tools
5. Layout and marking tools
6. Leveling and plumbing tools

*(a) Claw hammer.*

*(b) Sledge hammer.*

**FIGURE 1-1:** *Hammers.*

*(a) Nailing hammer, steel handle.*

*(b) Framing hammer.*

**FIGURE 1-2:** *Hammer claws.*

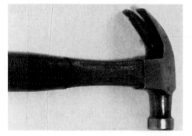

*(a) Belled.*

*(b) Knurled and plain.*

**FIGURE 1-3:** *Hammer faces.*

7. Measuring tools
8. Sharpening tools
9. Smoothing tools
10. Wrecking tools

On occasion we may find a tool which belongs in more than one of these groups.

## Assembling Tools

This group includes such tools as *hammers, screwdrivers, wrenches, nail sets,* and *staplers.*

**Hammers.** Hammers are classified according to the type of work done with them. Two of the most common classifications are claw hammers and sledgehammers. The claw hammer is used for driving nails and the sledgehammer is for driving stakes [see Fig. 1-1(a) and (b)].

Claw hammers are made with either curved claws for nail pulling or straight claws for ripping and wrecking [see Fig. 1-2(a) and (b)]. The face of a nail hammer may be belled, plain, or knurled (see Fig. 1-3). The weight of a hammer is usually 13 oz (370 g) for light work, 16–20 oz (455–570 g) for general work, and 22–28 oz (625–800 g) for framing work. You should choose the hammer for the job you have in mind—for framing work the heaviest hammer is used for driving large nails. On the other hand, for finishing work a light hammer is best.

Hammer handles may be made of wood, steel, or fiberglass. The wooden-handled hammer is preferred by some workers as it has more give or spring. Most prefer the steel- or fiberglass handled hammers, which are very strong and less likely to break (see Figs. 1-1 and 1-3). Steel-shanked hammers may be furnished with leather or plastic grips, and fiberglass hammers have plastic grips.

Claw hammers should never be used for purposes other than driving or pulling regular nails. Extensions such as sections of pipe should never be slipped over the handle to give more pulling power. If the nail is very hard to pull, use a block, a bar, or a nail puller (see Fig. 1-4).

When a hammer is being used, the handle should be gripped near the end so the entire length of the handle provides leverage. You should not hold a hammer high on the handle near the head as that way, there is no power behind the swing. Hold the handle firmly, use short strokes to start the nail, and then drive it home with longer strokes. When driving small nails with short strokes, use only your wrist and forearm in your swing. Spikes need the force of your entire arm to drive them easily (see Fig. 1-5).

FIGURE 1-4: *Block to assist pulling.*

FIGURE 1-5: *Hammer grip.*

**Screwdrivers.** Screwdrivers are most common in three types: *flat blade,* for use with slotted screws; *Robertson,* for use with Robertson head screws, which have a square pocket in the head; and *Phillips,* for use with Phillips head screws, which have an intended cross in the head (see Fig. 1-6).

The blades of screwdrivers are made in a number of widths and thicknesses to accommodate various sizes of screws (see Fig. 1-7). Some—called *stubbies*—are made with very short blades and handles for use in hard-to-get-at places (see Fig. 1-8).

Slotted head

Robertson head

Phillips head

FIGURE 1-6: *Screw head types.*

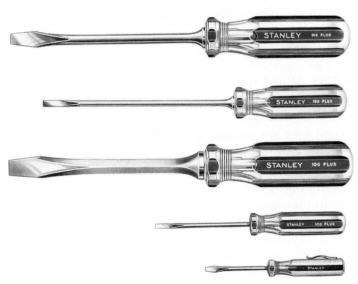

FIGURE 1-7: *Plain-handled screwdrivers.*

Robertson screwdrivers are made in a variety of lengths with four tip sizes—Nos. 0, 1, 2, and 3—to fit the standard sizes of screw sockets (see Fig. 1-9).

Phillips screwdrivers are also made in a variety of lengths and four tip sizes—Nos. 0, 1, 2, and 3—to fit a number of screw sizes (see Fig. 1-10).

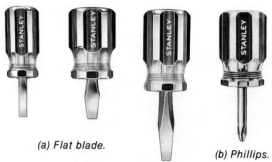

*(a) Flat blade.*

*(b) Phillips.*

**FIGURE 1-8:** *"Stubby" screwdrivers.*

**FIGURE 1-9:** *Robertson screwdriver.*

**FIGURE 1-10:** *Phillips screwdrivers.*

**FIGURE 1-11:** *Nail set.*

*(a) Hand tacker.*

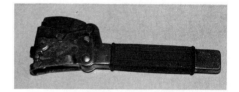

*(b) Hammer type stapler.*

**FIGURE 1-12**

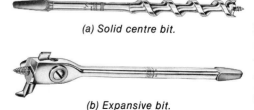

*(a) Solid centre bit.*

*(b) Expansive bit.*

**FIGURE 1-13:** *Wood bits.*

**Nail Sets.** Nail sets are designed to drive nail heads below the surface of the wood. The diameter of the tip is the size, ranging from $\frac{1}{16}$ in. (1 mm) to $\frac{3}{16}$ in. (5 mm). The shank is usually knurled for better grip (see Fig. 1-11).

**Staplers.** Staplers perform a variety of operations formerly done by hand nailing (see Fig. 1-12). They provide an efficient method of attaching building paper, vapor barrier, ceiling tile, and roofing materials. Staplers are convenient to use as they leave one hand free to hold the material in place.

### Boring Tools

Included in this group are the tools which actually cut holes in wood or metal—*bits* and *drills*—as well as the tools which hold and turn them—*bit braces* and *push drills*.

**Wood Bits.** Wood bits are made in several styles; two of the more common ones are illustrated in Fig. 1-13, a solid center bit and an expansive bit.

Wood bits are commonly made in sizes ranging from $\frac{1}{4}$ to $1\frac{1}{4}$ in. (6–31 mm) in diameter, increasing in size by increments of $\frac{1}{16}$ in. (1.5 mm). A common set, suitable for most tool boxes, will include bits from $\frac{1}{4}$ to 1 in. (6 to 25 mm). Holes over 1 in. (25 mm) in diameter are commonly bored with an *expansive bit* (see Fig. 1-13), in which an adjustable blade can be set to drill a hole of any size up to its maximum capacity. The bit is equipped with two blades, one boring up to $1\frac{1}{2}$ in. (38 mm) and the other from $1\frac{1}{2}$ to 3 in. (38–75 mm).

**Push Drill.** When holes smaller than $\frac{1}{4}$ in. (6 mm) are required in wood, some tool other than a wood bit must be used. One such tool is a push drill. This is a spring-loaded tool, made so that when pressure is applied, the bit turns in one direction; when the pressure is released, it turns in the opposite direction, cutting both ways. Bits are interchangeable, usually sold in sets of eight from $\frac{1}{16}$ to $\frac{3}{16}$ in. (1.5–4.5 mm). The top is removable so that a set of bits may be stored inside (see Fig. 1-14).

**Bit Brace.** Figure 1-15 illustrates a standard bit brace. It is used to hold and turn wood bits. This is a *ratchet* brace, which means that it can be set to drive in one direction only. This feature is helpful when one is boring in a position where a complete turn of the handle cannot be made.

FIGURE 1-14: *Push drill.*

FIGURE 1-15: *Hand brace with box ratchet. (Courtesy Stanley Tools)*

## Cutting Tools

Cutting tools include *saws, chisels, axes, snips,* and *knives.* In each of these major categories there are a number of styles or varieties, each adapted for a specific purpose.

**Saws.** Included in this category are *handsaws, backsaws, compass* saws, *coping* saws, *utility* saws, and *hacksaws.*

**Handsaws.** Two types of handsaws are made: one designed to cut across the fibers of wood—a *crosscut* saw—and the other designed to cut along the fibers—a *ripsaw.* The main difference between them is the method of shaping and sharpening the teeth.

Crosscut saws have teeth with the cutting edge sloped forward and filed at an angle, so that each tooth, as it is drawn across the wood, severs the fibers like a knife. Ripsaws have the front of the teeth at right angles, or very nearly so, to the blade. As a result the top of each tooth is a cutting edge and acts like a chisel (see Fig. 1-16).

Both crosscut saws and ripsaws are made with a tapered blade, that is, a blade that is thicker at the cutting edge than at the back so the saw will run more smoothly in the saw kerf (see

FIGURE 1-16: *Handsaw teeth.*

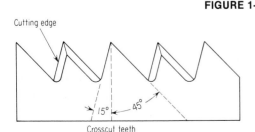

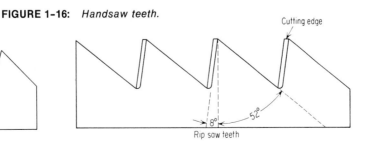

**FIGURE 1-17:** *Full tapered sawblade. (Courtesy Disston Inc.)*

Fig. 1-17). Crosscut saws are made in two sizes: *standard*, usually 26 in. (660 mm) long, and *panel*, about 20 in. (510 mm) long, with finer teeth for finish work.

All handsaws are designated by the number of teeth or *points* they have per inch. This number will vary from 5½ to 13, depending on the type of saw. The more teeth per inch, the smaller they will be and consequently the finer the cut they provide (see Fig. 1-18). Handsaws are available with hardened tipped teeth. The teeth on these saws are heat treated to harden the metal. These saws last much longer between sharpenings, but they are more difficult to sharpen (see Fig. 1-19).

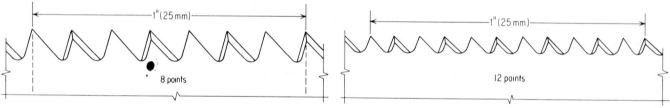

**FIGURE 1-18:** *Fine and coarse saw teeth.*

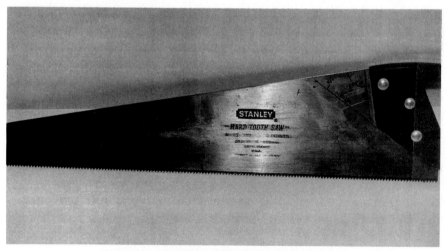

**FIGURE 1-19:** *Hardened tipped tooth saw.*

A new type of crosscut saw is available. The teeth are longer and are sharpened on the front and on the back side of the tooth (see Fig. 1-20). Sharpened this way, the saw cuts on the upstroke as well as on the down stroke, increasing the speed of cutting by up to 50%.

FIGURE 1-20: *Short saw.*

**Backsaws.** Backsaws are made with a stiff rib along the back and are intended for fine cutting and small work. Several styles are available, including the *standard* backsaw, 12–14 in. (300–350 mm) with 12–15 teeth per inch (TPI) [see Fig. 1–21(a)]. The *dovetail* saw, 10 in. (250 mm) long with 16 TPI, is a smaller version of the backsaw, with a lathe-turned handle in line with the spine. This saw is preferred by cabinetmakers for fine joint work [see Fig. 1–21(b)]. A *miter* saw is a long saw made to fit in a frame with guides to hold it in place (see Fig. 1–22). Its purpose is to cut angles or miters, and so the saw and its guides are on an adjustable arm which can be swung through an arc of 90°, up to 45° on either side of the right-angle position. It may be locked in any position to ensure an accurate miter cut.

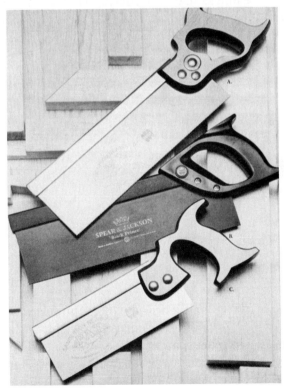

FIGURE 1-21

(a) Standard backsaws.

(b) Dovetail saw.

**FIGURE 1-22:** *Miter saw and frame. (Courtesy Stanley Tool)*

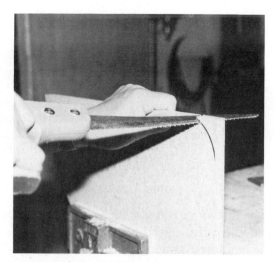

**FIGURE 1-23:** *Compass saw in use.*

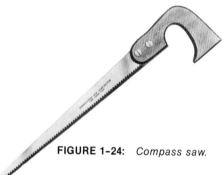

**FIGURE 1-24:** *Compass saw.*

**Compass Saws.** Compass saws are made with narrow, tapered blades and teeth designed to cut either along or across the grain. They are used for cutting holes or sawing along curved or irregular lines (see Figs. 1-23 and 1-24).

**Coping Saw.** A coping saw consists of a bow frame fitted with a very fine blade and is used for cutting thin, curved work. It is very useful in interior finishing work for making *coped* joints in small moldings, casing, baseboard, etc. (see Fig. 1-25).

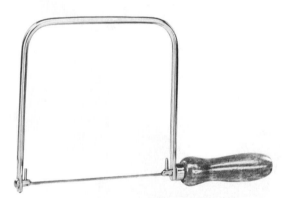

**FIGURE 1-25:** *Coping saw. (Courtesy Stanley Tools)*

**Utility Saw.** A utility saw consists of a thin, hard blade with small teeth, which is useful for cutting hard materials such as metal or plastic laminates or gypsum board or similar materials which tend to dull normal saw teeth. The one shown in Fig. 1-26 has a detachable handle which can be rotated into any position.

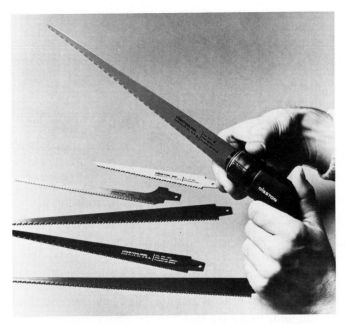

**FIGURE 1-26:** *Utility saw with detachable handle.*

**Hacksaw.** A hacksaw is an indispensable metal-cutting saw in your tool box. Most saws will adjust to take 10-in. (250-mm) to 12-in. (300-mm) blades, which will vary from 18 to 32 TPI, depending on the thickness of the metal being cut. The blade should be fine enough so that at least two teeth are in contact with the metal at all times (see Fig. 1-27).

**FIGURE 1-27:** *Hacksaw. (Courtesy Stanley Tools)*

**How to Use a Handsaw.** To begin a cut with a handsaw, rest the blade on the edge of the work, on the waste side of the cutting line. Steady the blade with your thumb [see Fig. 1-28(a)]. Draw the saw toward you slowly and carefully several times until a slight groove is formed. After the cut is started, use long, easy strokes with light pressure on the forward stroke. You will cut most easily with a crosscut if the saw is held at an angle of 45° to the work [see Fig. 1-28(b)]. After cutting has been started, be sure to place your body in a position that will enable you to see the cutting line. The saw, the forearm, and the shoulder should form a straight line at right angles to the work. Be

(a) Guiding blade with thumb.

(b) Cross-cut saw angle (45°).

**FIGURE 1-28:** *Using a handsaw.*

(c) Ripping saw angle (60°).

(d) Supporting work with sawhorses.

(e) Holding work in a vise.

sure to support the work properly [see Fig. 1–28(d)]. Resting it on sawhorses is preferable, but if they are not available, the work may be held in a vise [see Fig. 1–28(e)]. Be sure to support the piece that is being cut off so that it does not break away and splinter the underside of the stock.

When ripping is done, the saw should be held at an angle of 60° to the work [see Fig. 1–28(c)]. If the saw binds when you are ripping long stock, insert a wedge into the cut some distance from the blade.

When it is not being used, a saw should be hung up or placed in a tool box. Make sure other tools are not piled on top of the saw; there should be a place for all tools when they are not in use. A good saw is an important tool and deserves the best of care.

**Chisels.** Chisels are divided into two main classifications, depending on whether they are designed to cut wood or metal. Those intended for cutting wood are called *wood* chisels, whereas those used for cutting metal are called *cold* chisels (see Fig. 1–29).

(a) Wood chisel.

(b) Cold chisel.

**FIGURE 1-29:** *Chisel types.*

Chisel widths range from $\frac{1}{4}$ to 2 in. (6–50 mm), but $\frac{1}{4}$-, $\frac{3}{8}$-, $\frac{1}{2}$-, $\frac{3}{4}$-, and $1\frac{1}{4}$-in. sizes are most commonly chosen. Figure 1–30 illustrates a very satisfactory set of chisels for the tool box.

The companion tool for a chisel is a *mallet*—never a hammer. The softer head of a wooden or plastic mallet will not damage the head of your chisel as a hammer will (see Fig. 1–31).

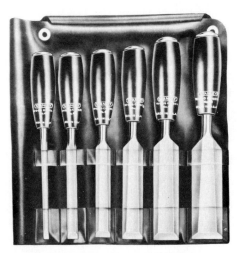

FIGURE 1-30: Chisel set. (Courtesy Stanley Tools)

FIGURE 1-31: Using mallet on head of chisel.

**Axes.** In more primitive types of construction the ax was a very useful tool. It was used for felling timber, hewing surfaces flat, cutting notches in logs, and many similar jobs. Today, however, with some changes in size, shape, and weight, the ax is being used quite differently. One type, short-handled and broad-bladed, is known as a *bench ax* or *hatchet*. It is used for rough cutting, stake sharpening, etc. [see Fig. 1-32(a)]. Another simi-

(a) Bench ax.

(b) Framing hatchet.

(c) Shingling hatchet.

FIGURE 1-32: Hatchets. (Courtesy Stanley Tools)

lar style with a hammer head and a nail slot in the back of the blade is a *framing hatchet* [see Fig. 1-32(b)]. An ax of different style, which has a narrow blade and slim head, is used for laying shingles. The distance between the head and adjustable pin is a standard exposure distance for shingles [see Fig. 1-32(c)].

**Snips.** Snips are specifically designed for cutting thin sheet metal, though they can be useful in cutting other materials such as aluminum or vinyl [see Fig. 1-33(a)]. The snips in Fig. 1-33(b) are excellent for cutting smaller circles and can be purchased for left- and right-hand curves as well as straight cuts.

(a) Snips. (Courtesy Stanley Tools)

FIGURE 1-33:

11

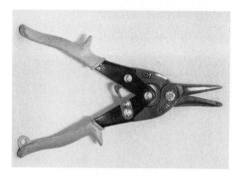

*(b) Aviation snips.*

**FIGURE 1–33:** *(continued)*

**Knives.** Utility knives are excellent tools for cutting thin veneers, sheathing paper, polyethylene, and gypsum board (see Fig. 1–34). A special hooked blade is designed for cutting asphalt shingles.

*(a) Utility knife. (Courtesy of Stanley Tools)*

*(b) Utility knife with a hooked blade. (Courtesy Stanley Tools)*

**FIGURE 1–34**

## Holding Tools

Included in this group are *pliers, C-clamps, bar* or *pipe clamps, adjustable hand screws,* and *vises.*

**Pliers.** Pliers are made in many sizes, shapes, and styles. Some common types are *adjustable, side-cutting,* and *locking.* The adjustable pliers may be put to any one of a large number of holding uses; the side-cutters are particularly useful for cutting wire, and the vise grip is excellent for holding material on which adjustable pliers may slip (see Figs. 1–35 and 36).

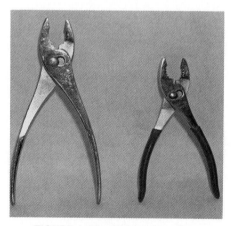

**FIGURE 1–35:** *Adjustable pliers.*

**C-clamps.** C-clamps are useful for holding small sections of lumber together, perhaps for gluing. They are made in a number of common sizes from 3 to 16 in. (75–400 mm), the size indicating the depth of the throat opening (see Fig. 1–37).

**Bar and Pipe Clamps.** These consist of a screw head and a movable tail block mounted on a bar or pipe. They are most useful for gluing pieces together, edge to edge. If pipe is used, almost unlimited lengths may be obtained by joining pieces of pipe together with couplings. A good set of tools should include at least two 6 in. (150 mm) C-clamps and a pair of 3 ft (1 m) bar or pipe clamps (see Fig. 1–38).

*(a) Vise grip.*

*(b) Sidecutting pliers.*

**FIGURE 1–36:** *Pliers.*

**Woodworkers' Vise.** This is a small, sturdy vise that may be clamped to a bench or sawhorse to hold work. It is particularly useful on a sawhorse to hold a door or a window sash while it is being dressed to size (see Fig. 1–39).

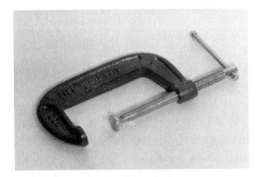

**FIGURE 1-37:** *C-clamp.*

**FIGURE 1-38:** *Pipe clamps.*

**FIGURE 1-39:** *Woodworker's vise in use.*

## Layout and Marking Tools

This group includes the *framing square,* the *combination square,* and the *quick square.* Others are the *butt gauge template* and the *chalk line.*

**Framing Square.** The standard framing square is a basic layout tool, and one of good quality is capable of providing a variety of information necessary for good roof framing and other layout operations. It has a 24 - in. (600 - mm) blade, 2 in. (51 mm) wide, and a 16 - in. (400 - mm) tongue, 1½ in. (38 mm) wide, with one

**FIGURE 1-40:** *Framing square.*

side designated as the face and the other as the back (see Fig. 1-40). This square is available in both imperial and metric measurements, both containing *rafter tables,* and cutting guides for all rafter cuts.

The framing square is especially useful for laying out wall plates and roof angles. Good squares are available in steel, aluminum, and painted surfaces. Aluminum is light and easy to handle but less likely to withstand rough usage than the others. Steel is strong and sturdy, but it may rust in wet weather unless care is taken. Painted squares are easy to read, but will scratch and rust if not handled with care.

**Combination Square.** This tool is a versatile one and, as its name implies, does the work of several simple tools. The blade slides in a slot in the head and may be locked in any position (see Fig. 1-41). One edge of the head is at right angles to the blade; another is at an angle of 45°. Some manufacturers include in the head two spirit bubbles so that the tool may be used for plumbing and leveling.

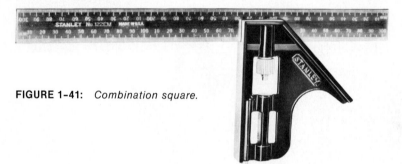

**FIGURE 1-41:** *Combination square.*

**Quick or Speed Square.** This tool is designed to provide a quick and repeatable means of laying out and cutting the various cuts on common, hip, valley, and jack rafters used in roof construction (see Fig. 1-42). This versatile layout tool features a movable locking arm that ensures fast, accurate measurements and a large frame to span wide boards. This tool can be used as a power saw guide, protractor, rafter square, and combination square.

**Butt Gauge Template.** This tool was designed for one specific purpose—to mark the location of a hinge gain. This tool not only marks the location of the hinge, but also cuts around the edge (see Fig. 1-43).

**Chalk line.** A chalk line is an easy way to mark long lines. The chalk-covered line is stretched, held close to the line to be marked, and snapped, as illustrated in Fig. 1-44. This action leaves a distinct line on the surface. A special reel rechalks the line each time it is wound into the case (see Fig. 1-45).

FIGURE 1-42:   *Quick or Speed square.*

FIGURE 1-43:   *Butt gauge template.*

FIGURE 1-44:   *Chalk line in use.*

FIGURE 1-45:   *Chalk line.*

## Leveling and Plumbing Tools

These are tools that are used to check the levelness or plumbness of structures being erected. In this category are the *spirit level, line level, plumb bob,* and *builder's level.* The last is an expensive instrument and is not a regular part of a carpenter's tool kit.

**Spirit Level.** This is really both a level and a plumb. The body is made from wood, aluminum, or magnesium, machined on top and bottom faces for accuracy. It contains three or more vial units, the bubbles in which indicate levelness or plumbness, depending on how the tool is held. Levels should be handled with

FIGURE 1-46: *Spirit level. (Courtesy Stanley Tools)*

great care to preserve their accuracy (see Fig. 1–46). For leveling or plumbing long lines, a straightedge should be used in conjunction with the spirit level.

**Line Level.** This is really a very small model of the spirit level, containing only a level bubble. It is used to hang on a building line to check its levelness (see Fig. 1–47).

FIGURE 1-47: *Line level. (Courtesy Stanley Tools)*

**Plumb Bob.** The plumb bob is an ancient but useful tool. It consists of a cone-shaped piece of steel or brass which hangs point down from a cord running from the center of the top (see Fig. 1–48). It is suspended from a point above and, when it comes to rest, will indicate a point on the earth directly below. It has many applications in construction when it is necessary to plumb down.

**Builder's Level.** See Chapter 3 for a description of the builder's level.

### Measuring Tools

Tools used for finding, laying out, and checking distances are included among the measuring tools. The more common ones include the spring-loaded pocket tape in lengths from 6 to 16 ft (2–5 m) [see Fig. 1–49(a)], and the rolled steel tape in lengths of 25, 50, and 100 ft (7.5, 15, and 30 m) [see Fig. 1–49(b)].

FIGURE 1-48: *Plumb bobs. (Courtesy Stanley Tools)*

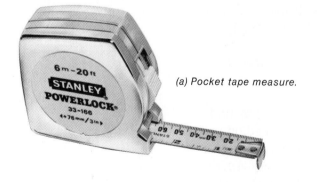

(a) Pocket tape measure.

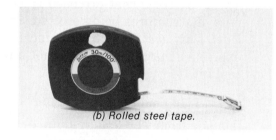

(b) Rolled steel tape.

FIGURE 1-49: *Steel tapes.*

### Sharpening Tools

This group of tools is not used in performing woodworking operations. Their function is to help keep the woodworking tools sharp. Included in this group are *triangular files, mill files, bit files, oilstones, slip stones,* and *emery stones.*

**Files.** Triangular files are made specially for filing handsaw teeth. They are designated by length and by their cross-sectional size or taper.

Mill files are flat, made in single and double cut, in three sizes of teeth: *bastard, second cut,* and *smooth cut.* They are used for jointing handsaws and for general filing. They are available in lengths from 4 to 16 in. (100–400 mm) (see Fig. 1–50).

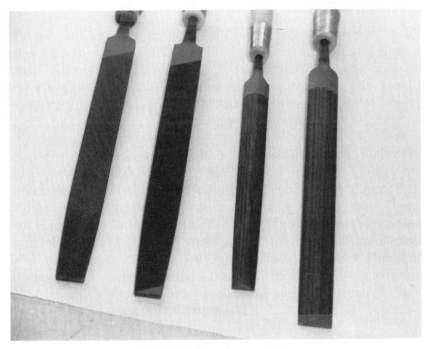

FIGURE 1–50: *Assorted files.*

Auger bit files are made specially for filing the cutting lips and spurs of wood-boring bits. One end has teeth on the flat faces but none on the edges, and the other end has teeth on the edges but none on the flat surfaces (see Fig. 1–51).

FIGURE 1–51: *Auger Bit file in use.*

**Sharpening Stones.** Of the three stones mentioned above, the slip stone is the finest, the oilstone is next, and the emery stone is the coarsest. A slip stone is used for sharpening gouges or other very fine edges and is sometimes used dry. The oilstone is used for sharpening plane blades and chisels and uses light oil as a lubricant. The emery stone is usually turned mechanically, either by hand or by electricity, and is used for grinding down

**FIGURE 1-52:** *Sharpening stones.*

plane blades, sharpening axes, and similar work. A small one which may be clamped to a bench or sawhorse is a useful addition to a tool kit (see Fig. 1–52).

## Smoothing Tools

There are four main types of tools in this group: *planes, scrapers, rasps,* and *sandpaper blocks.* The purpose of each is to produce smooth surfaces, and each has some specific uses. Planes and scrapers work on exposed, flat surfaces with the grain. Rasps are useful for curved surfaces, and sandpaper performs the final smoothing operation.

**Planes.** Surfacing planes are made in several sizes. A common one is a *block* plane, a small, light, one-hand tool usually 6 in. (150 mm) long [see Fig. 1–53(a)]. Its main uses are for surfacing small areas or for planing end grain. Another is the *smooth* plane, a common style about 9 in. (225 mm) long, used for smoothing and cleaning up surfaces [see Fig. 1–53(b)]. Perhaps the most widely used of all is the *jack* plane. About 14 in. (350 mm) long, with a 2 in. (50 mm) blade, it serves most general hand planing purposes [see Fig. 1–53(c)].

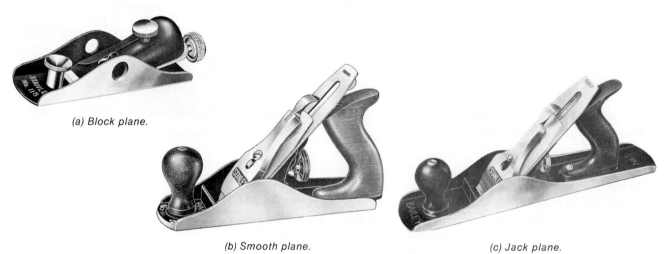

*(a) Block plane.*

*(b) Smooth plane.*

*(c) Jack plane.*

**FIGURE 1-53:** *Surfacing planes.*

**Scrapers.** A scraper is used for the same general purpose as a plane—to make a surface smooth—but it is used in a different way. Whereas a plane blade has a sharp edge which cuts its way through wood, a scraper works with the action of a claw. The edge is first sharpened in the same manner as a plane blade. Then that sharp edge is turned over into the shape of a hook. When the scraper is pushed or pulled across the surface of the wood, it scrapes off every thin shavings. Its work is limited to the final stages of smoothing a surface.

The simplest type of scraper is a thin piece of alloy steel with one sharpened edge. It may be held in one or both hands [see Fig. 1–54(a)]. It is used with both hands and is normally pushed away from the operator. Still another type consists of a wooden handle in which a narrow hooked blade is held [see Fig. 1–54(b)]. The paint scraper illustrated in Fig. 1–54(c) is useful in removing excess paint off the edge of a window pane.

**Rasps.** A wood rasp is a file-like tool used to shape and smooth surfaces which are irregular or difficult to reach with a plane or scraper (see Fig. 1–55).

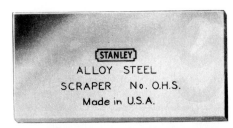

*(a) Hand scraper.*

*(b) Scraper.*

*(c) Paint scraper.*

**FIGURE 1-54:** *Scrapers. (Courtesy Stanley Tools)*

**FIGURE 1-55:** *Wood rasp.*

A modern version of the rasp is known as a *Surform* tool. It has a blade with a large number of small, razor-sharp cutting edges. Each cutting edge has its individual throat which allows the shavings to pass through the blade, thus eliminating clogging. These tools are made in several styles, each suited to a particular purpose [see Fig. 1–56(a)]. A couple of the uses to which these tools may be put are illustrated in Fig. 1–56(b).

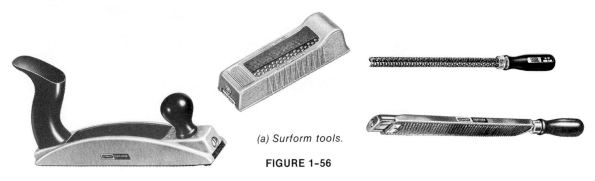

*(a) Surform tools.*

**FIGURE 1-56**

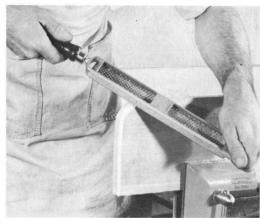

*(b) Using Surform tools.*

## Wrecking Tools

Tools belonging to this group are used to dismantle structures that have served their purpose. For example, concrete forms that have been used are taken apart with wrecking tools. The group includes the *rip chisel, ripping bar,* and *nail puller.*

**Rip Claw Hammer.** The claws on this style of hammer are made for ripping or prying (see Fig. 1–2). It may also be used, of course, for the same purpose as other hammers.

**Rip Chisel.** This tool is sometimes called a "wonder bar" and is similar to a regular ripping bar. The bar is much thinner, and the ends are sharpened like a chisel to make it much easier to remove baseboards, casings, or other material without damaging them [see Fig. 1–57(b)].

**Ripping Bar.** This tool, sometimes called a "goose neck" bar, is made both for pulling nails and for prying. It is made in several lengths, ranging from 12 to 36 in. (300–900 mm) [see Fig. 1–57(a) and (c)].

(a)

(b)

(c)

(d)

**FIGURE 1–57:**   *Wrecking bars.*

**Nail Puller.** A nail puller is made for one purpose only—pulling nails. It has a pair of movable jaws that clamp below the nail head and a curved lever arm that gives great pulling advantage. It is also fitted so that the jaws may be driven into wood to reach below the surface for nails whose heads do not protrude above (see Fig. 1–58).

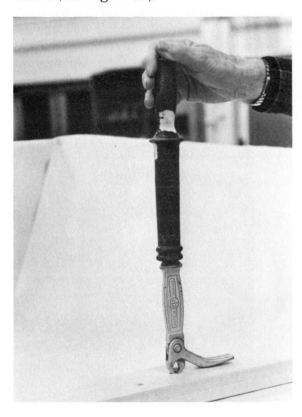

**FIGURE 1-58:** *Nail puller.*

## POWER TOOLS

In an age of speed and mass production, more power tools are being introduced into construction. There are power tools for every conceivable kind of job today, powered by electricity, compressed air, gasoline, or explosive powder. Some of them will do the job faster, and some will do it more accurately than can be done by hand; all lighten the load of manual labor involved.

All these tools are high-speed, and great care must be taken in their operation. Detailed instructions on how to set up and operate each one are issued by the manufacturer, and they should be followed explicitly.

With a couple of exceptions, the tools described here are held in the hand while being operated, and *great care and attention are necessary* in their handling and operation.

## Electric Power Tools

**Hand Electric Saw.** This tool is quite versatile. It may be used almost anywhere that an ordinary handsaw may be used. It will both crosscut and rip. The depth of cut is adjustable, and the bed may be tipped to permit angle cutting. It is available in a number of sizes, based on the diameter of the blade—from 6 to 10 in. (150–250 mm) (see Fig. 1–59). The electric hand saw is very convenient as it can be used for horizontal and vertical cutting and is also very transportable—it can be taken up on a roof for cutting. Portable electric saws are usually guided "freehand" so the accuracy of the cut is determined by hand guiding the saw (see Fig. 1–60).

*(a)*

*(b)*

**FIGURE 1–59:** *Hand electric saws. (Courtesy Skil Canada Ltd.)*

**FIGURE 1–60:** *Saw in use.*

The depth of the cut is adjusted by raising or lowering the base of the saw. The proper depth is equal to the thickness of the material plus the full tooth protruding through the work (see Fig. 1–61). The base can be set to cut at a bevel as shown in Fig. 1–62, allowing the operator to make compound cuts. Figure 1–63 shows the proper method for making a plunge cut—

**FIGURE 1–61:** *Depth of saw blade.*

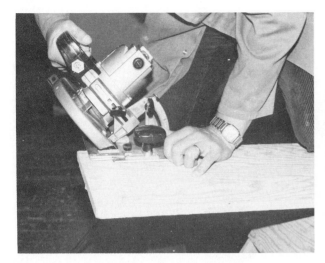

FIGURE 1–62: *Bevel cut.*

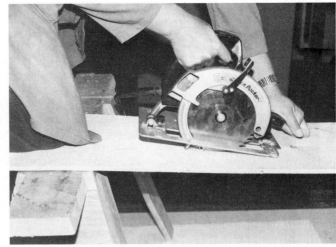

FIGURE 1–63: *Plunge cut.*

note that the front edge of the base is in contact with the work prior to starting the cut. Figure 1–64 shows standard types of blades. The chisel combination is a popular blade as it can be used for ripping as well as crosscutting and is also easy to re-sharpen. Carbide-tip blades are preferred by some as they stay sharp longer than a standard blade.

FIGURE 1–64: *Circular saw blade types.*

*(a) Belt sander.*

*(b) Orbital sander.*

**FIGURE 1-65:** *Electric sanders.*

**Electric Sanders.** Illustrated here are two of the many types of sanders on the market today. Figure 1-65(a) illustrates a belt sander for which belts of varying degrees of fineness are available. When this type of sander is being used, it must be kept constantly on the move, or it may leave deep depressions on the surface being sanded. The material must be supported so that it doesn't move while sanding.

Figure 1-65(b) is an orbital sander, designed to do fine sanding, although various grades of paper may be used. In the case of these and other types of sanders, they should be allowed to sand by their own weight only. Never press down on them while they are in operation.

**Electric Drills.** Electric drills are designed to receive straight-shanked bits and are made in several sizes, depending on the maximum diameter bit they will take. Figure 1-66(a) illustrates a drill that can be handled with one hand and will take bits up to $\frac{3}{8}$ in. (10 mm) in diameter. Figure 1-66(b) illustrates another light drill with trigger speed control and a reversing switch. This drill is specially designed to drive screws into gypsum dry wall. The drill will stop driving the screw when the head is slightly below the surface. Figure 1-66(c) shows a rechargeable drill which has the advantage of mobility without the use of a cord. Figure 1-66(d) shows a larger drill which is operated with both hands. It takes bits up to $\frac{1}{2}$ in. (13 mm) in diameter, and extra pressure may be exerted by pushing against the drill with the chest.

Electric drills utilize a variety of drill bits. The twist bit is the most common bit used, and a large range of sizes is available. When larger holes are required, either an auger bit or a speed bore bit is used (see Fig. 1-67). Numerous speciality bits are also available—screwdriver, masonry, spur-edged (see Fig. 1-67).

*(a) Electric drill [ $\frac{3}{8}$ in. (10 mm) size].*

**FIGURE 1-66**

(c) Rechargeable electric drill.

FIGURE 1-66

(d) Electric drill [ ½ in. (13 mm)].
(Courtesy Skil Tools)

(a) Twist.

(b) Auger.

(c) Speed.

(d) Spur.

(e) Speciality bits.

FIGURE 1-67: Electric drill bits.

FIGURE 1-68

(a) Electric router.

(b) Plastic laminate trimmer.

**Routers.** Electric routers are versatile tools because they will do many operations: *dadoing, rabbetting, bullnosing, fluting,* to mention only a few. Such a variety of operations is possible because many different bits may be used in the machine. Routers are made in a number of sizes, ranging from $\frac{1}{2}$ to $2\frac{1}{2}$ hp (0.37–1.85 kW) (see Fig. 1-68). A variety of router bits is available, producing numerous shapes and sizes of cuts (see Fig. 1-69).

**FIGURE 1-69:** *Router bits. (Courtesy Stanley Tools)*

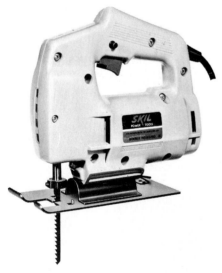

**FIGURE 1-70:** *Saber saw. (Courtesy Skill Tools)*

**Saber Saw.** This is an electric saw that can do all manner of jobs. It can do the work of a crosscut or ripsaw, band saw, keyhole saw, hacksaw, or jigsaw. It is particularly suited to jobs that are hard to get at with any other type of saw (see Fig. 1-70). Although it is quite light, it will cut lumber up to $1\frac{1}{2}$ in. (38 mm) thick. Figure 1-71 illustrates a variety of blades available for a saber saw.

The saber saw can be used to make straight or bevel cuts. Circles are easily cut with or without the use of a special guide (see Fig. 1-72). Plunge cuts are used in cutting internal openings. This is achieved by tipping the tool forward with the base resting on the material and the end of the blade just clearing the surface. Turn on the saw and lower it into the work until the blade comes through the other side (see Fig. 1-73).

**Reciprocating Saw.** Another type of all-purpose saw similar to a saber saw is the reciprocating saw. The saw has the blade extending out from the end, allowing it to get into places a saber saw cannot. The blade is longer as well, so cutting depth is increased (see Fig. 1-74).

| POINTS PER 1 IN. (25 mm) | | BLADE DESCRIPTION AND RECOMMENDED USE |
|---|---|---|
|  | 10 | Taper ground, clean cuts in paneling, formica, plastic and related materials. |
|  | 10 | Scroll cutting for wood, plywood, masonite and plastic, up to 5 mm thick. |
|  | 12 | Taper ground for smooth, clean finish cuts in wood, plywood, plastic and hardboard. |
| | 6 | Coarse tooth for extra fast cuts in wood, plywood and hardboard. Extra long. |
|  | 8 | Flush cutting for wood and plastic. |
|  | 18 | Metal cutting for non-ferrous metals up to 1/4"(6.5 mm) thick. |
| | 24 | Metal cutting for non-ferrous metals up to 1/8"(3 mm) thick. |
|  | 36 | Metal cutting for non-ferrous metals up to 1/16"(1.5 mm) thick. |
|  | 8, 12, 18 | General purpose assortment for wood: coarse, medium and fine. |
| | 8 | Coarse tooth wood cutting for heavy, fast cuts. |
| | 18 | Fine tooth wood cutting for smooth cuts in wood, plywood, plastic and counter top materials. |

**FIGURE 1-71:** *Saber saw blades. (Courtesy Stanley Tools)*

**FIGURE 1-72:** *Cutting a circle with a saber saw.*

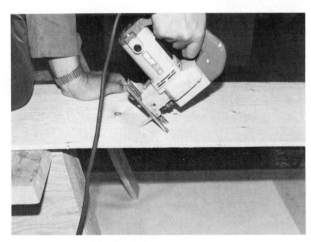

**FIGURE 1-73:** *Plunge cut.*

**FIGURE 1-74:** *Reciprocating saw. (Courtesy Skil Tools)*

**Electric Plane.** The electric plane is intended for jointing purposes, straightening edges, etc. It is particularly useful for working on doors or large window units. The fence may be tilted so that a bevel can be planed on an edge, as is necessary on the closing edge of a door (see Fig. 1–75).

**Electric Plate Cutter.** The electric plate, or wafer cutter, cuts a slot in wood to hold a wafer- shaped spline in a wood joint, providing a secure connection. This type of connection is commonly used in the fabrication of cabinets (see Fig. 1–76.)

**FIGURE 1–75:** *Electric plane. (Courtesy Skil Canada Ltd.)*

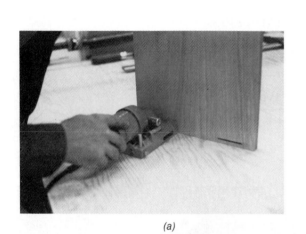

*(a)*

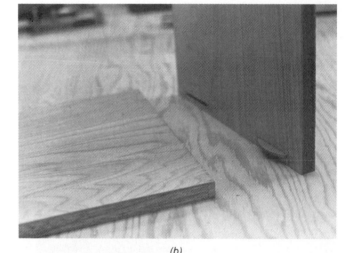

*(b)*

*(c)*

**FIGURE 1–76:** *Using an electric plate cutter to make a corner connection.*

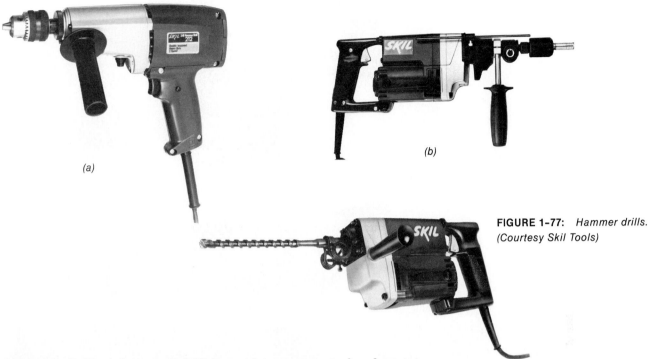

(a)

(b)

**FIGURE 1-77:** *Hammer drills. (Courtesy Skil Tools)*

**Hammer Drill.** A hammer drill is used to penetrate hard material such as concrete or stone and operates in such a way that it hammers at the same time as it turns the bit. Figure 1-77 illustrates three styles of drills and two different kinds of drilling operations.

**Power Screwdriver.** Various types of power screwdrivers are in use, some of them as attachments to an electric drill. The one shown in Fig. 1-78 is operated by rechargeable batteries.

**FIGURE 1-78:** *Power screwdriver.*

**Radial Arm Saw.** The radial arm saw is not a hand electric tool, but is operated from a table or bench and gets its name from the fact that the saw is suspended on a horizontal arm, which allows a great variety of movement. The saw can travel along the arm, pivot on the arm, and turn into a horizontal position; the arm itself will turn (see Fig. 1-79). The versatility of the tool is illustrated in Fig. 1-80, which shows it being used for ripping, and mitering as well as standard crosscutting. When crosscutting, mitering, or dadoing, the work is held firmly on the table and against the fence, and the saw is pulled through the work. Care should be taken with heavier materials so that the saw does not attempt to cut through the work too quickly. For ripping, the saw head is turned parallel with the table and locked into position. Lumber is then fed into the blade with care taken to feed the material in the opposite direction to the blade rotation.

**FIGURE 1-79:** *Radial arm saw.*

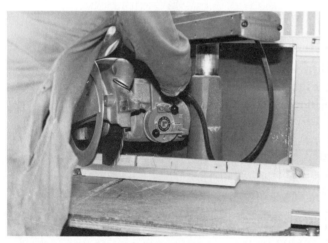

*(a) Miter cutting.*

*(b) Ripping.*

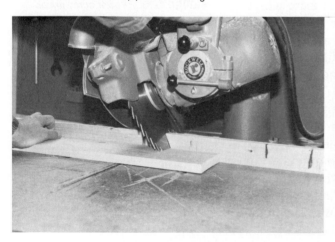

*(c) Compound miter.*

*(d) Crosscutting.*

**FIGURE 1-80**

**Miter Saw.** The miter saw is specially designed for cutting miters and is very useful for cutting moldings. The saw can be locked at 45° either left or right, or in a 90° position. A variety of materials can be cut—wood, plastic, and soft metals. Material being cut must be firmly held in place and carefully positioned prior to pulling the saw down through the material (see Fig. 1-81).

FIGURE 1-81: *Miter saw.*

FIGURE 1-82: *Table saw.*

**Table Saw.** This saw is primarily used for cabinetmaking and is sometimes used on projects where there are on-site-built cabinets. Carpenters will also use this saw for other finish work on a project. The saw is very useful for crosscutting, ripping, and dadoing. The size of the saw is determined by the diameter of the saw blade recommended for its use. Typical sizes are 8–21 in. (200–300 mm). The smaller sizes are often chosen for on-site work as they are easier to move through doorways (see Fig. 1-82). There are a number of kinds of saw blades available for the table saw. Be sure to select one with a blade of the correct diameter and arbor hole. Figure 1-83 illustrates the common types of blades.

*(a) Rip and cross-cut blades.*

*(b) Plywood and combination blades.*

FIGURE 1-83

*(c) Hardened tip and carbide tip blades.*

**Jointers.** The jointer is one of the most commonly used tools in a shop. Typical uses are for surfacing a board and jointing the edge. Jointers can also be used for cutting rabbets, bevels, or a taper. The size of the jointer is indicated by the length of the knives on the cutterhead. Care should be taken when using a jointer to keep the hand away from the area of the stock over the cutterhead. Use a push stick for smaller pieces (see Fig. 1–84).

*(a) Jointer.*

*(b) Combination jointer-thickness planer.*

**FIGURE 1–84**

### Gasoline-Powered Tools

A number of tools are run by small gasoline engines, including *paint sprayers, soil compactors,* and *chain saws.* The chainsaws are made in a variety of sizes, the size being determined by the length of the bar on which the saw chain runs. The one illustrated in Fig. 1–85 is a 14-in. (350-mm) saw. Such saws are useful for cutting heavy timbers, posts, etc. They have become quite common on framing jobs as they can be used anywhere without needing a power source. The saw cut is quite large, and the blade tends to tear at the wood, so care should be exercised in its use.

FIGURE 1-85: *Gas powered chain saw. (Courtesy Skil Power tools)*

## Pneumatic Tools

The most common pneumatic tools—those operated by compressed air—are *staplers, nailers,* and *drills.* Staplers are designed to drive staples and are used for fastening paneling, building paper, siding, and shingles. Fasteners used in staplers may be up to $3\frac{1}{2}$ in. (90 mm) with a maximum crown of 1 in. (25 mm) [see Fig. 1-86(a)].

Nailers are designed to drive various sizes and styles of nails up to a maximum of $3\frac{1}{2}$ in. (90 mm). They may be used almost anywhere that nails are required [see Fig. 1-86(b)].

Pneumatic drills are designed to duplicate the operations of electric drills. They are generally smaller in size and so can reach places electric drills are too cumbersome to fit. The common bits can be used in these drills [see Fig. 1-86(c)].

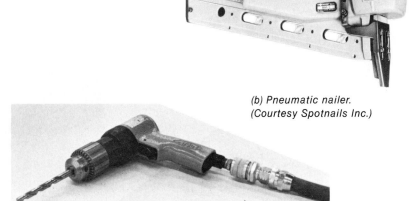

*(b) Pneumatic nailer.
(Courtesy Spotnails Inc.)*

*(a) Pneumatic stapler.
(Courtesy Spotnails Inc.)*

*(c) Pneumatic drill.*

FIGURE 1-86

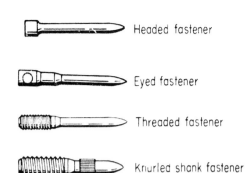

Headed fastener

Eyed fastener

Threaded fastener

Knurled shank fastener

**FIGURE 1-87:** *Power-actuated fasteners.*

## Power-Actuated Tools

In many situations, it becomes necessary to attach some object or material to a concrete, masonry, or steel surface. Not only is a special fastener necessary—one that is hard enough to penetrate the surface without bending—but special power is required to drive such a fastener into a hard material.

Tools designed to do such a job use an explosive charge contained in a small cartridge similar to a 22-caliber rifle cartridge. By this means, several types of pins and threaded fasteners (see Fig. 1-87) are driven into steel and concrete or masonry materials.

Cartridges of various energy levels are produced for use with fasteners of various lengths and materials of various densities. The energy level is designated by color: gray, brown, green, yellow, red, and purple denoting energy levels from low to high. Safety equipment should be used when using power-actuated tools—hard hat, safety glasses a must, and earmuffs (see Fig. 1-88).

*(a) Power actuated tool.*

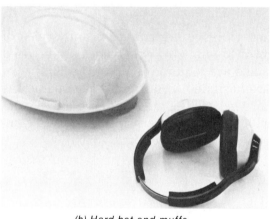

*(b) Hard hat and muffs.*

**FIGURE 1-88**

*(c) Shield and safety glasses.*

## CARE OF TOOLS

The success that one achieves with one's tools depends to a great extent on the care which one takes of them. No tool, no matter how expensive, will give good service unless it is given the proper attention. Tools must be kept sharp and in good general repair and must be protected against the weather and against rough usage.

### Sharpening Tools

While all cutting tools must be kept sharp, the ones which will probably need the most careful and constant attention are plane blades, chisels, and saws. Therefore, let us consider the sharpening procedures for these carefully.

**Plane Blade.** The first step is to shape the cutting edge. It may be square, or there may be a slight crown on it, depending on how it is to be used. If a surface is to be dressed flat, a crowned edge will be best, but for straightening an edge, a square edge is preferable.

Hold the iron at right angles to the grinding wheel, use light pressure, and grind slowly. If the edge is to be crowned, increase the pressure slightly at the ends of the blade. Test with a try square (see Fig. 1–89).

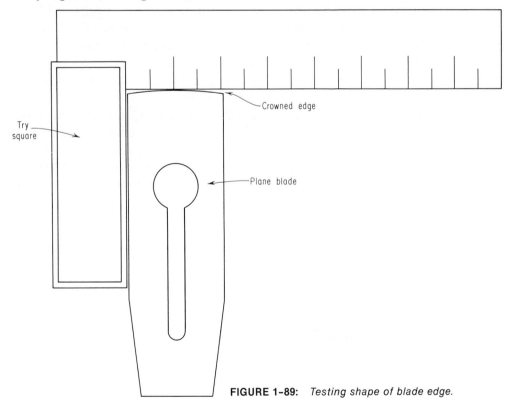

**FIGURE 1–89:**  *Testing shape of blade edge.*

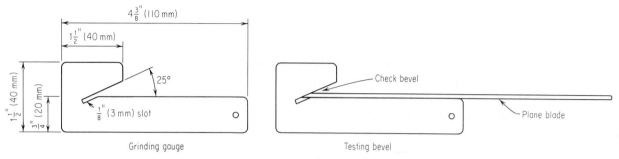

FIGURE 1-90: *Grinding gauge.*

At the same time the blade must be ground at the correct bevel, which for general-purpose blades will be 25°. Adjust the rest on the bench grinder so that when the plane iron is held on it, the correct angle will be ground. A simple gauge can be made to check the angle of the bevel (see Fig. 1-90 for particulars). When grinding, work the plane iron back and forth across the face of the stone using light, uniform pressure. Check the edge frequently and try to ensure that it becomes sharp throughout its entire length at the same time. The grinding operation leaves a burr on the back of the blade which must be removed by *whetting*. This, the next step in the sharpening process, is often done in two stages.

Two stones are generally used for whetting—an oilstone and a finer, Arkansas stone. Use the oilstone first. Apply a few drops of lubricant to start. A mixture of equal parts of light machine oil and solvent is recommended. Now set the bevel of the blade on the stone and raise the heel of the iron about 5°. Only the cutting edge of the beveled surface is in contact with the stone (see Fig. 1-91). Using a straight motion, whet the edge, taking care to hold the iron at a constant angle. After a few strokes, turn the blade over and rub it over the stone a few times, holding it perfectly flat. This action removes the burred edge which forms in whetting. Repeat this procedure until you have produced as sharp an edge as the stone will allow. The edge may be improved with a finer stone, so you repeat the whetting on the Arkansas stone.

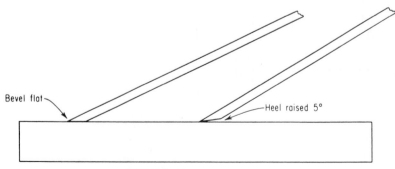

FIGURE 1-91: *Whetting a blade.*

The final step is *stropping* the edge on a piece of leather in much the same way that a barber would do with a razor blade. Glue a piece of heavy leather to a wooden block. Strop the cutting edge back and forth across the leather several times. The last remnants of the burr are removed, leaving an extremely fine, sharp cutting edge.

**Chisel.** The same procedure is used for sharpening a chisel as was used for a plane blade. The only difference is that the cutting edge of the chisel is always square. Try square and bevel gauge may be used in the same way as for plane blades.

**Handsaws.** Well shaped, sharp teeth are required to ensure that saws cut efficiently. Take care when selecting a sharpening shop to make sure that you get the quality of sharpening needed for fine workmanship. Always check your newly sharpened saws to see that a good job was done. Sight down the length of the saw to check that the teeth on both sides are of equal size. The V shape of a crosscut saw should be down the center of the saw (see Fig. 1-92).

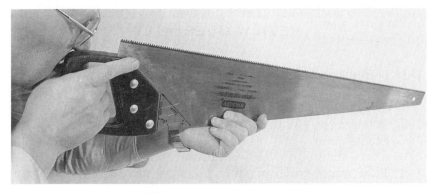

FIGURE 1-92: *Sighting a crosscut saw.*

Larger teeth on either side will cause the saw to pull to that side. Any "kinks" in the saw blade should be pointed out to the sharpening shop so that they can be straightened.

## Storing Tools

Proper storage facilities contribute considerably to the life of tools. Sharp-edged tools such as saws or chisels should be so placed in the tool box that the edges do not become damaged from contact with other tools. An excellent way to carry chisels or auger bits, for example, is to have them in a cloth roll with separate compartments for each bit or chisel. A plastic cap may be used for the saw blades, or they may be held separately, teeth down, in the tool box or kit. Take care of all your tools and you will be rewarded with longer use and better results.

**Handling Tools**

Equally important is how you handle and care for your tools *while on the job.* Saws and squares should never be dropped on the floor. Also, they should not be leaned against the leg of a sawhorse or bench unless you are sure that they are not going to slip and fall to the floor. Use some means of holding them securely. Planes should always be laid on the side—never on the bed of the plane. Don't let a great variety of tools get stacked up around you at work. When you have finished with one tool for a time, put it away where it will not be damaged.

Care in the handling of power tools is very important. This is true not only from the standpoint of damage to the tool but also from the possibility of danger to you. Careless or improper handling of a power tool may result in serious injury.

Develop a pride in your tools—in their appearance and condition—and you will find that you will be able to do a better job, that tool replacement will be less costly, and that you will be looked upon as a workman worthy of the name.

## REVIEW QUESTIONS

1–1. Name two *basic* differences between crosscut and ripsaw teeth in handsaws.

1–2. What is the advantage of having a handsaw with a tapered blade?

1–3. How many teeth per inch (25 mm) are there in an *eight-point* saw?

1–4. How does a backsaw differ from most other handsaws?

1–5. Why should the cutting angle of a chisel that is to be used for cutting hardwood be ground to 30°?

1–6. What are the two main differences between a shingling hatchet and a bench ax?

1–7. List four tables found on a framing square.

1–8. List the main differences between a speed bore bit and an auger bit.

1–9. Matching test: Place the number found beside each item in column 1 in the blank space to the left of each phrase in column 2 with which it matches.

|  |  |
|---|---|
| *Column 1* | *Column 2* |
| 1. Bit extension | _____ Acts as a depth gauge |
| 2. Push drill | _____ For drilling deep holes |
| 3. Bit file | _____ Has 16-in. (400-mm) tongue |
| 4. Combination square | _____ Cutting irregular lines |
| 5. Compass saw | _____ Ground straight across |
| 6. Rafter square | _____ Has one safe edge |
| 7. Butt gauge | _____ To lay out hinge gains |
|  | _____ Has an interchangeable blade |
|  | _____ A spring-loaded tool |

# 2
# CONSTRUCTION EQUIPMENT

During the course of construction, a variety of equipment is often employed, in addition to the hand and power woodworking tools used in the actual erection of the building.

## SOIL TESTING EQUIPMENT

In some cases it may be desirable to determine the types and depth of soil strata to be encountered before excavation takes place. This is usually done by digging or boring a test hole, as illustrated in Chapter 3.

## EARTH-MOVING EQUIPMENT

Earth-moving equipment includes such machines as the *bull-dozer* and the *backhoe* (see Fig. 2–1 and Chapter 4), used for excavating, and a *front-end loader* (see Figs. 2–1 and 2–2), used for moving and loading earth.

**FIGURE 2-1:** *Backhoe with a bucket.*

**FIGURE 2-2:** *(a) Front-end loader.*

**FIGURE 2-2:** *(b) Tractor with bucket for moving earth. (Bobcat)*

## CONCRETE EQUIPMENT

**FIGURE 2-3:** *Portable concrete mixer. (Courtesy Western Equipment Ltd.)*

Conventional foundations require the use of a concrete mixer, varying from the small, *portable mixer* shown in Fig. 2-3 to a *transit-mix truck*, like that illustrated in Fig. 2-4.

At the site, concrete may have to be transported from mixer to the forms, and this may be done by the use of wheelbarrows, power buggies, a concrete pump (see Fig. 2-5), or lifting buckets (see Fig. 2-6), and concrete in the forms may be consolidated by the use of an *internal vibrator,* such as the one shown in Fig. 4-86. A number of tools are used in finishing concrete slabs, including a *bull float,* illustrated in Fig. 2-7, *hand trowels* and *edgers,* and a *power trowel,* such as that illustrated in Fig. 2-8.

**FIGURE 2-4:** *Transit-mix truck.*

**FIGURE 2-5:** *Concrete pump.*

**FIGURE 2-6:** *Lifting bucket.*

**FIGURE 2-7:** *Bullfloat.*

**FIGURE 2-8:** *Concrete power trowel.*

## SOIL BREAKING AND COMPACTION EQUIPMENT

At some sites, it may be necessary to break up the surface to facilitate excavation, and this may be done by the use of a *jack hammer*, illustrated in Fig. 2–9. A *rammer* (see Fig. 2–10) may be used to compact backfill and a *plate vibrator* to compact a subgrade (see Fig. 2–11). Vibratory rollers may be used to compact and smooth earth and asphalt surfaces at the site (see Fig. 2–12).

**FIGURE 2-9:** *Jackhammer in use. (Courtesy Wacker Corp.)*

**FIGURE 2-10:** *Rammer compacting backfill. (Courtesy Wacker Corp.)*

**FIGURE 2-11:** *Vibro-compactor at work. (Courtesy Wacker Corp.)*

**FIGURE 2–12:** *Vibratory roller.*

**FIGURE 2–13:** *Wooden pole scaffolds.*

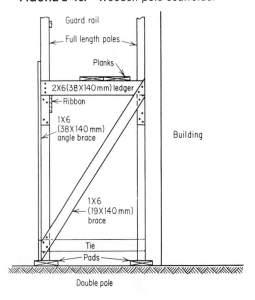

Double pole

## SCAFFOLDS

As construction progresses, *scaffolding* or *staging* is required to reach work areas which are beyond the normal reach of a workman standing on the ground. Scaffolding consists of elevated platforms, resting on rigid supports and strong and stiff enough to support workmen, tools, and materials safely.

Scaffolding may be made of wood or metal, the wooden ones normally being made on the job, while metal scaffolds are manufactured articles, made in a variety of styles.

### Pole Scaffolds

The most common wooden scaffolds are *pole scaffolds,* made in either *single-* or *double-pole* style scaffolds. Double-pole scaffolds have two legs per section (see Fig. 10–13), while the single-pole scaffold has but one. In both cases, 2 × 6 in. (38 × 140 mm) minimum *ledgers* support the platform, usually made up of two or more planks, at least 10 in. (235 mm) wide. 1 × 6 (19 × 140 mm) angle braces and a ribbon under the ledger join scaffold sections together. Figure 2–13 gives recommended minimum sizes of materials used in the construction of such scaffolds. The horizontal distance between scaffold sections should not exceed 10 ft (3 m) and the maximum height for such scaffolds should be limited to 20 ft (6 m). Bearing pads should always be placed under the bottom ends of the poles in order to obtain maximum stability, and double-pole scaffolds should be tied to the building at intervals for greater safety.

### Manufactured Scaffolds

Manufactured scaffolding is easily assembled and dismantled. Adjustments can easily be made to facilitate different heights, and they are very mobile. Many types of scaffolds are available, including brackets, ladder jacks, metal pole, climbing, sectional, tower, and swing stage.

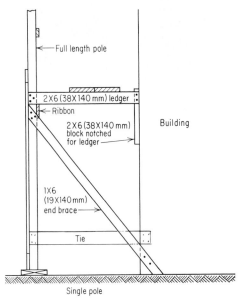

Single pole

### Brackets

Planks can be supported by special brackets which are fastened to the studs in wall construction and to the roofing members in roof installations (see Fig. 2–14). Brackets are very convenient as they can be quickly erected and they require little material. Brackets are also easily moved from one job site to another. Roof brackets are fastened with nails through the sheathing into the rafters (see Fig. 2–15). They can be removed without pulling the nails so damage does not happen to the roof covering.

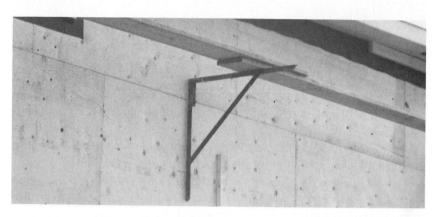

**FIGURE 2-14:**   *Wall bracket.*

### Ladder Jacks

Ladder jacks are commonly used by siding applicators and are especially convenient as they do not need fastening to the wall. This allows for placing of finish with little or no interference (see Fig. 2–16). A ladder jack is a device for hanging a plank from a ladder. Ladder jacks are convenient when only one workman is involved. Two ladders and a single plank are all that is required.

**FIGURE 2-15:**   *Roof bracket.*

**FIGURE 2-16:**   *Ladder jack.*

## Tube and Clamp Scaffold

A tube and clamp scaffold is similar in design to a single-pole wooden scaffold except the poles are made of aluminum in most cases. This makes for a very light pole to which the metal ledger is clamped. The other end is nailed to the wall at the desired height. Metal poles are also used for the required bracing (see Fig. 2–17). A wooden pad is used under the leg so that it doesn't sink into the ground.

**FIGURE 2-17:** *Tube and clamp scaffold.*

**FIGURE 2-18:** *Climbing or adjustable scaffold.*

## Climbing or Adjustable Scaffold

One type of adjustable scaffold looks similar to a single-pole metal scaffold but works on much the same principle as ladder jacks. A 2 × 4 (38 × 89 mm) is used as the vertical pole. It is fastened to the roof so that it does not rotate. Metal brackets are fastened to the support with horizontal ledgers for supporting the plank. These brackets are adjustable and can be moved up or down the support as the inner end is not fastened to the wall (see Fig. 2–18).

Another type of adjustable scaffold that has come on the market is a workhorse. It is supported by four legs and is easily moved on each of these legs individually. The height that it can be used is limited to about 6 ft (2 m) unless diagonal bracing is attached to the legs (see Fig. 2–19).

FIGURE 2-19:   *A workhorse.*

## Sectional Scaffolds

Sectional scaffolding is made up of tubular material in double-pole style, as illustrated in Fig. 2-20. A standard unit consists of two end frames and two crossed braces with holes at each end [see Fig. 2-20(b)]. An end frame has threaded studs attached to the legs which fit into the holes in the brace ends. Braces are held in place by wing nuts so that the assembled unit appears as illustrated in Fig. 2-20(c)]. To increase the length of a scaffold, additional sets of end frames are added, using two additional crossed braces for each end frame used. To extend the height, one standard unit is mounted above another. Coupling pins [Fig. 2-20(g)] are inserted into the top of the tubular legs of the lower unit, and the legs of additional end frames are slipped over the top half of the coupling. Additional crossed braces can be used horizontally on any unit to give it greater rigidity. By adding units as indicated, scaffolds of any length or height may be assembled [see Fig. 2-20(d)].

FIGURE 2-20:   *Tubular metal scaffolding.*

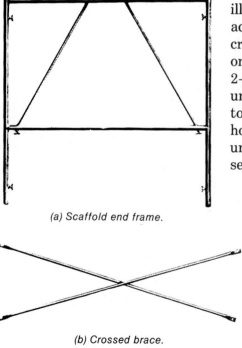

*(a) Scaffold end frame.*

*(b) Crossed brace.*

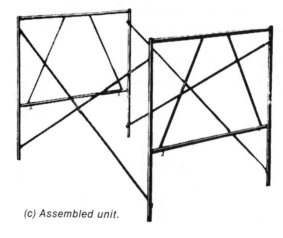

*(c) Assembled unit.*

(e) Metal scaffold plank.

(f) Guard rails.

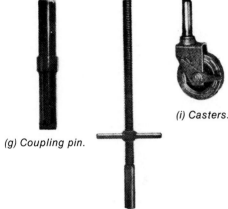

(g) Coupling pin.

(h) Screw jack.

(i) Casters.

(d) Assembled scaffolding.

(k) Metal scaffolding.

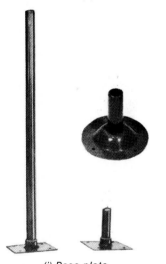

(j) Base plate.

**FIGURE 2-20:**   (continued)

Nonskid metal planks, like the one shown in Fig. 2–20(e), which span a standard unit, are available with this type of scaffold, or wooden planks may be used if desired.

Base plates [see Fig. 2–20(j)] fit into the bottom of frame legs to form the footing for a scaffold, the short one for level surfaces and the long one to compensate for uneven ground. Casters [see Fig. 2–20(i)] fitted with safety brakes, may be used in place of base plates on hard surfaces when it is necessary to move the assembled scaffold from one position to another. *Screw jacks* [see Fig. 2–20(h)] are available for use with base plates or casters where floors are uneven or where a fine adjustment in height is required.

Steel scaffolding of this type is made with the utmost consideration for safety, but of course care must be exercised in its erection and use. The following rules should be observed by erectors and workmen:

1. Provide sufficient sills or underpinning in addition to standard base plates on all scaffolds to be erected on fill or otherwise soft ground.
2. Compensate for unevenness of ground by using adjusting screws rather than blocking.
3. Be sure that all scaffolds are plumb and level at all times.
4. Anchor running scaffold to the wall approximately every 28 ft (8.5 m) of length and 18 ft (6 m) of height.
5. Adjust scaffold until braces fit into place with ease.
6. Use guard rails on all scaffolds, regardless of height.
7. Use ladders—not the cross braces—to climb scaffolds.
8. Tighten all bolts and wing nuts which are a part of the scaffold.
9. Use horizontal bracing to prevent racking of the structure.
10. All wood planking used on a scaffold should be of sound quality, straight grained, and free from knots.
11. When using steel planks, always fill the space because steel planks tend to skid sideways easily.
12. Handle all rolling scaffolds with additional care. Use wheel brake locks.
13. Do not extend adjusting screws to full extent.
14. Horizontal bracing should be used at the bottom, at the top, and at intermediate levels of 18 ft (6 m).

In addition to its many conventional uses, sectional scaffolding may be used as temporary *shoring* or support for various parts of a building under construction, as illustrated in Fig. 2-21.

**FIGURE 2-21:** *Sectional scaffolding used as shoring.*

For interior work a smaller sectional scaffolding can be obtained. It is equipped with casters and will fit through a standard doorway. Height adjustments are quickly made, making it convenient for different ceiling heights (see Fig. 2–22).

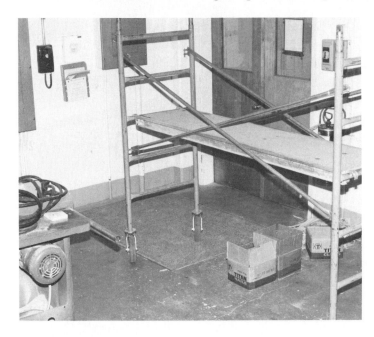

FIGURE 2-22:   *Rolling scaffold.*

## Tower Scaffold

Another commonly used type of metal scaffolding is the *tower* scaffold, shown in Fig. 2–23. A standard unit is made up of a pair of metal towers, tied together with both horizontal—*stringer*—braces and crossed braces (see Fig. 2–23). Pairs of towers are then tied together with stringer braces to form a continuous scaffold of any desired length. Each tower supports a *carriage*, on which rests a workman's plank platform or, in the case of scaffolding intended for use by masons, two platforms, one for the tradesmen and one for laborers and materials. A *winch* is attached to each tower to raise the platform to the required height.

The height of these scaffolds can be increased by adding sections to the ends of towers, thus producing scaffolds which will reach to any desired height.

The same rules of safety which apply to the erection and use of sectional scaffolding also apply to the use of tower scaffolds.

FIGURE 2-23:   *Tower scaffold in use. (Courtesy Morgen Mfg. Co.)*

## Swing Stage Scaffold

Swing stage scaffolds are platforms, complete with guardrail and toeboard, suspended from the roof of the building by a

FIGURE 2-24:  *Swing stage scaffold.*

block-and-tackle system attached to each end. By this means, the workers on the platform can adjust the height of the scaffold as required (see Fig. 2-24). Such scaffolds are intended for workmen using only light equipment, working high above the ground.

FIGURE 2-25:  *Heavy duty aluminum ladder.*

## LADDERS

Several types of aluminum and wooden ladders are used on construction projects. They include *step ladders,* ranging in height from 4 to 18 ft (1.2–6 m); and *extension ladders,* in lengths up to about 32 ft (10 m). Heavy duty aluminum ladders only, should be used on construction sites (see Fig. 2–25).

### Safety Rules for Ladders

1. Always check a ladder for defects before use.
2. In use, place the ladder so that the distance from its bottom end to the wall is at least one-quarter the length of the ladder, unless the top end is secured.
3. Extension ladders should extend at least 3 ft (1 m) above the landing against which the top end rests.
4. Check to see that both rails rest on solid, level footing.
5. Equip the bottom ends of the rails with *safety shoes* if the ladder is to be used on hard surfaces that may allow it to slip.
6. Lubricate locks and pulleys on extension ladders, keep fittings tight, and replace worn rope.
7. Do not allow paint, oil, or grease to accumulate on ladder rungs or rails.

## MATERIALS HOIST

Some type of equipment is required to lift materials which are to be applied to a building from a scaffold or used on the roof, and normally a *hoist* of some sort will be employed for the purpose.

For relatively low lifts, a *fork lift* on a tractor or front-end loader may be satisfactory. Platform hoists are used to handle loads up to 400 lb (180 kg) and heights up to 44 ft (13.5 m). They are used by all trades in industrial, residential, and commercial construction (see Fig. 2–26). For greater heights, an *elevator-type materials lift,* a mobile crane, or a tower crane may be necessary.

(a) Hydraulic swing hoist.      (b) Forklift hoist.

**FIGURE 2–26**

## REVIEW QUESTIONS

2–1. Explain the basic difference between a double-pole and a single-pole scaffold.

2–2. (a) Name three groups of workmen for whom "light trade" scaffolds are made.
   (b) Name three groups for whom "heavy trade" scaffolds are made.

2–3. Matching test: Place the number found beside each item in Column 1 in the blank space to the left of each phrase in column 2 with which it matches.

|  | *Column 1* | *Column 2* |
|---|---|---|

*Column 1*

1. Backhoe
2. Bobcat
3. Concrete pump
4. Concrete vibrator
5. Bullfloat
6. Power trowel
7. Transit-mix truck
8. Plate vibrator

*Column 2*

_____ Small tractor used to level fill in tight places

_____ Used to consolidate concrete

_____ Tractor used to level a building site

_____ Used to excavate water and sewer lines

_____ Used to place concrete

_____ Used to mix concrete on route to a construction site

_____ Used to level a concrete slab

_____ Ideal for breaking up rock and concrete

_____ Used to compact the base under a concrete slab

_____ Puts the final finish on a concrete slab

**2-4.** What are two advantages of ladder jacks?

**2-5.** What is the purpose of a life line on a swing stage scaffold?

**2-6.** List three advantages of metal scaffolding over wooden scaffolding.

**2-7.** Explain why more scaffold planks are needed on scaffolds being used by bricklayers or stone masons.

# 3

# THE BUILDING SITE

## SITE INVESTIGATION

The erection of a building, large or small, necessitates a good deal of prior study and planning, both in connection with the building itself and with the site on which it will be built.

This study, commonly referred to as *site investigation*, will vary widely as to method and degree, depending on the type, size, and proposed use of the building to be constructed. Planners in the light construction area will likely be most interested in surface aspects of the site and the subsoil at relatively shallow depths. On the other hand, planners of large, heavy buildings are usually interested in the nature of the subsoil at considerable distance below the surface and are concerned with the surface chiefly from the standpoint of site area and adjacent buildings.

### Site Investigation in Light Construction

The surface aspects of the site with which planners in the light construction field will be concerned include

1. Presence or absence of trees and shrubs
2. Contours of the site
3. Elevation of the site in relation to the surrounding area
4. The size, shape, and proximity of surrounding buildings

Particularly in the case of planning for residential construction, the presence of trees and their size often influence the design of the building. The number and kinds of trees and shrubs present will also help to determine the type of equipment necessary to clear the site. In some cases, it may be deemed necessary to remove all the trees, while in others the architect may wish to retain some trees as part of the overall design.

Whether the site is flat or rolling and whether it slopes in one direction and, if so, in what direction in relation to the front of the building are important questions for the designer. For example, a slope or small hill may enable him/her to introduce ground level entrances to the building at different levels of the building. The amount of slope and its direction will also determine the amount and disposition of fill which may have to be brought to the site.

The level of the area under study, in relation to that of the surrounding area, requires consideration. If it is low in comparison to the surrounding land, the level will probably have to be raised by adding fill. On the other hand, care must be taken that runoff from elevated land does not cause damage to surrounding property.

In the case of residential buildings particularly, it is usually desirable that they conform in a general way to those around them. For example, a tall, narrow building in the midst of a group of low, rambling ones would probably look out of place.

## SOIL INVESTIGATION

Soil investigation, carried out in connection with light construction projects, will consist basically of tests to determine the kinds of soil to a depth of twice the building height below the surface, the level of the water table in the soil, where frost is a problem, the depth of frost penetration, and any very unusual soil characteristics.

The type or types of soil present will indicate the bearing strength of the material and will help determine the excavating equipment best suited for the job and what measures, if any, must be taken to prevent cave-in of the excavation. Depending on the type of soil, the excavated material will either have to be removed from the site and replaced by other soil, or stored to be used for backfilling and landscaping. Soil type will also indicate whether or not frost penetration is a serious problem. Some very fine clay soils expand substantially when subjected to moisture, and care must be taken when these are encountered at the foundation level of a building.

The level of the water table—the natural water level in the soil—will determine whether particular precautions, (e.g., the installation of weeping tile) must be taken to drain water away from the foundation. It may also influence the waterproofing techniques used on the exterior of the foundation walls.

Testing for the presence of a number of aggressive chemical substances, particularly sulfates of calcium, sodium, or magnesium, in the groundwater or soil are important considerations in the study of soils on the site. When soil or water containing appreciable amounts of these sulfates comes in contact with concrete, the sulfates react chemically with hydrated lime and hydrated calcium aluminate in the cement paste. This causes considerable expansion in the paste, resulting in corrosion and disintegration of the concrete.

To prevent this deterioration, concrete which will be in contact with these sulfates should be made using cement which has a low content of calcium aluminate. If the soil contains over 0.10% sulfates or the water contains over 150 ppm (parts per million) water-soluble sulfate, sulfate-resistant cement should be used.

Penetration of the soil by frost may have serious consequences under certain conditions. When moisture is present in any of several fine-grained soils, freezing may result in the formation of ice lenses and consequent heaving of the soil. Under these conditions, it is desirable to have the footings for a building below the frost line. Possible alternatives are to eliminate the soil moisture by draining it away or to replace the offending soil with one which is not affected by frost action—gravel or coarse sand.

The method of soil testing commonly used in this type of construction work is done by boring. Machine augers may be used, and soil is brought to the surface for analysis in a *disturbed* condition (see Fig. 3-1). Disturbed samples are generally

**FIGURE 3-1:**  *Soil test operation.*

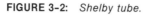

**FIGURE 3-2:** *Shelby tube.*

used for soil grain size analysis, for determining the specific gravity of the soil, and for compaction testing. For determining other properties of soils such as strength and permeability, it is necessary to obtain an *undisturbed* sample. The most common method of obtaining an undisturbed sample is to push a thin *Shelby tube* into the soil, thereby trapping the sample inside the tube (see Fig. 3-2).

Another danger which must be considered, although it is sometimes very difficult to detect without special equipment, is the presence of underground watercourses or springs. Such watercourses normally flow to some natural outlet, but when the soil is disturbed and natural outlets dammed off, often difficulties result. Water begins to collect underground, the hydrostatic pressure builds up, and eventually the water must break out somewhere. Often it will be through the basement floor. If there is the slightest hint of an underground water flow, drainage tile must be installed.

## AVAILABLE SERVICES

Are services such as electricity, sewer, water, gas, and telephone available? The answer will affect plans and preparations for the building. If a sewer line is already installed, it will be necessary to know its depth in order to get a drop from the building to the sewer line. A trench will have to be dug across the property to the building. If no sewer line is in, it will be necessary to find out what the level of a future line will be or, if none is available, to make plans for a private sewage disposal system.

Is there a water main in the immediate area? If so, what is, or will be, the location of the water connection for the site concerned? This location will determine where the water line will enter the building. If there is no main, plans must be made for a well or other water supply.

The availability of electricity will have an effect on the actual construction work. If there is none, the work will all have to be done by hand or by gasoline engine power. If there is electricity near at hand, a number of power tools may be used which could substantially reduce the time required for building.

If there is gas in the area, it should be ascertained where it is likely to enter the building, so that gas appliances may be located as conveniently as possible. If there is no gas, some other means of supplying heat must be found. It may be that more electrical power must be provided.

It will be necessary to find out from some civic authority the grade level at the site. The level at which the street and sidewalks will be put in must be known before the excavation and landscaping are planned. The grounds in front of the building should be level with or slope toward the sidewalk or street.

## ZONING RESTRICTIONS

Most urban areas have zoning laws which restrict specified areas to certain uses. They may be industrial, business, local commercial, multiple-family dwelling area, or single-family dwelling area. In addition, a building in a particular area may be required to have a specified minimum number of square feet of floor space. Regulations stimulate how far back from the front property line the house must be and the minimum distance it must be away from the side property line. Often minimum lot areas are defined and the maximum area of a lot which a building may cover. The setback for garages, whether front-drive or lane-drive, is specified in many cases.

These regulations will vary to some degree from city to city and from community to community. However, the basic reasons for having these restrictions are the same, namely, the preservation of certain standards and the protection of the citizens to whom they apply. Therefore, it is quite essential, when one is contemplating the erection of a building, that he/she be familiar with the regulations which apply to that community.

## SITE LAYOUT

When the design work for a building has been completed, plans are drawn to indicate in detail how the building is to be constructed. In many cases a *site plan* is included to show the exact location of the building on the property. When no site plan is included, more freedom of location may be possible, subject to the local or regional building regulations that will specify the minimum allowable proximity of the building to front and side property lines. In residential construction, for example, the front *setback* is frequently a minimum of 20 ft (5.4 m), while the side clearance might be 4 ft (1.22 m) or 10% of the width of the lot. These regulations should be checked before proceeding with any proposed construction.

**FIGURE 3-3:** *Lot layout.*

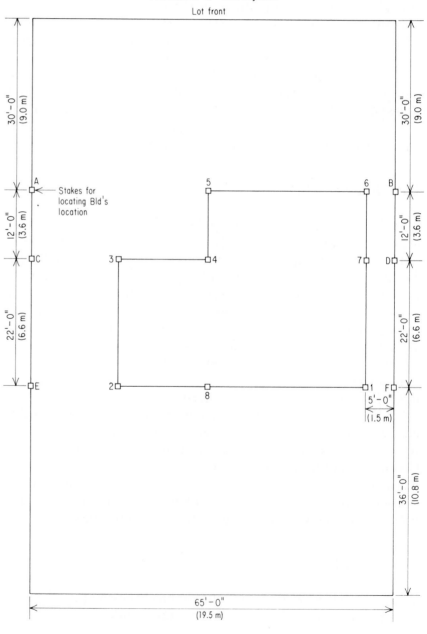

Armed with a set of plans, the builder must first lay out the position of the building on the site. In some areas it is necessary to employ a registered surveyor to locate the building stakes. If it were to be built on the surface of the ground, it would be a relatively easy matter to set stakes at the corners and other important points in the building by accurate measurements from the property lines, but in most situations some soil at least will be removed from the surface, and stakes would be lost during excavation. It is therefore necessary to set the stakes back from the excavation so they will remain in place after the digging is completed. These stakes are usually set at the lot property line (see Fig. 3–3). The distance to the building corners will be indicated on the stakes. The amount of digging or cut will also show on these stakes (see Fig. 3–4). After the digging is completed, the corners of the building are located in the bottom of the excavation. Footing forms can be set from these corners.

**FIGURE 3-4:**  *Building stakes.*

For larger buildings an alternate method using batter boards is sometimes utilized (see Fig. 3–5). Batter boards are kept back some distance from the actual building location and so are not disturbed during excavation work. Then, when excavating is complete, building lines are strung from one batter board to another, and each intersection of two building lines represents a point on the building. These points can be established in the excavation by dropping a plumb bob from the line intersections to the ground below.

A batter board is located by driving a stake at the approximate position of each point to be established and then building

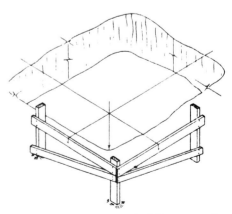

**FIGURE 3-5:**  *Locating building corner in excavation from batter boards.*

**FIGURE 3-6:** *Builder's level.*

**FIGURE 3-7:** *Transit level.*

a batter board to cover each position, placed well back from the area to be excavated. Then by accurate measurements and sometimes with the aid of leveling instruments (see Figs. 3-6, 3-7, and 3-8), the necessary reference points are placed on the batter boards where they may be marked by a nail or by making a shallow saw kerf on the top edge of the bar.

## LEVELING INSTRUMENTS

A *leveling instrument* is usually employed to lay out a building site. The basic types of levels used during the site layout are the *builder's level* (see Fig. 3-6) and the *transit level* (see Fig. 3-7). A *laser level*, as illustrated in Fig. 3-16, is very effective in determining levels on a construction site.

The builder's level turns in a horizontal plane only, while the transit level moves in both horizontal and vertical planes, making it much more versatile. Some instruments are leveled by means of leveling screws, while others are automatic—they simply require a small bubble to be centered in a circular dial by means of a single adjustment in order to level them.

## Builder's Level

The leveling instrument illustrated in Fig. 3-6 consists of a *telescope tube* containing an *objective lens* in front, which can be focused by means of a *focusing knob* on the side. The telescope is mounted in a *frame* and has attached to it a *bubble tube* very similar to a small spirit level. The telescope and bubble tube are leveled by means of three *leveling screws,* turned against a *leveling head.* The screws are adjusted until the bubble is centered in the dial, regardless of the direction in which the instrument points.

At the rear end of the telescope there is an *eyepiece,* containing a small lens and an *eyepiece ring* which can be turned to focus the lens. A pair of *cross hairs* is mounted in front of the eyepiece lens, and they are brought into sharp focus by the adjustment of the eyepiece ring.

At the bottom of the frame there is a *graduated horizontal circle* and a *vernier scale,* used to read horizontal angles accurately. The instrument may be held in any horizontal position by tightening a *horizontal motion clamp screw.* It can then be brought into fine adjustment by a *horizontal motion tangent screw.*

## Transit Level

A transit level telescope is pivoted in the frame and held in the horizontal position by a *locking lever.* When it is unlocked, the telescope may be tilted through a vertical arc and held in a tilted position by a *vertical motion clamp screw.* A fine adjustment to the position can then be made by the *vertical motion tangent screw.*

Attached to the telescope is a *graduated vertical arc* which moves as the telescope is tilted. Fixed to the frame is a *vertical vernier scale,* used to read the degree of tilt accurately.

The entire instrument is carried on a *centering head* which sits in a circular opening in the leveling head and allows lateral movement of the instrument within the confines of the opening when the leveling screws are loosened slightly. With some instruments a *plumb bob* is hung from the underside of the centering head and this lateral movement aids in the final centering of the instrument over a pin in the ground. Other instruments use an *optical plummet* (a visual sighting arrangement) to center over a pin (see Figs. 3-7 and 3-8).

FIGURE 3-8: *Transit level equipped with EDM (Electronic distance measuring equipment).*

## LEVELING

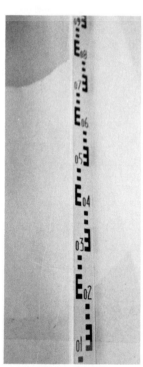

FIGURE 3-9: *A metric levelling rod.*

Once the instrument is leveled, it is ready for use, and a *leveling rod* or a thin pole is required to establish levels. A leveling rod, usually made in two or more sections, is marked off in feet (meters) and subdivided, often by the decimal system into smaller fractions of a foot (meter) (see Fig. 3-9).

Some rods are equipped with a sliding *target* (see Fig. 3-10), which is adjusted until the horizontal line coincides with the horizontal cross hair and then locked in position. The reading is then taken *at the horizontal line.* To take a level sight on a rod with target, proceed as follows:

1. Have a colleague hold a leveling rod with target at some convenient distance away [50-100 ft (15-30 m)] from the leveled instrument.

2. Aim the telescope at the rod by sighting along the top.

3. Now sight through the eyepiece and adjust the focus by turning the focusing knob. Adjust the instrument until the object is centered as closely as possible. Tighten the horizontal motion clamp screw and adjust with the horizontal motion tangent screw until the vertical cross hair is centered on the rod.

4. Have the rod man adjust the target up or down until the horizontal cross hair coincides with the horizontal line on the target. He can now take the reading indicated on the rod.

FIGURE 3-10: Target rod.

FIGURE 3-11: Using a transit to establish a straight line.

If, for example, the reading taken in the procedure outlined above were 3.625 ft (1.105 m), it would mean that the horizontal cross hair is the distance above a point of known elevation on which the rod is standing. This is commonly known as the *height of instrument* (H.I.) for that position.

Now have the rod moved to a second position and again take a reading, e.g., 4.746 ft (1.447 m). Since the *line of sight* of the instrument is level, the bottom end of the rod must be 4.746 − 3.625 = 1.121 ft (0.342 m) lower in the second position than it was in the first. In other words, the *difference in elevation* of the ground between the two positions is 1.121 ft (0.342 m).

## Use of a Level to Establish Batter Board Heights

To use a level in building layout, there are several basic operations. First, establish a common level at a number of different locations. Second, determine the elevation of a point or series of points, relative to a point of known elevation—a *benchmark* or a *datum point*. A benchmark is a fixed point of elevation in relation to sea level and a datum point is a temporary benchmark.

Third, run a straight line. Fourth, measure a given angle or establish an angle of a given size.

### Use of a Transit Level to Establish Building Lines

A transit is extremely useful for setting a number of points in a straight line—piers for a pier foundation or for resetting the building lines at the bottom of an excavation. The setting of these points can be achieved with a builder's level, but a transit is much more convenient, especially when a difference in elevation is involved.

Set the instrument directly over the reference point and level the instrument. Release the telescope level lock and swing the instrument in the desired direction and align the cross hair on the desired stake. Tighten the horizontal circle clamp so the telescope can only move in the vertical plane. Moving the telescope up or down will locate a number of points in a straight line (see Fig. 3–11). This same process will easily establish a line in the bottom of an excavation from reference points outside of the excavation (see Fig. 3–12).

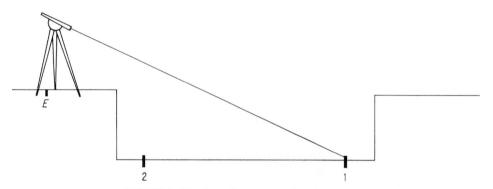

**FIGURE 3–12:** *Locating corners in a basement.*

### Using an Instrument to Turn a Horizontal Angle

To lay out an angle with a builder's level, set the instrument directly over the required point on the ground. This point is commonly marked with a nail driven in the top of a stake. Turn the instrument and sight on station B (see Fig. 3–13) and set the horizontal circle at zero to align with zero on the vernier scale. Swing the instrument to the required angle to locate station C. The line of sight must be dropped with a plumb line to the ground level to establish the exact point (see Fig. 3–14). This dropping is not necessary when a level transit is used as it can be rotated on a vertical plane.

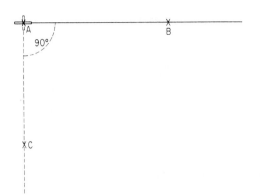

**FIGURE 3-14:** *Dropping line of sight to ground level when using a builder's level.*

**FIGURE 3-13:** *Turning a 90° angle with a transit or a level.*

Right angles can be established without the use of an instrument by using the right-angle method illustrated in Fig. 3-15. Once the layout is complete, work can progress on the building foundation.

**FIGURE 3-15:** *Checking diagonals.*

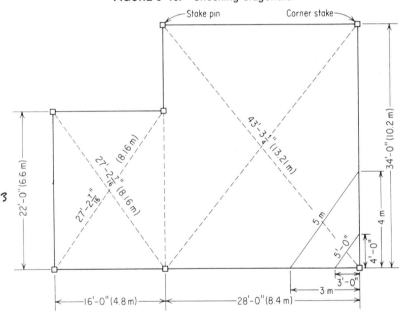

## Laser Level

The laser level is a one-person measurement system. It self-levels when set on a horizontal surface or when set on a tripod, allowing the worker the freedom to move around the construction site. The range of the laser is much greater than the normal builder's or transit level. The level emits a narrow beam of light that can be used for accurate references for elevation work and as a vertical reference for line and plumb control. The level rotates the beam in a level plane, and workers can measure distances from this beam using a laser rod or a tape measure to set forms or floor systems (see Fig. 3–16). The level can also be used in a vertical mode to set a plumb line. The laser level's accuracy is especially effective on a warm day since atmospheric refraction doesn't affect the beam as it does the line of sight of a standard transit or builder's level.

**FIGURE 3–16:**  *Laser level.*

## REVIEW QUESTIONS

3–1. Give two reasons for inspecting a residential building site before any plans are drawn.

3–2. Who is responsible for the location of property corner stakes?

3–3. Explain what is meant by *front setback.*

3–4. What do National Housing Standards say about
    (a) The retention of existing trees on a lot on which a building is to be built?
    (b) The handling of topsoil on a lot?

3–5. Explain how the approximate corners of a building are located.

3–6. Give two reasons why batter boards should be set to a common level.

3–7. Explain how you would use a leveling rod and level to determine the difference in elevation of two points.

3–8. Why is it important to keep batter boards back several feet from approximate building corners?

3–9. Explain how a corner is located in the excavation from building lines.

3–10. What is the purpose of each of the following parts of a transit level?
    (a) Objective lens
    (b) Eyepiece ring
    (c) A vernier scale
    (d) Horizontal motion tangent screw
    (e) Centering head

3–11. A leveling instrument is set up in the center of the building site illustrated in Fig. 3–3. A rod reading taken at position A is 3.156 ft (1.125 m). Readings taken at positions B, C, and D are recorded as 3.287, 5.246, and 5.718 ft (1.187, 1.904, and 1.988 m), respectively.
    (a) What is the difference in the elevation between point A and each of the other three points?
    (b) In what direction does the lot slope?

# 4

# THE FOUNDATION

The foundation is the supporting base upon which the super-structure of a building is built; it anchors the building to the earth and transmits the loads of that building to the soil beneath. It is therefore of the utmost importance that the foundation be strong, accurately built to size, plumb and level, and of such dimensions that its loads are spread over an area of undisturbed soil large enough to support them safely. Any errors made in the size, shape, or strength of the foundation may lead not only to construction difficulties but may also contribute to instability and future movement.

A building falling into the category of light construction may be constructed on any one of a number of types of foundation, depending on its size, use, location, the prevailing climatic conditions, and the type of soil in the area.

## FOUNDATION TYPES

The types of foundation most commonly used include *concrete full basement foundation, concrete surface foundation, slab-on-ground foundation, pier foundation,* and *preserved wood foundation.*

## FOUNDATION EXCAVATION

Regardless of the type of foundation to be used, some earth removal will be necessary, the amount depending on the type of foundation, type of soil, depth of frost penetration, soil drainage conditions, and the proposed use of the building.

For a full concrete or preserved wood basement foundation, the excavation may be of some considerable depth, while for a slab-on-ground, relatively little earth removal may be required. For a surface, pier, or slab foundation, the excavating may be confined to holes or trenches.

In any case, the top soil and vegetable matter must be removed, and, in localities in which termites occur, all stumps, roots, and other wood debris must be removed to a minimum depth of 12 in. (300 mm) in unexcavated areas under a building.

National building codes specify the *minimum depths* of foundations based on the type of soil encountered and on whether or not the foundation will contain an enclosed heated space. In general, for rock or soils with good drainage, there is no depth limit, but for soils with poor drainage and where there will be no heated space, the minimum depth will normally be 4 ft, 0 in. (1200 mm) or the depth of frost penetration, whichever is greater. The depth of frost penetration in a particular area is established by the local building authority. A stake driven to the proper level, a nearby manhole cover, or other permanent location of known elevation may be used as a reference point from which to measure the depth to be excavated.

The first step in carrying out an excavation is to stake out the area to be excavated. This will include not only the area covered by the building, already established (see Chapter 3), but enough extra space that people may move about outside the foundation forms (see Fig. 4-1). The deeper the excavation, the more necessary it is to allow outside working room. Generally, 2 ft, 0 in. to 3 ft, 0 in. (600–900 mm) on all sides will be sufficient.

**FIGURE 4-1:**  *Excavation space around foundation forms.*

The type of soil involved will also have an influence on the excavation limits. If it is firm and well packed and has good cohesive qualities, it may be possible to excavate and leave perpendicular earth walls standing at the outlined limits. However, if the soil is loose or becomes loose as it dries out, it will be necessary either to *slope the sides* of the excavation, up to about 45°, depending on the type of soil, thus increasing the excavation limits, or to *shore* the sides.

If space does not permit sloping, then shoring becomes necessary. If the excavation walls will hold up, then temporary walls—*cribs*—may be placed against them.

If the soil is very loose, it may be necessary to drive cribbing into the ground around the perimeter of the area and excavate inside it. This type of cribbing may be interlocking sheet piling or wooden or steel piles behind which some type of sheathing is placed as the excavating proceeds.

Another problem involved is the disposal of the earth from the excavation. If the top soil is good loam, it may be required for landscaping on the site after construction, in which case it should be stripped and piled by itself. The remainder of the earth must be disposed of according to circumstances. If some of it is required for backfilling, it should be piled at the site, out of the way of construction. If space does not permit storage, excavation machinery should be used which will allow direct loading onto trucks for removal (see Fig. 4-2).

**FIGURE 4-2:** *Excavating with bucket on wheeled tractor. (Courtesy Hough Machine Co.)*

## EXCAVATING PROCEDURES

The type of machinery used to do the excavating work will depend on the area and depth of the excavation, the type of soil involved, and the available space outside the excavation.

Shallow excavations may be dug with a *bulldozer blade* provided that there is room around the excavation to deposit the soil or another machine to load it onto trucks. Deeper excavations may be carried out with a front-end loader on a tracked or rubber-tired tractor (see Figs. 4–2 and 4–3).

**FIGURE 4–3:**   *Tracked front-end loader.*

**FIGURE 4–4:**   *Power shovel (back hoe).*

Another excellent machine for excavating, particularly for light construction, is a *power shovel* (see Fig. 4–4). It can dig either shallow or deep excavations with straight, vertical walls and a level floor.

Power trenchers are very useful for the walls for houses with crawl spaces or with slab on grade when the soil is stable enough to resist caving. This is especially suited to shallow foundations.

## FOUNDATION CONSTRUCTION

When the excavation has been completed, the work of constructing the foundation can begin. For foundations involving cast-in-place concrete, forms have to be built. For others, gravel must be laid and compacted. In each case, the building lines must be established on the excavation floor with a transit or by dropping a plumb from lines strung on batter boards (see Fig. 4–5).

**FIGURE 4-5:** *Batter boards.*

## CONCRETE FULL BASEMENT FOUNDATION

A *full basement* foundation of concrete is one of the most common types of foundation used in residential construction, because of the extra usable space provided. It consists of walls of cast-in-place concrete or concrete block, not less than 8 in. (200 mm) thick and of such a height that there will be at least 7 ft, 10 in. (2350 mm) of headroom. The walls usually encompass an area of the same dimensions as the floor plan of the building and enclose a floor and livable space.

The walls are supported on *continuous footings* wide enough that the building loads are supported safely by the soil beneath them. Interior loads are carried on one or more *beams*, supported on posts resting on individual *post footings* (see Fig. 4-6).

**FIGURE 4-6:** *Concrete basement.*

## Footing Forms

Forms for the continuous perimeter footings and the interior post footings are the first requirement in the construction of a full basement foundation.

Minimum footing widths for light buildings are given in Table 4–1. The thickness of the footing must not be less than the projection beyond the supported wall or post, except where the footing is suitably reinforced and, in any case, must not be less than 6 in. (150 mm).

**TABLE 4-1:**   *Minimum footing widths for light construction*

| *Number of floors supported* | *Minimum widths of strip footings [in. (mm)]* | | *Minimum area of column footings [ft² (m² )]* |
| :---: | :---: | :---: | :---: |
| | *Supporting external walls* | *Supporting internal walls* | |
| 1 | 10 (250) | 8 (200) | 4.5 (0.4) |
| 2 | 14 (350) | 14 (350) | 8 (0.75) |
| 3 | 18 (450) | 20 (500) | 11 (1.0) |

(Courtesy National Research Council.)

Notes: 1. For each story of masonry veneer over wood-frame construction, width of footings supporting exterior walls are to be increased by 2½ in. (65 mm).

2. For each story of masonry construction other than the foundation walls, width of footings supporting exterior walls must be increased by 5 in. (130 mm).

3. For each story of masonry supported by the footing, the width of footings supporting interior walls must be increased by 4 in. (100mm).

4. Sizes of column footings shown in the table are based on columns spaced 9 ft, 9 in. (3 m) o.c. For other column spacing, the footing areas must be adjusted in proportion to the distance between columns.

The type and thickness of material required for footing forms will depend on their size and on whether they are to be constructed above or below ground level (see Fig. 4–7). If they are to be set above the ground level, they should be built of 1½ in. (38 mm) lumber to withstand the pressure of the freshly placed concrete. Footings below ground level may be made from lighter material.

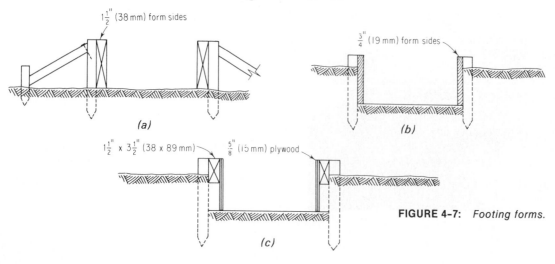

**FIGURE 4-7:**   *Footing forms.*

To lay out and construct footing forms for footings above grade level, proceed as illustrated in Figs. 4–8 through 4–11. These forms can be leveled using a builder's level, a spirit level, or a line level. Forms constructed of 1-in. (25-mm) boards should be held with stakes placed 2–3 ft (600–1000 mm) apart. When 2-in. (38-mm) material is used, the stake spacing may be increased.

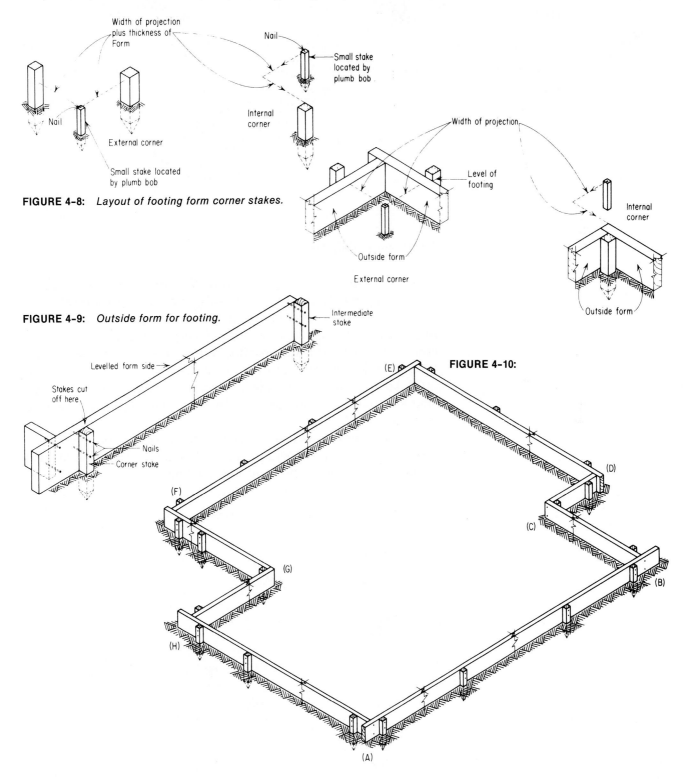

**FIGURE 4-8:** *Layout of footing form corner stakes.*

**FIGURE 4-9:** *Outside form for footing.*

**FIGURE 4-10:**

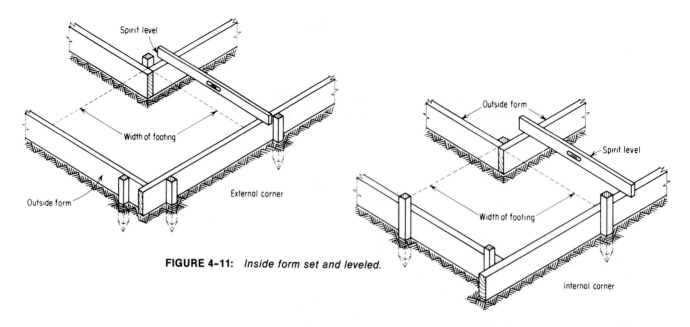

**FIGURE 4-11:** *Inside form set and leveled.*

## Footing-to-Wall Ties

Most concrete walls are poured directly into the footing with no special keying. When walls are subjected to high lateral pressure, some means should be provided to tie the wall to the footing. One method is to insert short pieces of reinforcing into the concrete footing during pouring to provide a tie. These dowels are placed along the centerline at intervals of 4 ft, 0 in. projecting 3 to 4 in. above the footing. Another method involves setting a tapered wooden keyway form into the top of the footing (see Fig. 4-12).

If the keyway is coated with a thick coating of asphalt before the wall is cast, it will provide a barrier against penetration of moisture between the wall and footing.

**FIGURE 4-12:** *Footing-to-wall ties.*

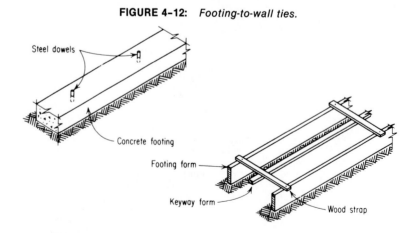

## Post Footings

Individual footings, usually square in plan, are required for the posts which will support the center beam (see Fig. 4-6). The minimum area of such footing is given in Table 4-1, and the depth will normally be a minimum of 6 in. (150 mm) for unreinforced footings. If the column is to be of wood, a layer of polyethylene should be wrapped around the bottom end to protect it from moisture (see Fig. 4-13). Footings for fireplaces and chimneys are normally placed at the same time as other footings. Footings vary in size depending on the soil-bearing capacity and the load they carry.

## Bearing Wall or T-Footing

In place of the conventional center beam, supported by posts, it is common practice to use a *bearing wall*, normally made of a 2 × 6 in. (38 × 140 mm) wood frame (see Chapter 5 for framing details).

The wall is supported on a continuous footing, similar in dimensions to the outside wall footings but with a raised center portion to keep the bottom of the bearing wall plate above the level of the basement floor (see Fig. 4-14).

The bottom part of the form is similar to that used for sidewall footings, while the center section is formed by suspending a narrow form the same width as the bearing wall (see Fig. 4-15).

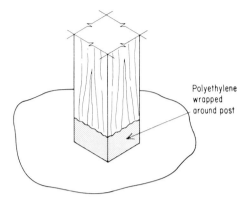

FIGURE 4-13: *Polyethylene around base of wood post.*

Polyethylene wrapped around post

FIGURE 4-14: *T-footing.*

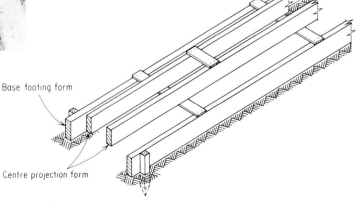

FIGURE 4-15: *T-footing form.*

Base footing form

Centre projection form

## Stepped Footings

Stepped footings are used on steeply sloping lots and where the attached garage or living areas are at basement level. The vertical part of the step should be poured at the same time as the footing. The bottom of the footing should be set level on undisturbed soil below the frost line. The vertical portion of the step should be a minimum of 6 in. (150 mm) thick and the same width as the footing. The vertical portion of the step should not exceed 2 ft (600 mm), and the horizontal portion should not be less than 2 ft (600 mm). In very steep slopes or while building on rock, special footings may be required (see Fig. 4–16).

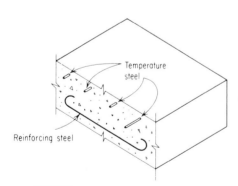

FIGURE 4–16:   *Stepped footing forms.*

FIGURE 4–17:   *Reinforced footing.*

In residential construction, loads are seldom heavy enough that reinforcement is necessary in the footings. But other types of light construction may require reinforced footings, and, in such cases, the reinforcement should be in the form of *deformed rods* with hooked ends, placed *across the width* of the footing. There should be about 3 in. (75mm) of concrete below the reinforcement, and the ends of the hooks should not be closer than 1 in. (25 mm) to the side form (see Fig. 4–17). Post footings are reinforced in the same manner, except that in some cases two layers of bars may be placed to run at right angles to one another—*two-way reinforcement.*

## Wall Forms

When the footing concrete has hardened and at least partially cured, the forms are removed, and the job is ready for the erection of wall forms. There are many methods of building them, and here only a few of the well-known ones will be discussed.

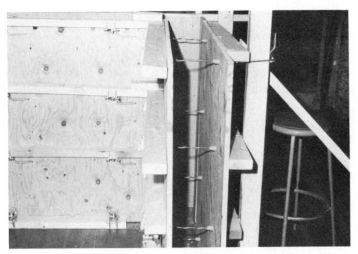

**FIGURE 4-18:** *Wall form section.*

Wall forms all contain the same basic features, although they may vary as to the details of construction and hardware required. The main component is the *sheathing*, which will give the concrete its desired shape. The sheathing is stiffened and aligned by horizontal *walers,* which, in turn, are supported by *bracing.* The two sides of the form are fastened together by a system of *ties* and are held at their proper spacing by *spreaders* (see Fig. 4–18).

A commonly used forming system involves the use of ³⁄₄-in. (19-mm) *plywood panels without any framework, ties* with loops or slots in their ends, and *brackets* or *bars* which are inserted through the tie ends on the outside of the forms. Single *walers* are used to align the forms (see Fig. 4–19).

**FIGURE 4-19:** *Typical form ties.*

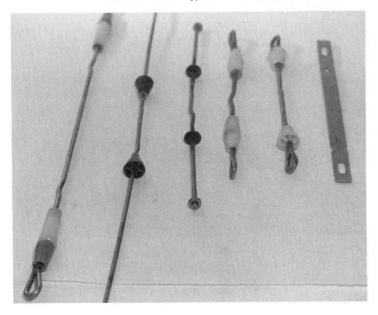

**FIGURE 4-20:**   *(a) Corner rod.*

**FIGURE 4-20:**   *(b) Corner angle.*

Panels are held together at the corner by a vertical rod running through a series of metal straps with looped ends, which are bolted along the panel edge, as illustrated in Fig. 4-20. A metal angle nailed to the panel edges can also be used to hold the panels together at the corner (see Fig. 4-20).

The erection of a wall form by this method is quite simple. First, the plywood panels are slotted to receive the tie ends. The number of ties required will depend on the rate of placement and the temperature, but commonly accepted tie spacings for a 4-ft (1200-mm) rate of placement at 70°F (21°C) are as follows:

For a 2 ft × 8 ft (600 × 2400 mm) panel, the *two* end slots are 8 in. (200 mm) from the top and bottom of the panel and 6 in. (150 mm) from the edges. The remainder are in line, 16 in. (400 mm) o.c.

For a 4 ft × 8 ft (1200 × 2400 mm) panel, the *three* end slots are spaced 16 in. (400 mm) o.c., 8 in. (200 mm) from top, bottom, and edges. The remainder are in line, 16 in. (400 mm) o.c. All panels are treated with oil or other form coating.

The panels are erected as follows:

1. Snap a chalk line on the footing ¾ in. (19 mm) inside the foundation wall line.
2. Nail a 2 × 4 plate to the footing on that line with concrete nails (see Fig. 4-21).
3. Hinge the inside corner panels together with a rod and stand them in place (see Fig. 4-22).
4. Nail them to the plate with 2-in. (50-mm) nails and plumb and brace them temporarily.

**FIGURE 4-21:** *Plate fastened to footing.*

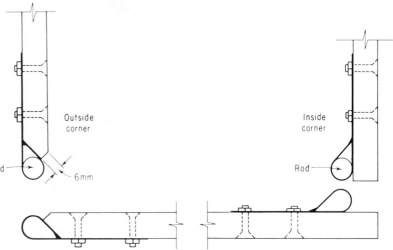

**FIGURE 4-22:** *Corner straps for plywood forms.*

5. Set all the inside panels in place and nail two 2 × 4 (38 × 89 mm) members to them horizontally, one at the top and one at the center (see Fig. 4–23).

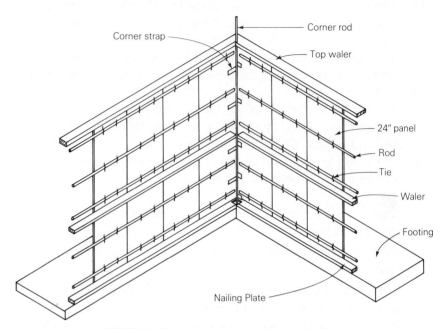

**FIGURE 4-23:**  *Inner panels and walers in place.*

6. Place the ties in the slots and insert the rods or bars as shown in Fig. 4–24.

**FIGURE 4-24:**  *Bars placed in tie ends.*

7. Put outside corners together and set them in place, using temporary wooden spreaders to maintain proper spacing.

8. Place the remainder of the outside panels, guiding the tie ends through the slots as each is erected.

9. Insert the inside rods or bars.

10. Finally, align the outside form and brace it as required from the two single walers.

In a cast-in-place floor system the inside forms are set and firmly held in position first (see Fig. 4–25). The outside forms are a little longer to allow fastening to the outside of the floor frame (see Fig. 4–26). When a straighter wall is required, a system of wall forms using 2 × 4 walers is recommended (see Fig. 4–27). Strongbacks give vertical stiffness to the forms. This system is more rigid and will not deflect as much due to the concrete pressure. The bottom waler is fastened to the footing as shown in Fig. 4–28. Figure 4–29 illustrates the method used to support the walers and how corners are supported.

**FIGURE 4–26:** *Outside forms in cast-in-place system.*

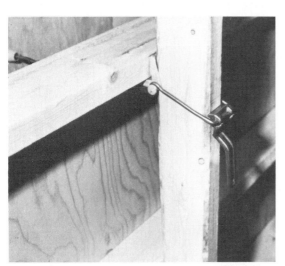

**FIGURE 4–25:** *Inside forms set in cast-in-place system.*

**FIGURE 4–27**

*(a) Single waler system with vertical strongback.*

*(b) Double waler system.*

*(b) Waler bracket and tie.*

**FIGURE 4-28:** *Fastening bottom waler (single waler system).*

*(a) Corner support.*

FIGURE 4-29

## Beam Pocket Form

In designs in which the floor frame is to be built on top of the foundation (box sill), it is necessary to provide a pocket in two opposite foundation walls in which the ends of the center beam may rest [see Fig. 4-30(b)]. It is formed by a box, wide enough to allow for an air space around the end of the beam [see Fig. 4-30(a)] and deep enough to allow for a bearing plate under the end of the beam and for the top of the beam to be 1½ in. (38 mm) above the top of the foundation wall.

FIGURE 4-30: *Beam pocket in concrete foundation.*

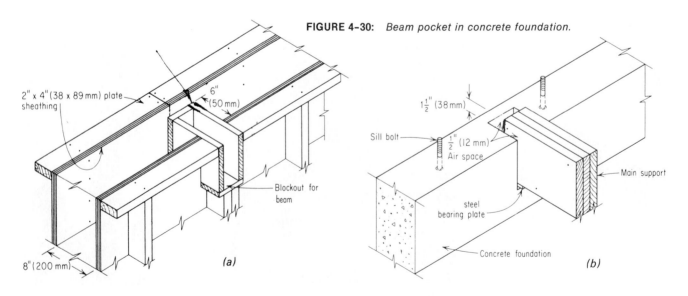

## Sill Plate Bolts (Wood Floor Frame)

Also, in cases where box sill construction is used, the floor frame must be anchored to the foundation walls. This is done by bolting a 2 × 6 (38 × 140 mm) *sill plate* to the top of the foundation and nailing the floor frame to it. The anchors are ½-in. (12.7-mm) bolts, spaced approximately 4 ft (1200 mm) o.c., set into the concrete [see Fig. 4-30(b)] to hold the sill plate in position. They may be set after the concrete has been placed and before it has hardened, or they may be suspended from wood straps nailed across the top of the form before concrete is placed.

## Sill Plates (Steel Floor Frame)

Several different methods are used for setting a sill plate in a foundation wall if the plate is to support a steel floor frame. If the building is to have conventional wood siding or similar finish, a 2 × 4 (38 × 89 mm) sill plate is set into the top *outside* edge of the wall form and held in place by straps, as illustrated in Fig. 4-31. Anchor bolts are suspended from the sill, to be cast into the concrete.

If the foundation wall is to support brick veneer exterior finish, the sill plate is cast into the top *inside* edge of the wall (see Fig. 4-32).

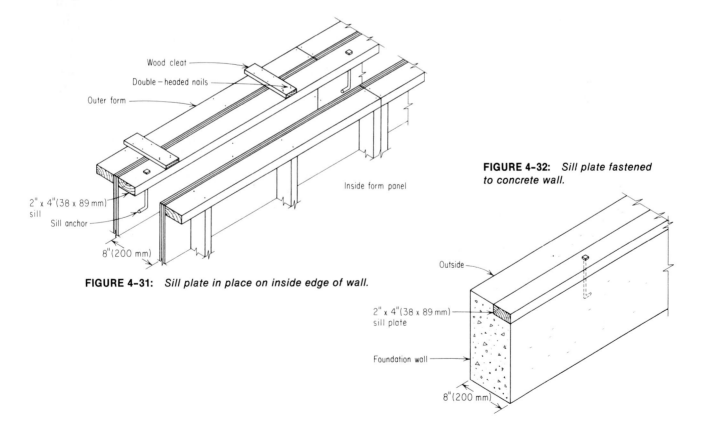

Wood cleat
Double – headed nails
Outer form
2" x 4"(38 x 89 mm) sill
Sill anchor
8"(200 mm)
Inside form panel

**FIGURE 4-31:** *Sill plate in place on inside edge of wall.*

**FIGURE 4-32:** *Sill plate fastened to concrete wall.*

Outside
2" x 4"(38 x 89 mm) sill plate
Foundation wall
8"(200 mm)

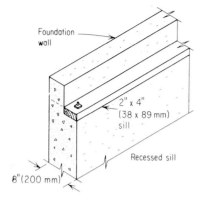

**FIGURE 4-33:** *Recessed sill plate.*

The design may call for the top of steel joists to be flush with the top of the foundation. The sill plate must then be *recessed* below the top of the wall by the depth of the joists (see Fig. 4-33).

### "Cast-in" Wood Floor Frame

Another method of anchoring the floor frame to the foundation is the *cast-in joist* system. Instead of resting on top of the foundation, the ends of the floor joists and the beam ends are treated and embedded in the concrete (see Fig. 4-34).

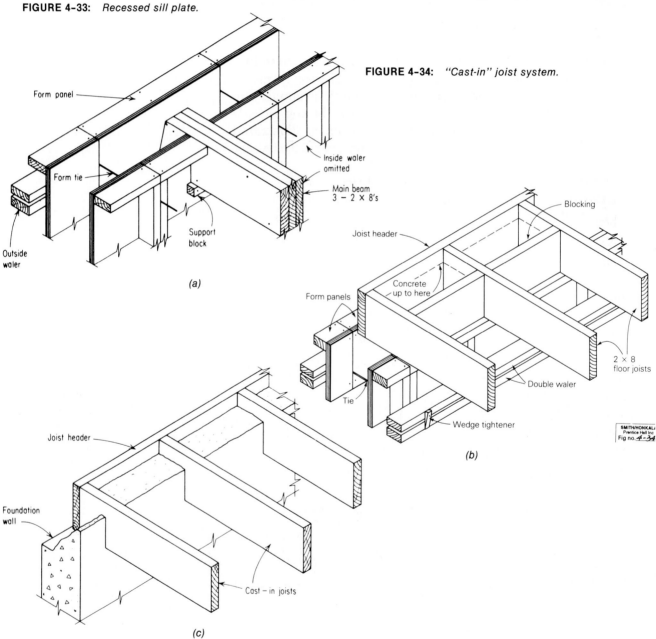

**FIGURE 4-34:** *"Cast-in" joist system.*

As a result, the beam and floor joists must be set in place before concrete is placed. the procedure is as follows:

1. Treat the ends of the beam and one end of each joist with wood preservative.
2. Cut notches in two opposite inside wall forms, the width and depth of the beam, and nail a support block at the bottom of each notch (see Fig. 4-34).
3. Lay out the joists with one end resting on the center beam and the other on the wall forms.
4. Lay off the header joists according to the specified joist centers and nail the joists to them at these locations (see Fig. 4-35).

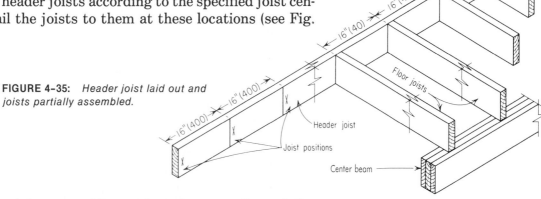

**FIGURE 4-35:** *Header joist laid out and joists partially assembled.*

5. Position the joist assembly so that the outer face of the header joists is flush with the inner face of the outside form.
6. Nail *blocking* flush with the inner face of the form sheathing.

## Door and Window Openings

Openings for doors and windows may be blocked out in two ways. One method is to secure the door or window *frame* into the form in its correct position. Wood frames must be made to coincide with the wall thickness, and metal frames are produced to fit various wall thicknesses. Wood frames should have nailers secured to their outside surface so that they will not be able to move in the wall (see Fig. 4-36). Wood frames must also be braced diagonally, horizontally, and vertically so that the pressure of the concrete will not change their shape during placing.

**FIGURE 4-36:** *Window frame set into forms.*

Another method of forming openings is to set *rough bucks* into the form. A rough buck is a frame made from 2-in. (38-mm) material with *outside dimensions* equal to those of the frame to be used. *Wedge-shaped nailers* are nailed to the outside of the buck as illustrated in Fig. 4–37. After the concrete is placed and hardened and the forms removed, the rough buck is also removed, leaving the key embedded in the concrete. The door or window frame is then inserted into the opening and held in place by nailing it to the nailer.

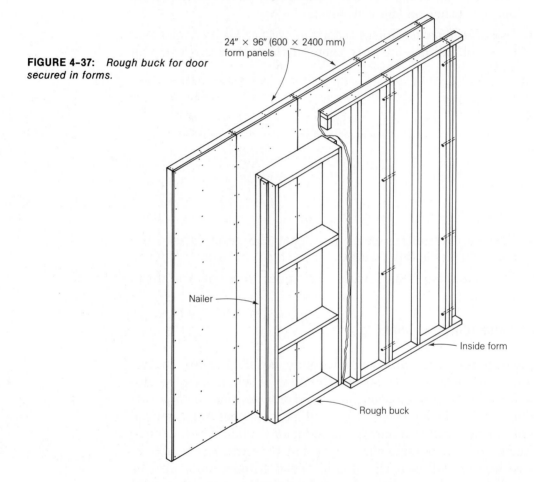

**FIGURE 4–37:** *Rough buck for door secured in forms.*

## CONCRETE BLOCK FOUNDATION WALLS

*Concrete block* is the name given to a type of masonry unit made from a mixture of expanded shale or clay, some fine aggregate and cement, with or without color added. A great variety of blocks are available, in a wide range of types, shapes, and sizes, each for a specific purpose. Figure 4–38 illustrates some of the common shapes used in basement construction. Concrete block is mainly used for foundations or for exterior walls in light construction. Regardless of the use to which blocks are to be put, a basic requirement for good results, both from the standpoint of structural stability and good appearance, is good mortar.

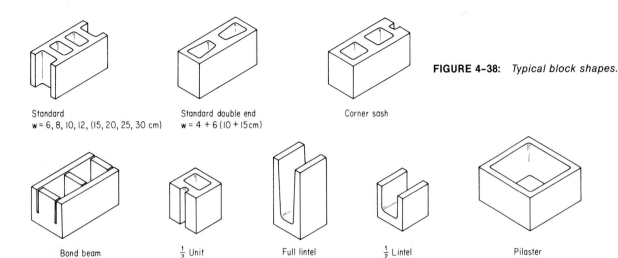

**FIGURE 4-38:** *Typical block shapes.*

Standard
w = 6, 8, 10, 12, (15, 20, 25, 30 cm)

Standard double end
w = 4 + 6 (10 + 15cm)

Corner sash

Bond beam

½ Unit

Full lintel

½ Lintel

Pilaster

## Mortar

Mortar serves a number of purposes, the main one being to *join the masonry units together* into a strong, well-knit structure. In addition, mortar is required to *produce tight seals between units*, to *bond to steel reinforcement*, *metal ties*, and *anchor bolts*, to *provide a bed* which will accommodate variations in the size of units, and to *provide an architectural effect* by the various treatments given to mortar joints in exposed walls.

Masonry mortar is composed of one or more *cementatious materials* (normal portland cement, masonry cement, and hydrated lime), clean, well-graded *masonry sand*, and enough *water* to produce a plastic, workable mixture. In addition, *admixtures* (accelerators, retarders, and water-reducing agents) may be added for some special purpose.

A number of mortar types are recognized, based on strength and composed of varying amounts of cement and hydrated lime, by volume. Table 4–2 indicates the types and the proportions of ingredients in each case.

To obtain good workability and allow the development of the maximum strength possible, mortar ingredients must be thoroughly mixed. Whenever possible, the mixing should be done by machine, except when only a small quantity of mortar is required.

**TABLE 4-2:** *Mortar types by cement and lime proportions*

| | | Parts by volume | | |
| Specification | Mortar type | Portland cement | Masonry cement | Hydrated lime or lime putty |
| --- | --- | --- | --- | --- |
| | M | 1 | 1 | — |
| | | 1 | — | ¼ |
| | S | ½ | 1 | — |
| | | 1 | — | Over ¼ to ½ |
| For plain masonry | N | — | 1 | — |

Note: The total aggregate will not be less than two and one quarter or more than three and one half times the total volume of cementitious material.

**FIGURE 4-39:** *Face-shell bedding.*

**FIGURE 4-40:** *Full mortar bedding.*

**FIGURE 4-41:** *Test lay-up for spacing.*

Mixing time should be from 3 to 5 minutes after all ingredients have been added. A shorter mixing time may result in poor-quality mortar, while a longer mixing time may adversely affect the air content of mortars made with air-entraining cements.

If the mortar becomes stiff because of water evaporation, it may be *retempered* by the addition of a little water and thorough remixing. However, if the stiffness is due to partial hydration, the material should be discarded. Mortar should be used within 2 hours after the original mixing if the temperature is above 80°F (26°C) or within 3 hours if the temperature is below that point.

Two methods are used for applying mortar to concrete masonry units. One is to apply the mortar to the two long edges only. This is known as *face-shell bedding* (see Fig. 4-39). The other is to apply mortar to the cross webs as well as the face shells, and this is known as *full mortar bedding* (see Fig. 4-40).

## Laying Blocks

The first step in laying blocks is to locate accurately the positions of the corners of the building on the footings and establish the line of the outside of the wall. This can be done by taking the dimensions from the plans and snapping chalk lines on the footing to indicate the corners and building lines. Then the first course may be laid without mortar to ascertain what spacing is required between blocks (see Fig. 4-41), although, in general, that spacing should be ³⁄₈ in. (10 mm) in order to maintain a 16-in. (400-mm) module, center to center of mortar joints.

Now remove the blocks, spread a full bead of mortar long enough to accommodate at least three blocks, and lay the corner block, making sure that it is *to the line, plumb,* and *level*. Butter the ends of the face shells of the second block, bring it over its final position, and set it down into the mortar bed, while at the same time pressing it against the previously laid block to ensure a tight vertical joint (see Fig. 4-42).

**FIGURE 4-42:** *Full mortar bed for first course.*

Now butter the ends of several blocks, as shown in Fig. 4-43, so that they can be laid up in quick succession. After several blocks have been laid each way, use a straightedge and level to make sure that the blocks are *aligned*, brought to the *correct level*, and *plumb*, as illustrated in Fig. 4-44.

After the first course is laid, build up the corners as shown in Fig. 4-45. Use a tape to ensure that the bedding joints are maintained at the same thickness for each course, so that the four corners will remain level with one another. Use the straightedge and level frequently to make sure that the corners are plumb and level (see Fig. 4-46).

**FIGURE 4-43:** *Mortar on block ends.*

**FIGURE 4-44:** *Block aligning, leveling, and plumbing.*

**FIGURE 4-45:** *Building up corners.*

**FIGURE 4-46:** *Plumbing and leveling corners.*

**FIGURE 4-47:** *Line from corner to corner.*

When the corners have been built up, the walls are completed between them. To do so, a line is run from corner to corner, along the top edge of the course to be laid (see Fig. 4-47). The line is held by a *line holder* attached to each corner and adjusted so that the line is at the correct height—level with the top of the block. The line is then drawn as tight as possible to provide a horizontal guide for the blocks in the course.

The bed joint mortar is then laid, and the ends of enough blocks buttered to complete the course. Set each block carefully and tap it down until it comes to the line (see Fig. 4-47).

**FIGURE 4-48:** *Closure block set in place.*

The final block in each course is the *closure* block. Butter all the edges of the opening and the four vertical edges of the closure block. Set it carefully into place (see Fig. 4-48) and make sure that the mortar is pressed firmly into the joint. Finally, remove any extruded mortar that appears on both the exterior and interior faces of the wall.

After the mortar is set hard enough that it can just be dented by the thumb nail, the joint may be *tooled*—shaped and compacted. Figure 4-49 illustrates the tooling of a concave joint.

Joint reinforcing is usually placed in the bed joint of every second or third row in a block wall to provide a tie between the units in the wall. They are usually galvanized sections of wire, generally of the truss or ladder type (see Fig. 4-50).

**FIGURE 4-49:** *Concave mortar joint.*

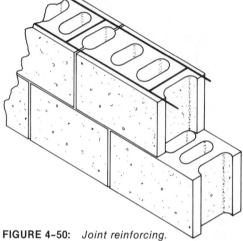

**FIGURE 4-50:** *Joint reinforcing.*

### Plate Anchored to Block Wall

When a wooden plate is to be fastened to the top of a block wall, anchor bolts are used. They should be ½ in. (12 mm) in diameter, 18 in. (450 mm) long, and not more than 4 ft (1.2 m) apart. Lay a piece of metal lath over the cell in which the bolt will be set, two courses below the top of the wall, as shown in Fig. 4-51. When the wall is complete, fill the cell with concrete and set the bolt in place so that at least 2 in. (50 mm) project above the wall.

### Lintels

The wall load over door and window openings in block construction must be supported by a horizontal member which spans the opening and is carried on solid bearing at each end. Such a member is called a *lintel*, and it may be provided by two different methods. One is to use a precast concrete lintel, designed for the span, with its ends resting on the block at each side of the opening (see Fig. 4-52).

**FIGURE 4-51:** *Setting anchor bolts in block wall.*

The other method involves the use of *lintel blocks* that are laid across the top of the opening and filled with reinforced concrete. Lintel blocks must be supported until the concrete has hardened, and this may be done in one of two ways. One is to set the window frame in place and use it to support the blocks, and the other is to provide a temporary support, which will be removed when the concrete has reached its design strength.

FIGURE 4-52: *Precast lintel in place.*

## Watertight Block Walls

To ensure that block walls below grade will be watertight, they must be parged and sealed. Parging consists of applying two ¼-in. (6-mm) coats of plaster, using the same mortar that was used for laying the blocks (see Fig. 4-53). Dampen the wall before applying the plaster in order to get a better bond. The first coat should extend from 6 in. (150 mm) above the grade line down to the footing. When it is partially set up, roughen with a wire brush and then allow it to harden for at least 24 hours. Before the second coat is applied, the wall should be dampened again and the plaster kept damp for 48 hours.

(a)

(b)

(c)

FIGURE 4-53: *Parging block wall.*

In poorly drained soils, the plaster should be covered with two coats of an asphalt waterproofing, brushed on (see Fig. 4-54).

In heavy, wet soils, the wall may be further protected by laying a line of drainage tile around the outside of the footing to prevent a buildup of moisture in the area (see Fig. 4-54).

*(a) Waterproofing below grade.*

*(b) Weeping hose.*

**FIGURE 4–54**

### Pilasters

A pilaster is a type of *column*, incorporated into a block wall for the purpose of providing additional lateral support and/or providing a larger bearing surface for beam ends carried on the wall.

In concrete block construction, the pilaster is formed by means of a *pilaster block*, one of which is illustrated in Fig. 4–38. Pilaster blocks may be filled with reinforced concrete to give them additional strength.

## CONCRETE SURFACE FOUNDATION

A surface foundation also consists of concrete or block walls, but they extend into the earth only far enough to reach below the top soil or below the frost line in areas where frost penetration is a problem. Surface foundations are especially popular in regions where there is little exposure to freezing temperatures since this type of foundation is less expensive than a full basement. The crawl space can be either treated as heated area or ventilated in systems where the floor system is insulated. Forms for a concrete surface foundation are the same as those for a full basement, except the wall forms are not as high. Masonry surface foundation walls are built in the same way as full masonry basements.

### Heated Crawl Space

All crawl spaces must be at least 1 ft (300 mm) high. When equipment installed in the crawl space requires servicing, this space must be at least 2 ft (600 mm) high. In some cases this area is enlarged to provide storage space for the building. This space is usually accessed from the interior of the building. Intermediate floor supports are provided by pouring strip T-footings in the interior of the excavation (see Fig. 4-55). A short bearing wall is built on this footing extending up to support the underside of the floor frame (see Fig. 4-56). Rigid insulation is applied to the interior or exterior of the foundation wall and under the concrete floor. In areas affected by termites, the insulation should be placed on the inside. Termite barriers, as illustrated in Fig. 4-57, are usually placed on the outside of the wall at the base of the floor frame to provide protection from damage. Stepping the top of the foundation wall (see Fig. 4-58) provides additional protection to the floor frame. A moisture barrier (polyethylene) is often placed under the concrete slab to ensure a dry floor. Another method of providing support for the

**FIGURE 4-55:**  *Concrete surface foundation.*

**FIGURE 4-56:**  *Bearing wall supporting floor frame.*

FIGURE 4-57: *Termite barrier.*

FIGURE 4-58: *Ledge for floor joists.*

FIGURE 4-59: *Post footings.*

floor frame is to pour several post footings in the excavation and set posts and beams to support the floor system (see Fig. 4-59).

## Ventilated (Unheated) Crawl Space

In an unheated crawl space the method used to build the foundation is the same as for a heated crawl space. The only differences are that only the floor above the crawl space is insulated and no insulation is put under the concrete slab or on the foundation walls. The insulation between the joists can be supported with a covering such as an air barrier house wrap, preventing the wind from stripping the heat out of the insulation. The space must also be ventilated to prevent deterioration of the framing members. The working conditions are somewhat restrictive and the actual installation of the insulation can be difficult and time consuming. In general, unheated crawl spaces are not recommended in colder regions.

## SLAB-ON-GROUND FOUNDATION

Many residential buildings are built without basements. This is very common in southern regions where it is not necessary to excavate to reach a frost line. Two types of concrete floor construction are the *combined slab and foundation* and the *independent concrete slab and foundation walls.*

## Combined Slab and Foundation

The combined slab and foundation consists of a shallow perimeter footing or beam that is placed at the same time as the concrete floor slab. This type of foundation is especially useful in

**FIGURE 4-60:** *(a) Slab-on-ground foundation.*

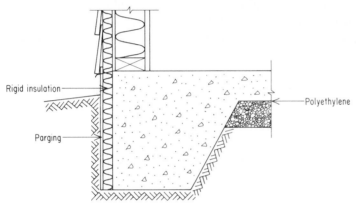

Rigid insulation

Parging

Polyethylene

**FIGURE 4-60:** *(b) Combined slab and foundation.*

southern regions where frost penetration is not a problem and where good predictable ground conditions exist (see Fig. 4-60). The footing is reinforced, and the bottom of the footing should be at least 12 in. (300 mm) below grade line. This thickening of the slab may also occur under interior load-bearing walls. The outside edge of the slab can be stepped as illustrated in Fig. 4-61 to provide not only a support for a brick veneer, but also protection from water penetration.

**FIGURE 4-61:** *Stepped edge on slab.*

**FIGURE 4-62:**  *Insulating edge of slab.*

Insulation of this type of concrete slab is done by placing a strip of rigid insulation around the outside edge of the slab, as illustrated in Fig. 4–62. Rigid insulation is also placed under the entire surface of the slab.

### Independent Concrete Slab and Foundation Walls

An independent slab-on-ground foundation consists of perimeter footings and stub walls surrounding a reinforced concrete slab cast directly on the ground. The walls will extend down to solid undisturbed soil below frost level (see Fig. 4–63). However, in areas of deep frost penetration, it may be impractical to extend the footings down to below the frost line, and instead the footing is placed on a well-drained gravel pad at least 5 in. (125 mm) in depth.

The slab must not be less than 4 in. (100 mm) in thickness, supported by at least 5 in. (125 mm) of clean, coarse, well-packed gravel or similar granular material.

**FIGURE 4-63:**  *Independent slab and foundation wall.*

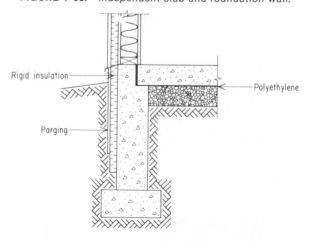

Forms for the footings for the perimeter bearing wall will be identical to those for a surface foundation and normally will be built in a shallow trench.

Walls may be cast-in-place concrete or concrete blocks and, in many cases, may not exceed 16–32 in. (400–800 mm) in height. If concrete walls are specified, forms for them will be similar to those for other concrete walls except for the height. Cast-in plates at the top of the wall are easily fastened inside the form prior to casting, providing a base connection for framed walls (see Fig. 4-64). A ledge is usually formed in the wall to receive the slab. Inserting slab reinforcing into the concrete wall will also provide support (see Fig. 4-65). Placing piers inside the perimeter walls will give the slab additional support (see Fig. 4-66). Continue the reinforcing from the piers into the slab, providing a positive tie.

**FIGURE 4-64:**  *Connection at top of foundation wall.*     **FIGURE 4-65:**  *Reinforcing inserted into concrete wall.*

**FIGURE 4-66:**  *Pier supports for concrete slab.*

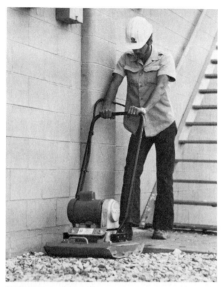

**FIGURE 4-67:** *Power compactor at work. (Courtesy Wacker Co.)*

When the walls are complete, the earth within them is leveled and compacted to within approximately 9 in. (225 mm) of the top of the wall. A layer of gravel is added and compacted to a level within 4 in. (100 mm) from the top. Compaction is usually carried out by a power-driven compactor, similar to that shown in Fig. 4-67.

Two very important considerations with this type of foundation are *moisture control* and *insulation,* and Figs. 4-60 and 4-63 illustrate typical slab constructions with these two factors in mind.

A continuous waterproof membrane is laid over the entire compacted gravel surface to prevent the migration of moisture into the slab from below. Six-mil polyethelene is often used for this membrane. A strip of rigid insulation at least 2 in. (50 mm) thick is applied to the outer exposed wall surface with asphalt adhesive. Then rigid insulation is laid on the entire surface. This insulation may only be placed around the perimeter or may be eliminated in warmer regions. Where it is used on exterior surfaces, it should be covered with a ½ in. (12 mm) of cement parging on wire lath. Finally, welded wire mesh or ⅜ in. (10-mm) steel placed 24 in. (600 mm) on center in both directions is placed over the whole surface, and then concrete is placed over the reinforcing.

## PIER FOUNDATION

**FIGURE 4-68**

A pier foundation is one in which the building is constructed on a number of beams, with each supported by several *piers* or posts of pressure-treated wood, masonry, or concrete. Each post rests on an individual concrete footing or is used without a footing when the soil has sufficient bearing capacity (see Fig. 4-68).

Pier footings should be taken down to below the frost line or placed on well-drained gravel pads.

*(a) Pier foundation.*

*(b) Post footing.*

Forms for pier footings are usually built in individual excavations, square in plan, and may be *rectangular* or *stepped*. The footing area is based on the amount of load carried by each one and the type of soil on which it rests. The construction of these footing forms is illustrated in Fig. 4–69.

Footings which are to support wooden piers should have a base plate set in the center of the top surface to anchor the pier in place (see Fig. 4–70). Mortar is sufficient to anchor the masonry pier to the footing.

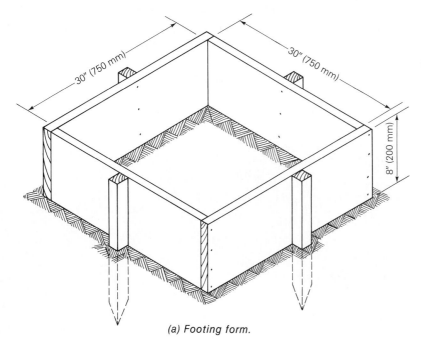

**FIGURE 4-69**

30" (750 mm)

30" (750 mm)

8" (200 mm)

(a) Footing form.

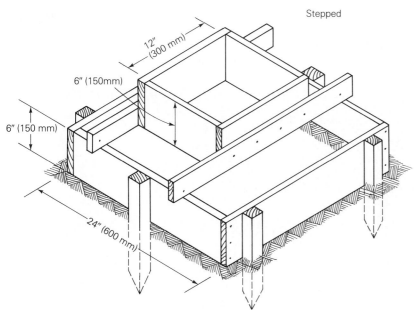

Stepped

12" (300 mm)

6" (150mm)

6" (150 mm)

24" (600 mm)

(b) Stepped footing form.

**FIGURE 4-70:** *Base plate.*

## PRESERVED WOOD FOUNDATION

A preserved wood foundation is a complete *wood-frame founda-tion* system, built with preservative-treated lumber and in-tended for buildings falling into the light construction category. In this system, all wood exposed to decay hazard is pressure-treated with chemical preservatives which permanently impreg-nate the wood cells to the degree that makes the wood resistant to attack by decay organisms and termites.

It can be built as a *full basement* foundation (see Fig. 4–71) with a *concrete slab floor, wood sleeper floor,* or *suspended wood floor* or as a *surface* foundation (see Fig. 4–72).

**FIGURE 4-71**

*(a) Preserved wood foundation with pressure-treated plank footings. (Courtesy of Forest Industries of B.C.)*

*(b) Preserved wood foundation with concrete footings.*

**FIGURE 4-72:** *Surface foundation.*

## Site Preparation

After the excavation has been completed to the desired level, service and drain lines and a sump, if necessary, are installed and the trenches backfilled and compacted. In some localities, the sump pit may be replaced by a 4 in. (100 mm) perforated, vertical standpipe, at least 24 in. (600 mm) high, surrounded by 16 in. (400 mm) of washed, coarse gravel. The standpipe should extend up through the floor and be capped by a cleanout plug. No drainage system is required for unexcavated crawl spaces if the final grade inside the crawl space is equal to or higher than the grade outside.

Next, 5 in. (125 mm) of clean gravel is laid on undisturbed soil over an area extending 12 in. (300 mm) beyond the dimensions of the building and leveled. The gravel under all *footing plates* is compacted at least 12 in. (300 mm) beyond the edges of the plates to provide good bearing for loads.

## Footings

Continuous wood footings, consisting of the *wood footing plates* and the *compacted gravel bed* beneath them, are the most practical and economical for this type of foundation, since they eliminate the building of forms and placement of concrete (see Fig. 4-73).

Wood footing plates are placed directly on the leveled, compacted gravel bed, butted together at end joints and wall intersections. The treated lumber can be ordered in specified lengths

**FIGURE 4-73:** *Continuous wood footings.*

**FIGURE 4-74**

(a) Post footing.

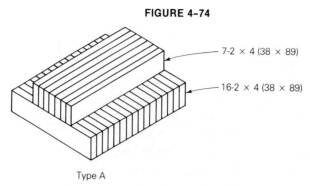

7-2 × 4 (38 × 89)

16-2 × 4 (38 × 89)

Type A

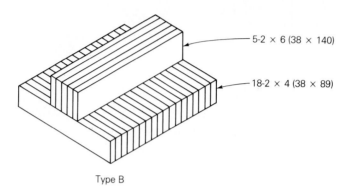

5-2 × 6 (38 × 140)

18-2 × 4 (38 × 89)

Type B

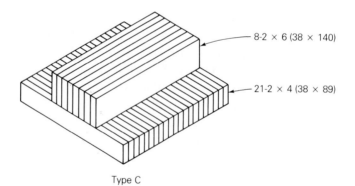

8-2 × 6 (38 × 140)

21-2 × 4 (38 × 89)

Type C

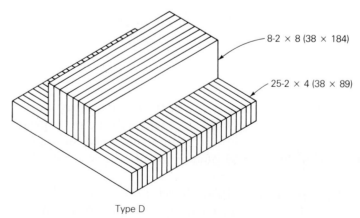

8-2 × 8 (38 × 184)

25-2 × 4 (38 × 89)

Type D

(b) Wood post footings.

to suit the footing layout, and members may extend beyond the line of the wall at corners to avoid the cutting of plates wherever possible. However, if members must be cut, the exposed ends must be thoroughly saturated with wood preservative.

*Concrete footings* can be used under wood foundation walls instead of wood footings. They are more convenient on sloped lots, where stepped footings are necessary (Fig. 4–75). They can be placed on a gravel bed or directly on undisturbed soil. When they are placed on undisturbed soil, drainage should be provided through the footing, as illustrated in Fig. 4–76. The width of concrete footings supporting exterior walls should be the same width as those indicated in Table 4–1.

**FIGURE 4-75:** *Concrete footing under wood foundation.*

**FIGURE 4-76:** *Concrete footing on undisturbed soil.*

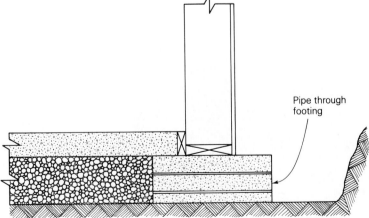

Pipe through footing

When a beam and posts are used to support the interior loads rather than a bearing wall, post footings may be either concrete or preservative-treated wood. Concrete footings are similar to those in conventional foundations, and Fig. 4–74 illustrates the construction of wood post footings for various loading conditions. Post footings may be set on undisturbed soil below the gravel bed to avoid the top of the footings interfering with the basement floor.

### Foundation Walls

Wood foundation walls, consisting of a *frame of studs* with *single top and bottom plate, sheathed with plywood* and all treated with preservative, may be prefabricated in sections in a shop or completely assembled on site. Where plywood sheets are applied horizontally, *blocking* is required between studs at the plywood joint. In addition, all plywood joints are caulked with sealant (see Fig. 4–77). Double top plates are required where the floor joists are offset more than 2 in. (50 mm) from the foundation studs.

**FIGURE 4–77**

*(a) Prefabricated foundation walls.*

*(b) Blocking at plywood joints.*

*(c) Sealant at joints.*

For full basement construction, walls are 8 ft (2.4 m) high for slab and sleeper floors and 10 ft (3.0 m) high for suspended wood floors. The size and spacing of studs depend on the *building loads, species* and *grade of lumber,* and the *height of backfill,* which in turn depends on the depth of the excavation. The thickness of plywood used for sheathing depends on the *direction of face grain* (that is, whether the face grain is parallel or perpendicular to the studs), the *stud spacing,* and the *height of the backfill.*

Most governing authorities require that (1) size and spacing of members in a pressure-treated wood *foundation* are determined by using engineering principles, (2) that the foundation be inspected by a *professional engineer* or a *registered architect,* and that the plans and specifications are stamped by a *registered engineer or architect.*

Plywood may be fastened to the frame with hot dipped galvanized nails or corrosion resistant staples, minimum length 2 in. (50 mm). Nails and staples are spaced 6 in. (150 mm) o.c. along outside edges and 12 in. (300 mm) o.c. along intermediate supports. Framing and fastening requirements for openings in wall panels for windows or landings of split level entrances are given in Fig. 4-78.

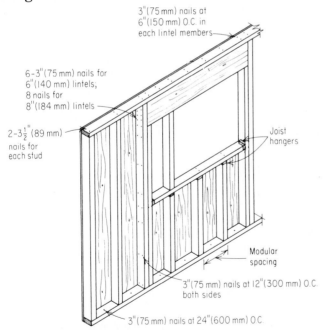

**FIGURE 4–78:** *Nailing requirements at openings in preserved wood foundation wall.*

All joints between plywood panels below grade are sealed by pressing the plywood edge into a bead of sealant. The exterior of the foundation walls below grade is also covered with a 6-mil polyethylene membrane, extending from a minimum of 3 in. (75 mm) above the finished grade line to the bottom of the

**FIGURE 4-79:** *Polyethylene membrane.*

footing plate, where it should be cut off. The membrane *should not* extend under the gravel pad or under the footing plate (see Fig. 4–79).

The polyethylene is cemented to the sheathing at the top edge by a 6-in. (150-mm) band of adhesive (see Fig. 4–80). It is also protected at the grade level by a 12 in. wide (300 mm wide) strip of treated plywood, set with its top edge at least 3 in. (75 mm) above the finished grade line. A strip of sealant about 3 in. (75 mm) wide is applied to the top inside face of the plywood before it is nailed to the foundation wall.

The polyethylene sheet exterior protection is not required if all surfaces below grade are coated with two coats of bituminous damp-proofing material applied by brush or spray.

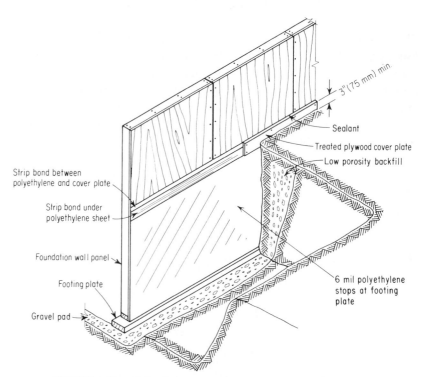

**FIGURE 4–80:** *Polyethylene membrane on exterior of preserved wood foundation wall.*

## Concrete Slab Floors

Concrete slab floors used in conjunction with wood foundations are similar to those used for conventional basement floors. Basically, they consist of a minimum 4-in. (100-mm) concrete slab, placed over a 5-in. (125-mm) gravel bed, with a 6-mil polyethylene moisture barrier between concrete and gravel.

To transmit lateral soil loads from the wall into the slab, the top edge of the slab must butt directly against the bottom ends of the wall studs. This may be done by fastening a continu-

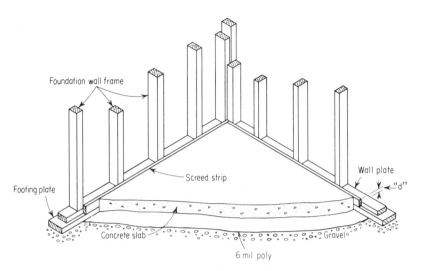

**FIGURE 4-81:** *Concrete slab floor in wood foundation basement.*

ous, treated wooden strip along the lower edge of the foundation wall (see Fig. 4-81) wide enough that distance "d" will be from 1 to 2 in. (25-45 mm), depending on stud spacing and depth of backfill. This strip can be used as a screed to level the concrete slab and will remain in place after the concrete has hardened.

## Wood Sleeper Floors

Wood sleeper floors (see Fig. 4-82) are damp-proofed by laying 6-mil, 4-ft-wide (1200-mm-wide) strips of polyethylene, over-lapped 4 in. (100 mm) at the joints—not a continuous mem-brane—over the leveled gravel bed.

The 2 × 4 in. (38 × 89 mm) treated wood *sleepers* are placed on the polyethylene cover at spacings of from 4 to 6 ft (1200-1800 mm), depending on the depth of the floor joists to be used. Then floor joists, 2 × 4 in. (38 × 89 mm) or wider, span between the footing plates and the sleepers with at least 1½ in. (38 mm) bearing on the footing plate. To achieve this, it may be necessary to use wider footing plates than the design requires.

**FIGURE 4-82:** *Wood floor frame on wood sleepers.*

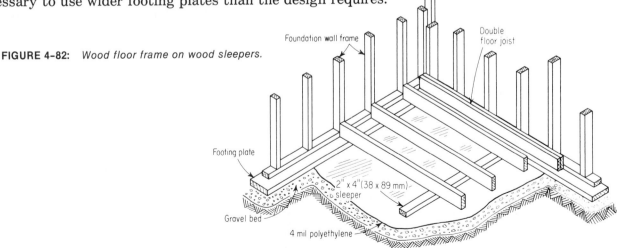

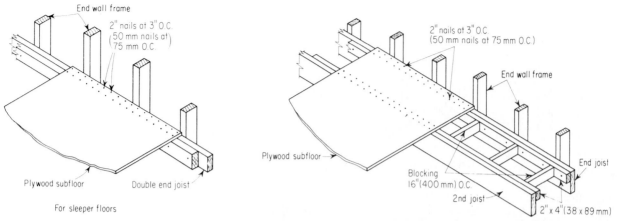

**FIGURE 4-83:** *Sleeper and suspended floors end nailing and extra framing.*

Joists are placed in line with foundation wall studs (see Fig. 4–82) and butt in line over the sleeper supports. They are toe-nailed to the sleepers and to the wall studs with at least two 3-in. (75-mm) nails at each junction.

Plywood subflooring is installed over the floor joists and acts as a diaphragm to resist lateral earth loads. For the thickness of plywood required, see Table 5–1, page 143.

To ensure the proper transfer of lateral soil loads from the *end* walls to the floor frame and plywood subfloor, it is necessary to provide additional nailing and, in some cases, additional framing. See Fig. 4–83 to illustrate this additional support.

## Suspended Wood Floors

Joists for a suspended wood floor are supported above the gravel base on a continuous 2 × 4 in. (38 × 89 mm) *ledger* at the foundation walls and by a low bearing wall at the inner end (see Fig. 4–84).

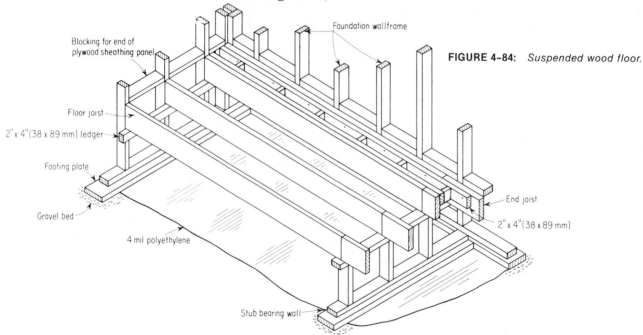

**FIGURE 4-84:** *Suspended wood floor.*

Joists are placed directly in line with the foundation wall studs and butted in line over the bearing wall (see Fig. 4–84). Plywood subflooring is applied over the joists and nailed as required in the same manner as for sleeper floors.

As was the case with wood sleeper floors, additional framing and nailing may be required to ensure the proper transfer of lateral soil loads to the floor (see Fig. 4–83).

## CONCRETE PLACING

Regardless of the care spent in building forms, the final test of the strength and durability of the foundation being built will lie in the quality of the concrete used. That quality will depend on a number of factors, all of major importance. They include the following:

1. Clean and well-graded aggregate and properly proportioned fine and coarse aggregate.

2. Clean water; water fit for human consumption is the best test.

3. The amount of water used in the mix per unit of cement—a matter of primary importance. This ratio to a large extent controls the strength of the concrete. The less water used, within limits, the stronger the concrete will be, and, conversely, the more water used, the less strength will be achieved. The ratio, expressed in pounds (kilograms) of water per pound (kilogram) of cement, will ordinarily vary from 0.40 to 0.70 lb/lb (kg/kg).

4. Whether or not *entrained air* is included in the mix. Entrained air consists of thousands of tiny, stable bubbles of air which are introduced into the fresh concrete to improve the *flowability* of the mix. Air entrainment does, however, result in some reduction in compressive strength.

Table 4–3 indicates the probable compressive strength which will be achieved, using a number of different water/cement ratios, both with and without entrained air.

**TABLE 4-3:** *Compressive strengths of concrete for various water/cement ratios*

| *Water/cement ratio [lb/lb (kg/kg) of cement]* | *Probable compressive strength after 28 days [psi (MPa)]* | |
| --- | --- | --- |
| | *Non-air-entrained* | *Air-entrained* |
| 0.40 | 5800 (40) | 4800 (33) |
| 0.50 | 4800 (33) | 3650 (25) |
| 0.60 | 3900 (27) | 2750 (19) |
| 0.70 | 3050 (21) | 1750 (12) |

The concrete may be mixed on the job, delivered ready-mixed from a concrete mixing plant, or delivered from a batching plant, mixed in transit. No matter which method is used, great care must be taken in placing the concrete in the forms:

1. Concrete should not be allowed to drop freely more than 48 in. (1200 mm). If the height of the form is greater than that, some type of chute is required so that the concrete may be conducted to at least within 48 in. (1200 mm) of the bottom.

2. Concrete should be placed in such a way that it will drop straight down, not bounce from one form face to the other.

3. Place in even layers around the form—don't try to place all in one spot and allow the concrete to flow to its final position.

4. Start placing at the corners and work toward the center of the form. All of these precautions will help to prevent *segregation*, the separation of the aggregates from the water-cement paste.

The placement of concrete can be improved by the use of a labor saving concrete pump. The hose from the truck at one location can be easily moved over the entire site, reducing the placement time. Special ramps and chutes are not needed to place concrete on a sloped or uneven site (see Fig. 4–85).

**FIGURE 4–85:** *Concrete pump.*

Concrete can best be consolidated in the form by vibration. This may be done either internally or externally. An internal vibrator (see Fig. 4–86) is inserted into the concrete and operated until consolidation has taken place. An external vibrator is operated against the outside of the form. Care must be taken not to overvibrate, because excess paste will be brought to the top or out to the face of the forms.

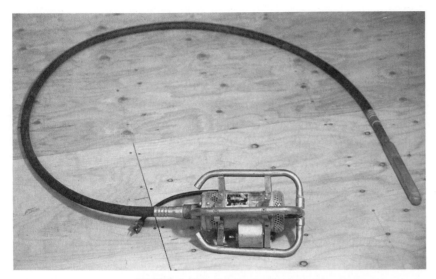

**FIGURE 4-86:** *Concrete vibrator.*

Proper curing of the concrete, that is, allowing it to gain its rated strength, is very important. Temperature and moisture conditions control the curing. Concrete cures best at a temperature of about 70°F (21°C) and cures very slowly below 40°F (5°C). Moist conditions are required for good curing. If the concrete is allowed to dry out soon after it is placed, it cannot be expected to gain the strength required of it. Keep the concrete warm and moist for as long as possible.

One means of keeping the concrete moist is to leave the forms in place. However, if it is necessary to remove the forms early in the curing process, care must be taken not to damage the green concrete.

There are occasions when it is necessary to have the concrete made with other than normal cement. If the land on which the foundation will rest contains alkali salts, concrete made with normal cement will set and cure poorly. In such cases, it is wise to specify alkali-resistant cement, which will produce concrete that will set and cure under alkaline conditions. Sometimes it may be necessary to have the concrete set and cure more quickly than is normally the case. If this is so, a special cement, called high-early-strength cement, should be used in making the concrete. Concrete so made will cure much more rapidly in its early stages than that made with normal cement.

## BASEMENT FLOOR

The concrete basement floor is placed in one layer after the proper base preparations have been completed. First a 5 in. (125 mm) layer of well packed gravel is placed under the floor.

A 6-mil polyethylene membrane is then laid over the gravel, initially to prevent the loss of water from the concrete to the base and eventually to prevent the migration of moisture upward through the slab. The level of the slab is established by measuring down from the underside of the joists or by placing screeds around the outside of the slab. A *screed* is simply a guide strip, the top of which represents the level of the finished floor. Stakes or screeds may be placed in the middle of the floor to establish the level at the middle of the floor (see Fig. 4–87).

**FIGURE 4–87:**   *Stakes to establish concrete floor level.*

The concrete is placed either with a concrete pump or by chute (see Fig. 4–88). It is then compacted and leveled with a straight edge and trued with a bullfloat, eliminating the ridges and filling the surface voids [see Fig. 4–89(a)]. Bullfloating should immediately follow the screeding and must be completed before any bleed water is present on the surface [see Fig. 4–89(b)].

**FIGURE 4–88:**   *Placing concrete by chute.*

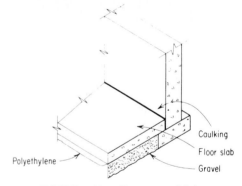

(a) Leveling with a straight edge.

(b) Bullfloating.

**FIGURE 4-89**

Machine floating is not done until the concrete has stiffened. This floating will depress the larger aggregates slightly below the surface, remove the imperfections, and compact the mortar at the surface in preparation for finishing. The final compaction and smoothing is achieved by steel troweling with a hand or a power-driven trowel (see Fig. 2-8).

## Concrete Joints and Reinforcement

The joint between floor and wall may require some special consideration. Since the floor is probably placed after the wall concrete has hardened, there is little bond between them, and eventually shrinkage will produce a crack around the perimeter. This crack may be a source of trouble if moisture collects under the footings, because the water will find its way up through the joint. Such an occurrence may be prevented by sealing the joint with an asphalt caulking compound (see Fig. 4-90).

The need for reinforcement will depend on the size of the floor and its use. Residential floors do not usually require reinforcing, but larger ones may. Reinforcing may be done for two reasons, one being to give the concrete greater strength in bending and the other to control contraction and expansion of the top surface due to temperature changes. In the first case, the reinforcement will be rod or heavy wire mesh placed near the bottom of the slab. In the second, it will be light wire mesh placed close to the top surface (see Fig. 4-91).

**FIGURE 4-90:** *Floor to wall joint.*

Caulking
Floor slab
Gravel
Polyethylene

**FIGURE 4-91:** *Reinforcing mesh.*

## CONCRETE STEPS

Entrance steps must be attached to the foundation wall by means of reinforcing placed during wall construction or bolts fastened through the wall after construction. The foundation for the step can be piers or a wall resting on a footing when needed or brackets fastened to the wall (see Fig. 4-92). Steps may be included and poured as part of the platform (see Fig. 4-93). When the steps are over 3 ft (1 m) wide, 2-in. (38-mm) material should be used for the risers, and additional support should be added when the width is over 6 ft (2 m), as shown in Fig. 4-93.

*(a) Wall to support step.*

*(b) Brackets for step support.*

**FIGURE 4-92**

**FIGURE 4-93:**  *Step forms.*

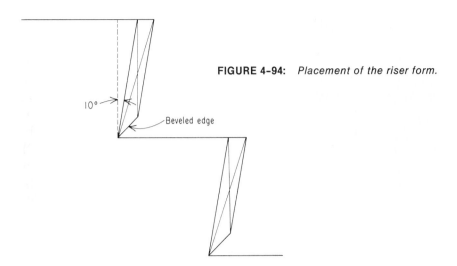

**FIGURE 4-94:** *Placement of the riser form.*

10°

Beveled edge

The risers of the steps should be set at an angle of about 10° to provide a nosing. The bottom edge of the riser should be beveled to permit troweling of the entire surface of the step (see Fig. 4–94).

Precast platforms and steps are commonly used, particularly where custom work is not required (see Fig. 4–92).

## SIDEWALKS AND DRIVEWAYS

Sidewalks and driveways are not usually poured until after construction of the building is complete. In some areas the slab may be poured directly in contact with the soil. If the base is subjected to moisture and frost action, a gravel base is advised. Concrete thickness can also be reduced from 5 in. (125 mm) to 3½ in. (90 mm) when put down on a 5-in. (125-mm) gravel base.

The forms for the slab should be set so that there is a drainage slope of at least 1:60. Reinforcing of deformed steel or welded wire mesh is commonly used to keep the floating slab together and to minimize cracking (see Fig. 4-95). Expansion joints are used when the slab comes in contact with a garage slab, curb, or public sidewalk or every 20 ft (6 m). Control joints act as a stress relief to limit uncontrolled cracking.

Construction joints usually form the edges of each day's work. They are located to conform to the slab jointing pattern and constructed to function as and to align with control or expansion joints (see Fig. 4-96). For sidewalks, the distance between joints should be equal to the width of the slab. Form sides are usually 2 × 4s or 2 × 6s so the edges can be kept straight (see Fig. 4-97).

Edges and expansion joints should be rounded with an edger. A jointing tool is commonly used to establish a control joint as well. The surface of the slab can be troweled, or when extra traction is required, a fine brush finish is used.

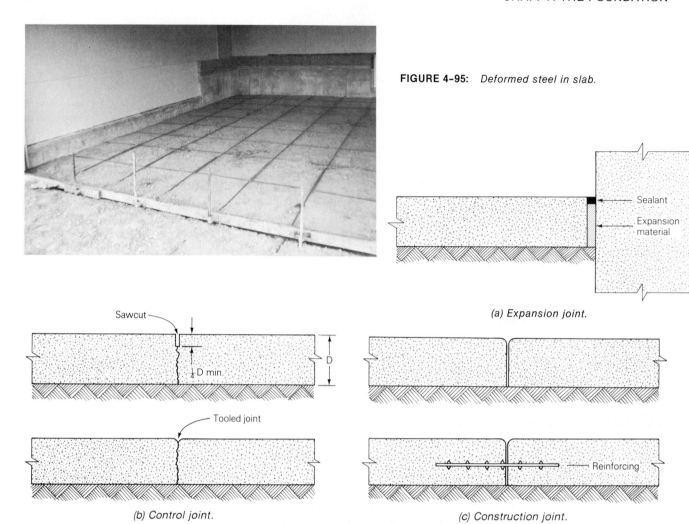

**FIGURE 4-95:** *Deformed steel in slab.*

*(a) Expansion joint.*

*(b) Control joint.*

*(c) Construction joint.*

**FIGURE 4-96:** *Joints in a concrete slab.*

**FIGURE 4-97:** *Sidewalk form.*

Recently, interlocking paving stones have been used for sidewalks and driveways. Numerous different shapes are available in a variety of colors (see Fig. 4-98). The unique geometric shape of the paving stones provides a completely interlocking surface which will transfer individual loads to adjacent stones, allowing the surface to move like a mesh. The flexibility of the system makes repairing the surface an easy procedure.

Interlocking concrete paving consists of a layer of *concrete pavers,* a *sand bedding layer,* and a compacted *sub*grade and is held in place by solid *curbs.* The thickness of the pavers can vary from 2⅜ in. (60 mm) to 4 in. (100 mm) depending on the type of traffic. The herringbone pattern provides the best locking effect, though other patterns are also used (see Fig. 4-99). The subgrade should be level, and the thickness depends on ground conditions and use of the area. The strength of the soil is measured in terms of the California bearing ratio (CBR). Minimum subgrade thicknesses are given in Table 4-4.

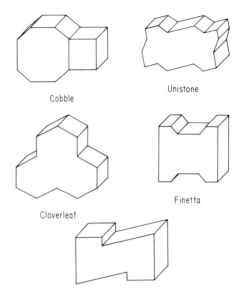

**FIGURE 4-98:** *Paving stone shapes.*

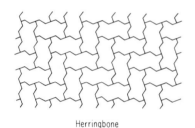

Herringbone

Parquet

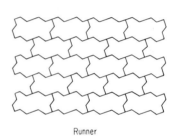

Runner

**FIGURE 4-99:** *Paving stone patterns.*

**TABLE 4-4:** *Minimum subgrade thickness*

| | Walk or patio | Driveway |
|---|---|---|
| CBR of greater than 8% (well-compacted rocky round, gravel, sandy loam, or sand with a small amount of silt) | Not required | Not required |
| CBR of 4–8% (sand, loam, and stiff clay not subject to moisture) | Not required | 3 in. (75. mm) |
| CBR of less than 4% (wet clays or soils which may easily deform when wet or subject to car traffic) | 3 in. (75 mm) | 5 in. (125 mm) |

The sand bedding layer should consist of well-graded concrete sand. Uniformity of the layer is important to achieve a good-quality surface. This layer should not be over 1½-in. (40 mm) thick after compaction and should not be used for leveling low spots (see Fig. 4-100). Solid curbs are needed around the perimeter to prevent moving and slipping of the stones. Curbs can be made of concrete, pressure-treated wood, lawn, compacted earth, or an existing building (see Fig. 4-101).

**FIGURE 4-100:** *Concrete paving stone structure.*

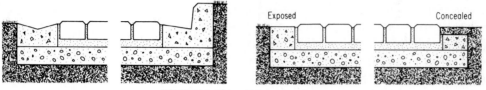

**FIGURE 4-101:** *Edge restraints.*

Construction procedures should conform to the following steps:

1. Ground should be cut out and shaped for area needed and then compacted.
2. Subgrade should be spread to the required level and compacted.
3. Edge restraint can be placed before or after placing of stones.
4. Sand is spread and screeded to a level that will result in proper level after compaction.
5. Lay stones starting from a straightedge and a corner directly onto screeded sand in pattern selected. Joints between stones should not exceed $\frac{1}{8}$ in. (3 mm), and the surface should have a 2% slope to provide drainage.
6. Vibrate stones with a plate vibrator to final level.
7. Spread dry sand over surface and brush into joints to complete the interlock.

Now that the concrete work and foundation are complete, the job is ready for the erection of the superstructure. If it has been carefully planned and carried out, the completion of the remainder of the building will be easier, with fewer chances of errors as work continues.

## REVIEW QUESTIONS

4-1. What is the general purpose of a building foundation?

4-2. Outline the essential difference between a full basement foundation and a surface foundation.

4-3. Explain the reason for placing foundation footings below the level of frost penetration.

4-4. How does a gravel pad under a slab foundation compensate for the fact that the foundation is not below the frost line?

4-5. Why is it necessary, in many cases, to make the excavation larger than the size of the foundation?

4-6. Why is cribbing used in excavating?

4-7. Explain the reason for coating a footing keyway with asphalt before a wall is placed on it.

4-8. What is the reason for placing a sill gasket under a sill plate before bolting it down?

4-9. Explain what is meant by *cast-in* joists.

4-10. What is the purpose of using screeds when placing a basement floor?

4-11. Explain the reason for using a bearing wall, rather than a center girder, to support interior floor loads.

# THE FLOOR FRAME

## COMPONENT PARTS

After the foundation has been completed, the next logical step in the construction of a building is the erection of the floor frame. This, as the name implies, is the part of the structure which carries the floor and interior walls, along with its supporting members. This floor frame consists of *bearing posts*, the beam which they support, the *floor joists* carried by the beam and foundation walls, the *bridging* between the joists, and the *subfloor*; sometimes a *bearing wall* will replace posts and beam. When the box sill or ladder type of construction is used, a sill plate or ladder becomes one of the components of the floor frame.

## POSTS AND BEAMS

Posts and beams are fundamental structural components of the floor frame which support approximately half the total load of the building and transmit it to end foundation walls and footings.

### Posts

The bearing posts may be made of either steel or wood. Wooden ones are sometimes one solid piece of timber but more often are built up of three or four pieces of 1½-in. (38-mm) material laminated together. The cross-sectional area depends on the load to be carried, but usually 6 × 6 (140 × 140 mm) will prove ample. One factor governing the size will be the width of the beam. One dimension of the post should be equal to that width in order to provide full bearing.

**FIGURE 5-1:**   *Steel adjustable post.*

A steel post, usually round, will be smaller in cross section than a wooden one. It must be capped by a steel plate to provide a suitable bearing area. Steel posts are manufactured which have a thread on the inside of the top end so that a short, heavy stem may be turned into them (see Fig. 5-1). Consequently, the post becomes adjustable in length. This is a decided advantage, because the post can be adjusted to the exact length required on installation, and later if the beam shrinks in its depth, the post can be lengthened to take up the shrinkage.

### Beams

Beams may be made of wood and steel. A wooden beam has been most popular for light construction. It is often built up of a number of pieces of $1\frac{1}{2}$-in. (38-mm) material laminated together, although it may be one solid piece of timber. When the beam is laminated, care must be taken in its construction. Pieces may be nailed, bolted, or glued and nailed together, the latter method providing the most rigid unit [see Fig. 5-2(a)]. A new type of beam is manufactured by gluing strands of wood together under pressure [see Fig. 5-2(d)].

Rarely will it be possible to find pieces long enough to reach from one end of the beam to the other, and consequently pieces must be end-jointed, usually with butt joints. Select or cut pieces of such a length that the joints will come directly over posts [see Fig. 5-2(b)]. When this is not possible, some codes will allow joints within 6 in. (150 mm) of the quarter point in the span [see Fig. 5-2(c)]. If only nails are used in laminating, they should be spaced not over 12 in. (300 mm) apart and staggered, one at the top and the next at the bottom of the beam, as illustrated in Fig. 5-2(b)]. On beams of extra depth an extra row of nails may be necessary along the center line.

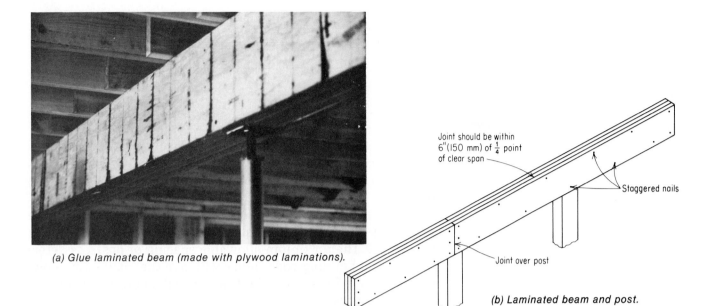

(a) Glue laminated beam (made with plywood laminations).

Joint should be within 6"(150 mm) of ¼ point of clear span

Staggered nails

Joint over post

(b) Laminated beam and post.

(d) Parallel strand beam.

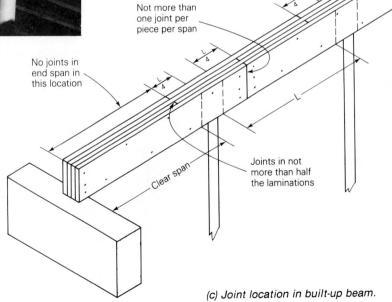

Not more than one joint per piece per span

No joints in end span in this location

Clear span

L

Joints in not more than half the laminations

FIGURE 5-2

(c) Joint location in built-up beam.

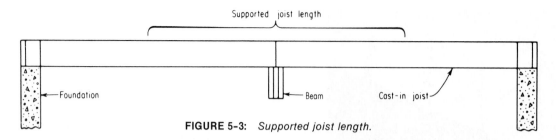

**FIGURE 5-3:** *Supported joist length.*

The size of the beam depends on the load which it must support, the species and grade of lumber, and the spacing of the posts. The load is determined by the *supported joist length*—one-half the width of the building (see Fig. 5-3). Using these factors, the maximum allowable *free span* of the beam or, in other words, the maximum allowable spacing of posts, is determined. Local building code tables will give the maximum allowable free spans for wooden beams that will support one or two residential floors.

The method for setting the bottom of the bearing post has already been discussed in Chapter 4. At the top end some provision must be made for adjustment, so that the beam will be held exactly level and also so that shrinkage in the depth of the beam can be taken up at a later date. This provision is made by placing two wedge-shaped pieces between the top of the post and the beam when the beam is raised to its correct level. Further compensation may be made for future shrinkage in the same way.

### Steel Beam

A steel beam for light construction may be a *standard* or *wide flange rolled shape* (see Fig. 5-4).

Several depths of rolled shapes are commonly used, the number of supports (posts) required being determined by the supported joist length. If the joists rest on top of the beam, a wooden pad is generally used to facilitate fastening the joist

*(a) Steel beam.*

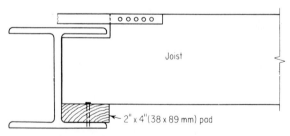

*(b) Steel beam supporting joist ends.*

**FIGURE 5-4**

*(c) Steel beam and post.*

**FIGURE 5-4:** *(continued)*

ends, and the height of the beam must be regulated accordingly [see Fig. 5-4(a)]. If the top of joists and beam are to be flush, the joist ends must be carried by the bottom flange of the beam, as illustrated in Fig. 5-4(b). In the latter case, the joists must be spliced over the beam by 2 × 2 (38 × 38) lumber at least 2 ft (600 mm) in length.

## BEARING WALLS

In a good many cases, posts and beam are replaced by a *bearing wall* as the primary support for a building. Such a wall will carry the load quite adequately and has the advantage of providing a wall framework if the basement space is to be divided into rooms.

As illustrated in Chapter 4, the bearing wall is supported by a continuous footing having a raised center portion to which the wall is anchored (see Fig. 4-15). The material must be 2 × 6 (38 × 140 mm), minimum, with top and bottom plates and studs spaced not more than 16 in. (400 mm) o.c. (see Fig. 5-5). At the midpoint between top and bottom, blocks must be fitted snugly between the studs, staggered if required, to facilitate nailing, as illustrated in Fig. 5-5. The double top plate will be level with the top of the sill plate or with the bottom edge of the joists, depending on whether box sill or cast-in construction is used.

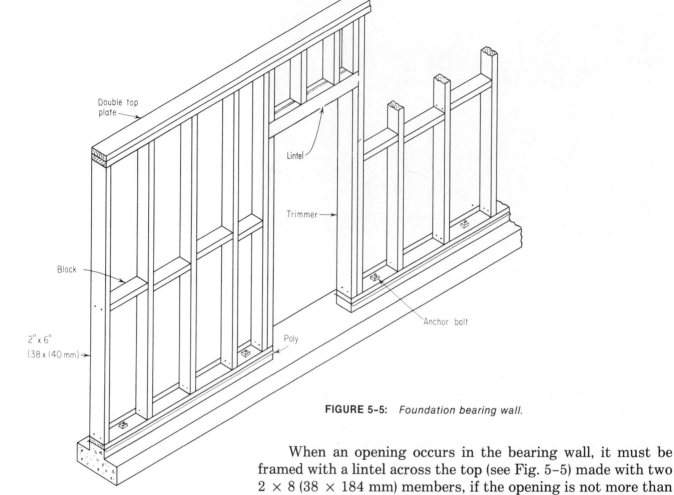

**FIGURE 5-5:**   *Foundation bearing wall.*

When an opening occurs in the bearing wall, it must be framed with a lintel across the top (see Fig. 5–5) made with two 2 × 8 (38 × 184 mm) members, if the opening is not more than 4 ft (1200 mm) wide.

## FOUNDATION WALL-FLOOR FRAME CONNECTION

When a concrete foundation wall is used, a wood sill is either anchored to or cast into the foundation wall to provide a nailing surface for the floor joists. The sill plate is anchored to the top of wall by casting anchor bolts or metal nailing strips into the concrete (see Fig. 5–6). A sill gasket is placed under the sill plate to seal the junction between the wood and concrete (see Fig. 5–7). This method is also used when the foundation wall is constructed with concrete blocks.

Another way to provide a good connection is to cast a wood ladder into the top of the foundation wall, as illustrated in Fig. 5–8. This frame work stiffens the top edge of the concrete form making it easier to straighten the top of the wall. In some areas floor joists are embedded into the top of the foundation wall providing a strong connection (see Fig. 4–34).

*(a) Sill plate anchored with anchor bolts.*　　　　　　*(b) Metal straps for anchoring sill plate.*

**FIGURE 5-6**

**FIGURE 5-7:** *Sill gasket.*

**FIGURE 5-8:** *Ladder-type sill plate.*

## JOISTS

*Floor joists* are the members that span from foundation wall to beam or in some cases from wall to wall, and that transfer the individual building loads to those members. These may be made of wood or steel. Wooden joists have been widely used, particularly in residential construction (see Fig. 5-9), but prefabricated wood joists are gaining in popularity (see Fig. 5-10). Steel joists are also used in some areas, particularly for long spans (see Fig. 5-11).

FIGURE 5-10:   *Prefabricated wood joists.*

FIGURE 5-9:   *Wood joists in residential construction.*

FIGURE 5-11:   *Steel joists in residential construction.*

## Wood Joists

Wood joists consist of 2-in. (38-mm) material, varying in widths from 6 to 12 in. (140–286 mm), depending on their load, length, spacing, and the species and grade of lumber. Common spacings are 12, 16, and 24 in. (300, 400, and 600 mm) o.c. Building codes give maximum spans for floor joists for residential construction (living quarters and bedrooms), based on lumber species and grade, joist spacing and, where applicable, type of ceiling.

For buildings other than residential, with heavier loads, the size of joists should be calculated by a competent authority.

## Joist Framing

Two systems are used for assembling joists—the *cast-in* system, previously described in Chapter 4, and the *box sill* system, in which the whole assembly is mounted on top of the foundation wall, secured to a plate or ladder sill.

In the box system, joists are held in position at the foundation wall by the *header joists,* running at right angles to the regular joists and bearing on the sill plate (see Fig. 5–12). At the inner end, the joists may be carried *on top* of the beam, or, where more headroom is needed under the beam, supported by joist hangers (see Fig. 5–13). Care must be taken to allow for shrinkage of the joist material when they are supported by a joist hanger. The top edge of the joists must be above the beam level, or differential shrinkage will cause an uneven floor (see Fig. 5–14).

**FIGURE 5-12:** *Joist framing at foundation wall.*

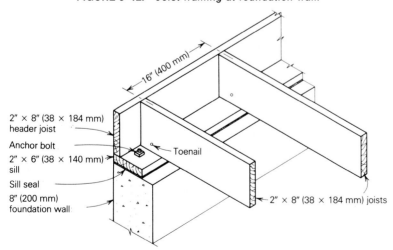

16″ (400 mm)

2″ × 8″ (38 × 184 mm) header joist

Anchor bolt

2″ × 6″ (38 × 140 mm) sill

Toenail

Sill seal

8″ (200 mm) foundation wall

2″ × 8″ (38 × 184 mm) joists

*(a) Lapped.*

*(b) Joist hangers.*

**FIGURE 5-13**

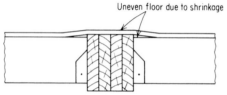

**FIGURE 5-14:** *Differential shrinkage.*

In locations where an extra load is imposed on the floor frame, such as where a non-loadbearing partition parallel to the joists should bear on joists or blocking between the joists, the blocking should be 2 × 4 (38 × 89 mm) lumber spaced 4 ft 0 in. (1.2 m) or less (see Fig. 5–15). When loadbearing partitions run parallel to the joists, they should be supported by beams or loadbearing walls in the basement. Loadbearing partitions at right angles to the floor joists should be located not more than 3 ft (1 m) from the joist support when the wall does not support an upper floor and not more than 2 ft (600 mm) when the wall supports one or more upper floors unless floor joists have been designed to carry the concentrated loads.

**FIGURE 5-15:** *Partition support.*

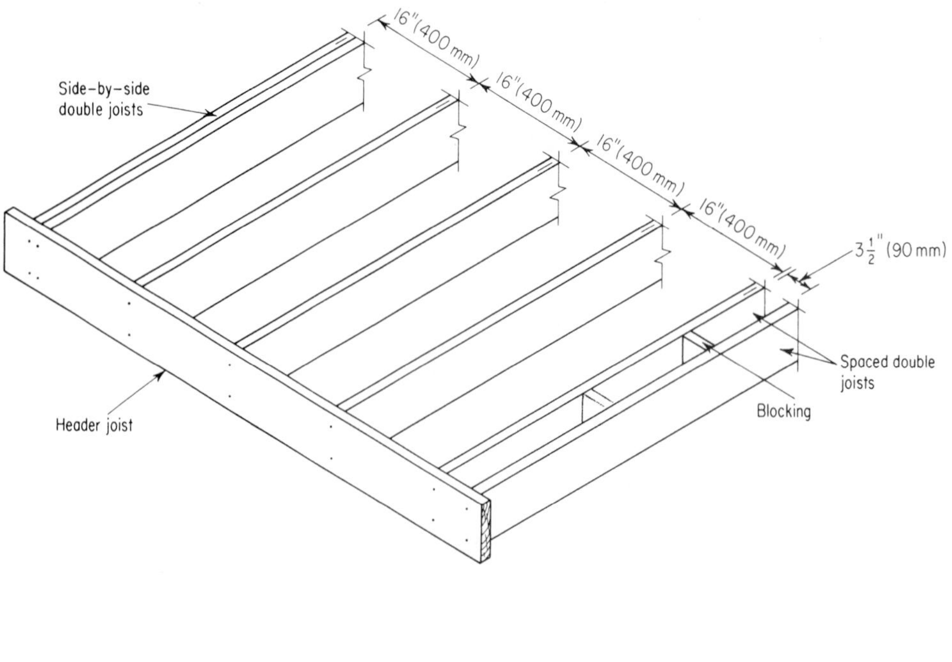

Openings in the floor frame for a stairwell or where a chimney or fireplace comes through the floor must be framed in the proper way. Trimmer joists are doubled if they support header joists more than 32 in. (800 mm) long. Header joists longer than 48 in. (1.2 m) should also be doubled. Trimmer joists that support header joists more than 6 ft (2 m) long and header joists that are more than 10 ft, 8 in. (3.2 m) long should be designed according to accepted engineering practice. Joist hangers are used to support long joist headers and tail joists (see Fig. 5–16). Most codes require that a chimney opening be at least 2 in. (50 mm) larger on all sides than the dimensions of the chimney and that the framing be kept back 4 in. (100 mm) from the back of a fireplace. See Chapter 8 for stairwell opening calculations.

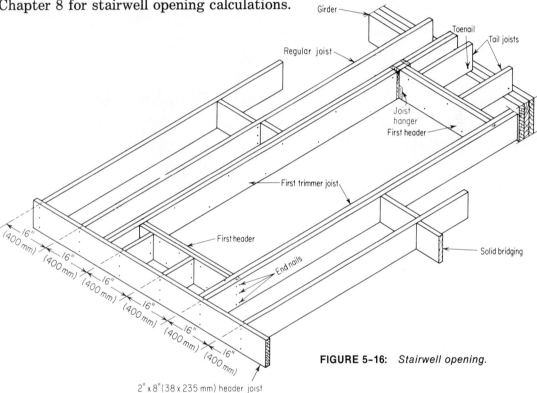

**FIGURE 5–16:** *Stairwell opening.*

## Bridging

It is important that joists be prevented from twisting after they are in place and, unless board type *ceiling* finish is installed on the underside, restraint must be provided, both at end supports and at intervals not exceeding 7 ft (2.1 m) between supports. At the end supports, the restraint is provided by toenailing the joists to the supports and by endnailing through the header joist.

The intermediate restraint is provided by *bridging,* which may be in the form of *solid blocking* between joists, *cross-bridging,* or *wood strapping.* The solid blocking will be pieces of

$1\frac{1}{2}$-in. (38-mm) material the same depth as the joists and may be *offset* one-half their thickness to facilitate endnailing (see Fig. 5–16). The crossbridging is made from 2 × 2 or 1 × 3 (38 × 38 mm or 19 × 64 mm) material, cut to fit as illustrated 5–17(a). Continuous wood strapping nailed to the underside of the joists or blocking between is the easiest way to provide intermediate joist restraint (see Fig. 5–17(b)). The use of bridging or a combination of bridging and strapping can increase the maximum span allowed with some sizes of floor joists. Check your local code restrictions for spans in your area.

*(a) Cross bridging.*

*(b) Block bridging.*

**FIGURE 5–17**

### Joist Assembly

Setting the joists in their proper location, nailing them securely in place, and providing the extra framing necessary for concentrated loads and frame rigidity are very important steps in the framing of a building. The procedure may be as follows:

1. Study the plans to check the location and centers of the joists. Note where they are to be doubled and if the doubling will be side by side or separated.

2. Select straight header joists and lay them off according to the plans. Be sure that joints in the header joist occur at the center of a regular joist (see Fig. 5–18). Note that if joists are to be *lapped* at the beam, the header joist lay-off on the two opposite sides of the building will have to be offset from one another by the thickness of the joists.

3. Check for the number of full-length regular joists required, square one end and cut them to length, unless they are to be lapped.

4. For box sill construction, toenail the header joists in place on the sill plate (see Chapter 4 for procedure in cast-in construction).

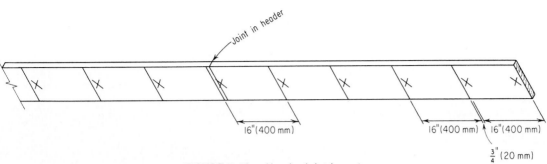

**FIGURE 5-18:** *Header joist layout.*

5. Where joist hangers are to be used, nail them in place on the beam, in line with the header joist layout.

6. Lay out all the regular joists on one side of the building, set them up in position *with the crown up,* and *endnail* into them through the header joist.

7. Repeat with the regular joists on the opposite side and if joists lap at the beam, nail the two together through the lap joint.

8. Check the plans for the location of floor openings; mark on the joist header the location of the trimmer joists; square the end and endnail in place.

9. Mark the trimmer joists for header positions (see Fig. 5-16); cut headers to exact length and endnail in place.

10. Add the second trimmer if doubling is required.

11. Add the second header if doubling is required.

12. Cut tail joists to exact length and nail them in place *on regular centers.*

13. Locate the position of walls running parallel to floor joists and nail blocking at that location (see Fig. 5-15).

14. Space the top edges of the joists properly over the beam using a 1 × 4 (19 × 89) nailing strip to hold them in place, and then toenail to beam (see Fig. 5-9).

15. Mark the centerline of the bridging with a chalk line [not more than 7 ft (2.1 m) from end supports] and nail bridging to the line.

## Prefabricated Wood Joists and Truss Systems

In recent years prefabricated wood joists and truss systems have become popular. Prefabricated systems provide greater clear spans and are lighter in weight and straighter than conventional framing. This will provide a flatter floor and straighter ceilings below, and as the chord members are wider than standard joists, the need for strapping is eliminated. Wood prefabricated members are in the form of a wooden I beam or a flat truss (see Fig. 5-19).

*(a) "I" beam floor joists. (Courtesy Jager Industries Inc.)*

**FIGURE 5-19**

*(b) Flat truss.*

Heating ducts, plumbing pipes, and electrical wires are easily incorporated into the joist systems. Trusses have many large openings, allowing room for services. Holes are easily cut into the webs of I beams of plywood or waferboard. Holes $1\frac{1}{2}$ in. (38 mm) can be cut anywhere in the web; larger holes can only be placed in the locations shown in Fig. 5–20. In an area where multiple holes are needed, a distance equal to double the larger hole's diameter is required between holes. Square or rectangular openings must have four times the long dimension between edges of the openings. Rectangular and square holes must be located in the mid-one-third of the span. Maximum hole length must not exceed twice the hole height.

**FIGURE 5-20:**  *Hole chart.*

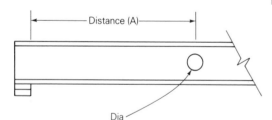

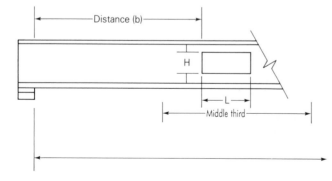

| Diameter or dimension H | Distance (A) | Distance (B) |
| --- | --- | --- |
| $1\frac{1}{2}$ in. (38 mm) | 0 in. (0 mm) | N.A. |
| 2 in. (50 mm) | 8 in. (200 mm) | 32 in. (800 mm) |
| 3 in. (75 mm) | 12 in. (300 mm) | 48 in. (1.2 M) |
| 4 in. (100 mm) | 16 in. (400 mm) | 64 in. (1.6M) |
| 5 in. (125 mm) | 20 in. (500 mm) | 80 in. (2.0M) |

In a prefabricated joist floor frame, the joist header can be either ³⁄₈ or ³⁄₄ in. (9.5 or 19 mm) plywood. The joists are fastened to the support by nailing through the flange eliminating the need for a heavy joist header (see Fig. 5-21). Stiffeners are used on one side or both sides of the joist over a support, depending on the weight it must carry (see Fig. 5-21).

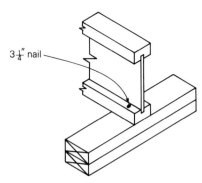

*(a) Fastening prefabricated joists.*

*(b) Fastening joist header.*

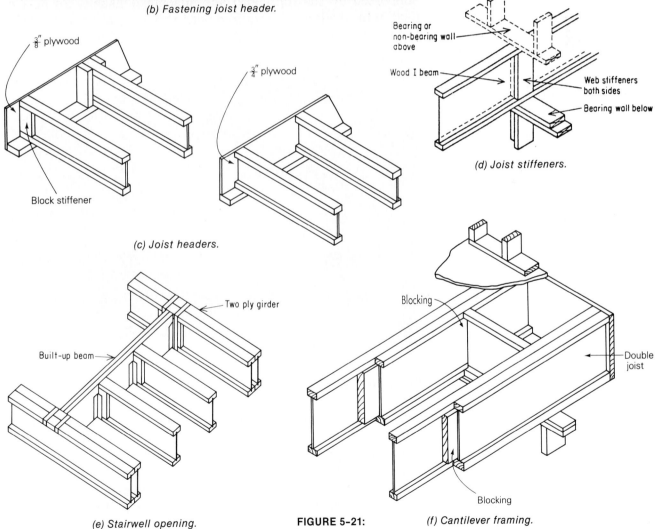

*(c) Joist headers.*

*(d) Joist stiffeners.*

*(e) Stairwell opening.*          **FIGURE 5-21:**          *(f) Cantilever framing.*

Placement of prefabricated joists is much easier and faster than standard joists since fewer are needed, they are much lighter, and they do not need to be supported until fastened to the joist header. Standard spacings for prefabricated "I" beam joists are 12, 16, 19.2, and 24 in. (300, 400, 480, and 600 mm). Bridging also can be eliminated when using "I" beam floor joists. Longer spans are available, reducing or eliminating the need for beams in the floor frame. The straightness of the joists and their lack of shrinkage also reduces the potential for squeaky floors. Care must be taken not to walk on the joists until they are adequately braced as they are unstable. Stairwell opening framing and cantilever framing details are illustrated in Fig. 5–21.

Another type of prefabricated joist floor system uses a member known as a *steel web truss.* Trusses upper and lower chords are 2 × 4s (38 × 89 mm), and the web members are made of tubular steel. Spans up to 38 ft (12.6 m) are possible depending on the loading and spacing of trusses. Trusses are supported by the top chord and spacing is usually 24 in. o.c. (600 mm). Bridging is required with this type of truss to make the entire bay act as a single unit (see Fig. 5–22).

**FIGURE 5-22:**   *Bridging open web joists.*

## Steel Joists

Steel joists of various kinds are available for use in place of wood joists and are particularly useful where relatively long spans are required. They are all prefabricated units, some made in various depths to suit various span requirements. Steel joists have greater loadbearing capacity than equivalently sized wood joists, and can be used with various other materials as illustrated in Fig. 5–23.

*(a) Steel joist with wood header joist. (Courtesy U.S. Steel Corp.)*

*(b) Steel joists with concrete floor.*

**FIGURE 5-23**

One type, the cold-formed steel joist, is made from sheet steel in several standard depths as shown in Fig. 5-24. The *nested joist section* is used as a trimmer joist at floor openings, and the *perimeter closure section* is used as a rim joist in an all-steel floor frame.

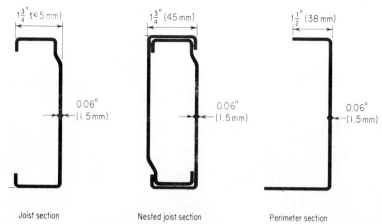

**FIGURE 5-24:** *Cold-formed steel joist shapes. (Courtesy Steel Co. of Canada)*

In an all-steel floor frame, the perimeter section is secured to the sill plate with screws or staples, and the regular joists are normally secured to the perimeter section (see Fig. 5-25) at 16 in. (400 mm) o.c. with screws. The other ends of the joists rest on the center beam or bearing wall and are provided with *web stiffeners* (see Fig. 5-25) in order to develop the required web strength.

**FIGURE 5-25:** *Steel floor framing.*

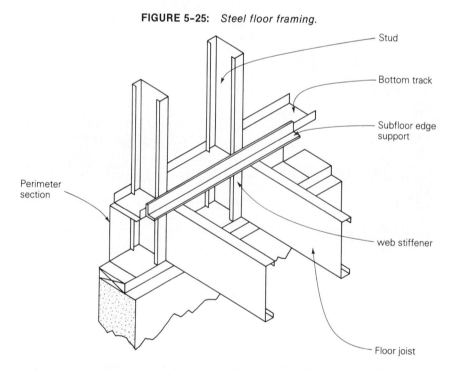

Floor openings in steel frame construction are framed in much the same way as in wood frame construction. The *nested joist section* is used in place of double trimmers and headers around the opening, and the tail joists are supported by *hangers* (see Fig. 5-26), held in place by screws.

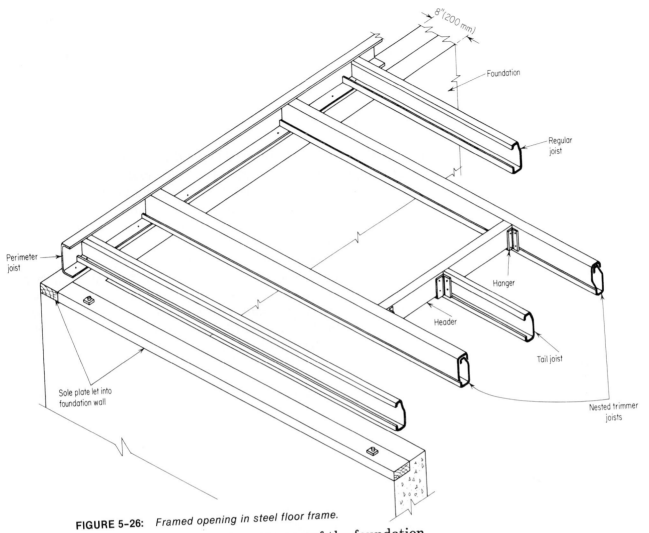

**FIGURE 5-26:** *Framed opening in steel floor frame.*

Steel joists may be *recessed* into the top of the foundation to provide a *flush floor*. The recessing may be done by lowering the sill plate into the top, inner edge of the foundation wall, as illustrated in Fig. 5-27. This method leaves part of the upper surface of the foundation exposed as a base for brick veneer exterior finish.

**FIGURE 5-27:** *Steel floor frame on recessed sill plate.*

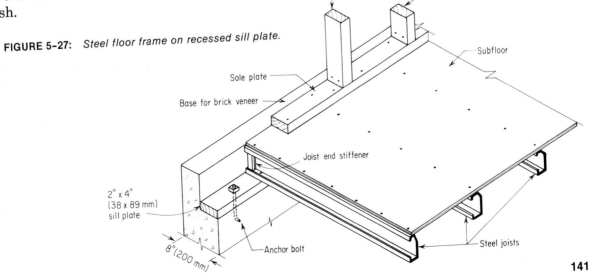

When the lowered sill plate method is used, joists are provided with end clips or stiffeners and secured to the sill plate by screws through their bottom edge.

## Floor Framing at Projections

Floor joists occasionally project beyond the foundation wall to provide support for bay windows or additional floor space in upper rooms. The cantilevered portion of the floor should not exceed $1\frac{1}{2}$ times the joist depth for bay windows or additional interior floor space. The space between the floor joists should be left open to allow for circulation of warm air so even floor temperature occurs throughout the room (see Fig. 5-28). When the floor joists are perpendicular to the projection, the framing is very easy as the joists need only to extend farther to support the projection (see Fig. 5-28). However, if the floor joists are parallel to the projection, cantilevered joists must be at right angles to the regular joists (see Fig. 5-29).

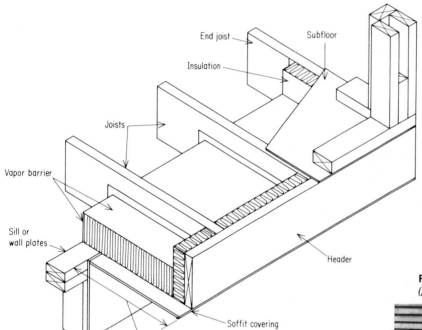

**FIGURE 5-28:** *Framing floor projections (joists perpendicular to projection).*

**FIGURE 5-29:** *Framing floor projections (joists parallel to projection).*

Framing for balconies can be framed in the same method as bay windows, but as less load is supported, the joists can project farther (see Fig. 5-29). Other methods of supporting balconies include building a beam into the foundation beyond the outer face of the wall, providing support for the balcony framing (see Fig. 5-30). Bearing posts can also be installed, transferring the load of the balcony to lower floors or foundations. The top level is often cut down for 2-in. decking, which still provides a break in the floor level and does not cause interference with the functioning of the balcony door (see Fig. 5-31).

**FIGURE 5-30:** *Support for balcony framing.*

## SUBFLOOR

Laying the subfloor is the final step in completing the floor frame. *Center match, common boards, plywood,* or *particle board* may be used for subflooring, and if one of the first two is specified, application should be at an angle of 45° to the joists (see Fig. 5-31).

The minimum thickness of subflooring should conform to Table 5-1, the *long dimension* should run *across* the joists, and the joints should be broken in successive rows (see Fig. 5-32). To provide a stiffer subfloor, the long dimension of the panel should be supported by *blocking* between the joists, or the panels used should have tongue and groove edges. The matching of the tongue with the groove in the plywood is easier to achieve if the tongue is fed into the groove. This allows for hammering the joints together without damaging the tongue. A block of 2 × 4 can be laid against the groove edge of the plywood and then hammered with a sledge hammer without damaging the panel edge.

**FIGURE 5-31:** *Balcony framing.*

Nails for plywood or particle board subflooring should be a minimum of 2 in. (50 mm) long, and spaced 6 in. (150 mm) o.c. along the edge of the sheet and 12 in. (300 mm) o.c. on intermediate supports. Annular ringed or spiral nails provide extra holding power. Staples of a minimum length of 2 in. (50 mm) can also be used at the same spacing.

**FIGURE 5-32:** *Plywood subfloor.*

**TABLE 5-1**

| | *Thickness of Subflooring, in. (mm)* | | |
|---|---|---|---|
| *Maximum spacing of supports, in. (mm)* | *Plywood and 0-2 grade waferboard and strandboard* | *Particleboard* | *Lumber* |
| 16 (400) | 5/8 (15.5) | 5/8 (15.9) | 11/16 (17) |
| 20 (500) | 5/8 (15.5) | 3/4 (19) | 3/4 (19) |
| 24 (600) | 3/4 (18.5) | 1 (25.4) | 3/4 (19) |

**FIGURE 5-33:** *Applying subfloor adhesive.*

Plywood or particle board subflooring is attached to steel joists with steel joist nails or self-drilling tapping screws, using a nailer for the nails or a power screwgun for the screws. Subfloor adhesive is extensively used to provide a squeak-free floor. A bead of adhesive is applied to the edge of the joist, as illustrated in Fig. 5–33, assuring a rigid tight connection.

## REVIEW QUESTIONS

5-1.  What is the advantage of using a steel bearing post to support the main girder in a floor frame?

5-2.  Define the following terms:
      (a) Clear span.       (b) Supported joist length.

5-3.  At what locations in a built-up wood beam are butt joints allowed in the laminations?

5-4.  Outline two primary reasons for using bridging.

5-5.  What are three ways of connecting a wood floor frame to a foundation wall?

5-6.  What are the main advantages of using prefabricated wood joists in a floor frame?

5-7.  An opening 3 ft, 6 in. (1050 mm) wide by 6 ft, 6 in. (1950 mm) long is to be framed in the floor of a building 32 ft (9.6 m) wide by 40 ft (12 m) long with a center beam. The opening is 3 ft (900 mm) from one side and 11 ft (3300 mm) from one end. What length would you cut?
      (a) The opening headers?
      (b) The trimmer joists?
      (c) The tail joists on the outside?

5-8.  Carefully draw two sketches to illustrate the differences between a box sill floor frame and a cast-in joist floor frame.

5-9.  Fill in the blanks with the word or phrase which makes the sentence correct:
      (a) Material for bearing wall studs must be at least _____ in. (mm) in width.
      (b) Joists spanning 16 ft (4.8 m) should have _____ rows of bridging.
      (c) Strap bridging is usually made from _____.
      (d) Common spacing for anchor bolts in sill plates is _____.
      (e) Joists may be carried on the side of a beam by a _____.
      (f) Nonload-bearing partitions running parallel to the floor joists are supported by _____, or _____ between the joists.
      (g) _____ bridging is usually used when the space between the joists is less than the regular joist spacing.

# 6

# THE WALL FRAME

There are two basic systems used for framing walls, namely the *platform* frame (see Fig. 6–1) and the *balloon* frame, shown in Fig. 6–2. Many of the members are the same in both, and the main differences lie in the method of starting the frame at the ground floor level, the length of the wall framing members, and the method of framing in the floor for the second story.

## COMPONENT PARTS, PLATFORM FRAME

As illustrated in Fig. 6–1, a frame begins on the subfloor. The bottom member is the *sole plate* to which are attached *regular studs* one story in length, special arrangements of studs at corners, extra studs to which partitions are attached—*partition junctions*—and other shorter members. On top of these vertical members is a *top plate* and on top of that a *cap plate*. Over door and window openings are *headers* or *lintels* and, supporting the ends of these, *trimmer studs*. The bottom of a window opening is framed by a *rough sill*, and the spaces between rough sill and sole plate and between header and top plate are framed with *cripple studs. Wall backing* is placed where sinks, drapes, etc., are to be attached to interior walls, and *sheathing covers* the exterior of the frame. Wall sheathing consisting of plywood, waferboard, strandboard, gypsum board, diagonal lumber, or fiberboard will eliminate the need for diagonal bracing.

## COMPONENT PARTS, BALLOON FRAME

A balloon frame begins down at the sill plate (see Fig. 6–2). Full-length *regular studs* and *corner posts* rest on the sill and are capped at the top by *top plate* and *cap plate*. At the first floor level, a $\frac{3}{4}$-in. (19-mm) *ribbon* is let into the studs, and the ends of the *first-floor joists* rest on it. *Partition junctions* are set in only one story high. *Firestops, window and door headers, trimmers, rough sills, cripple studs,* and *wall backing* are similar to those in a platform frame. *Sheathing* completes the frame.

**FIGURE 6-1**

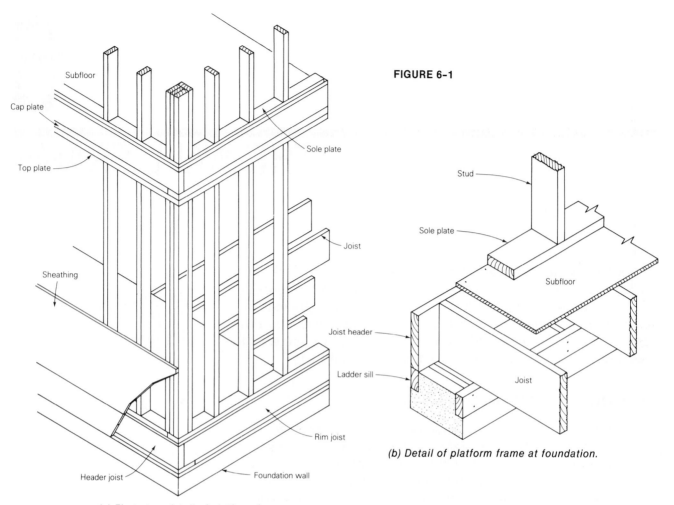

*(a) First-story detail of platform frame.*

*(b) Detail of platform frame at foundation.*

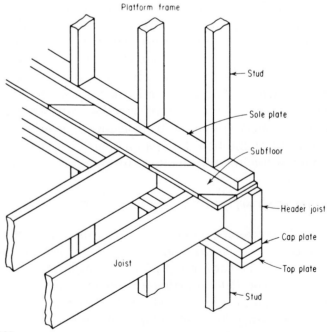

*(c) Detail of platform frame at second floor.*

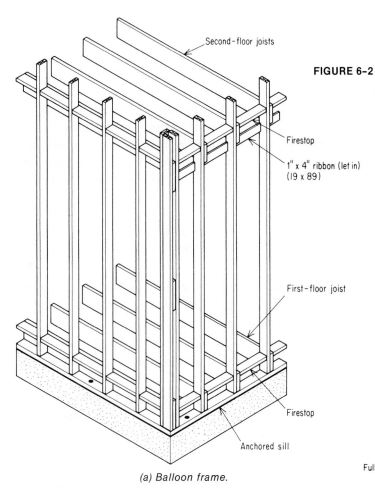

Second-floor joists

**FIGURE 6-2**

Firestop

1" x 4" ribbon (let in)
(19 x 89)

First-floor joist

Firestop

Anchored sill

(a) Balloon frame.

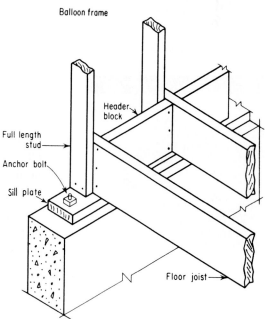

Balloon frame

Header block

Full length stud

Anchor bolt

Sill plate

Floor joist

(b) Detail of balloon frame at foundation.

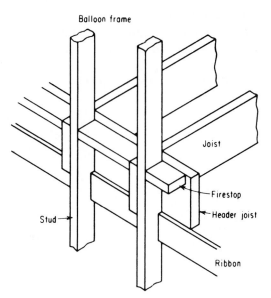

Balloon frame

Joist

Firestop

Stud

Header joist

Ribbon

(c) Detail of balloon frame at second floor.

## PLATFORM FRAME WALL CONSTRUCTION

### Plate Layout

The first step in the construction of a wall is to *lay out* on the sole plate—the base for a platform frame—the exact location of each member required in that wall. They will include *corner posts, regular studs, opening trimmers, partition junctions,* and *cripple studs.* Since the location of the members on the top plate will be identical, the two plates are laid out together. Proceed as follows:

1. Pick out straight stock for the plates; two or more pieces are probably required for each one. Set them out across the subfloor, side by side.
2. Square off one end of each plate, cut them to length; if more than one piece is needed, the end joints should come in the center of a stud position.
3. Check the plans for the locations of the centers of door and window openings. Mark these on the plates by a centerline, as illustrated in Fig. 6-3.
4. Measure on each side of the centerline one-half the width of the opening, and mark for trimmer studs outside these points (see Fig. 6-4). Use a "T" to indicate trimmer.
5. Outside the trimmer, lay off the position of a full-length stud (see Fig. 6-5). Use an "X" to indicate full-length stud.
6. Check the plans for positions of partitions that intersect the wall; mark the position and framing needed (see Fig. 6-6).
7. Locate the positions of all the regular centers, making sure the first space is ¾ in. (20 mm) smaller so panel sheathing joints will occur on studs [see Fig. 6-7(a)]; stud locations in an opening are marked with a "C" to indicate cripples.

**FIGURE 6-3:**   *Center line of opening.*

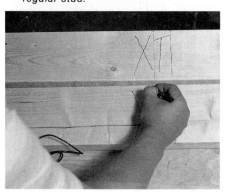

**FIGURE 6-4:**   *Locating trimmer and regular stud.*

**FIGURE 6-5:**   *Layout for rough opening.*

**FIGURE 6-6:**   *Layout for partition junctions.*

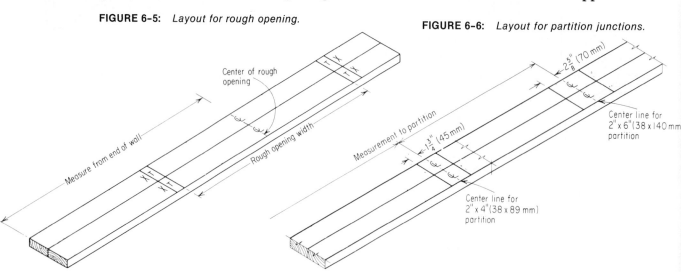

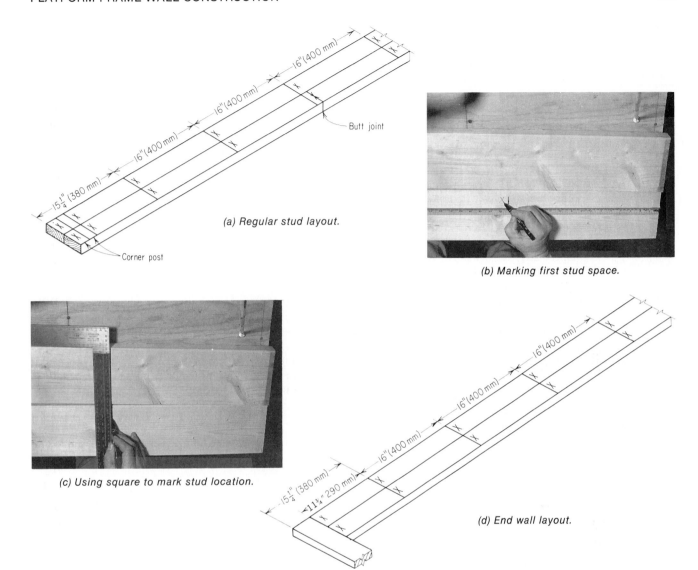

(a) Regular stud layout.

(b) Marking first stud space.

(c) Using square to mark stud location.

(d) End wall layout.

**FIGURE 6-7**

End walls must fit snugly between sidewalls when they are in place; therefore the plates must be two plate widths shorter than the end wall dimension. The first stud space must be smaller by the plate width minus one-half the thickness of stud, as illustrated in Fig. 6–7(d). The rest of the studs will be on regular centers from that point.

## Size and Spacing of Studs

The size and spacing of studs is determined by the *location* of the wall, its *height*, and the *load* which it will have to support. Table 6–1 indicates the size and spacing required for studs in both exterior and interior walls for a variety of loading conditions.

**TABLE 6-1:** *Size and spacing of studs*

| *Type of wall* | *Supported loads (including dead loads)* | *Min. stud size [in. (mm)]* | *Max. stud spacing [in. (mm)]* | *Max unsupported height [ft-in. (m)]* |
|---|---|---|---|---|
| Interior | No load | 2 × 2 (38 × 38) | 16 (400) | 7–10 (2.4) |
| | | 2 × 4 (38 × 89) (flat) | 16 (400) | 11–10 (3.6) |
| | Limited attic storage[a] | 2 × 3 (38 × 64) | 24 (600) | 9–10 (3.0) |
| | | 2 × 4 (38 × 89) | 24 (600) | 11–10 (3.6) |
| | Full attic storage[b] plus 1 floor, or roof load plus 1 floor, or limited attic storage [a] plus 2 floors | 2 × 4 (38 × 89) | 16 (400) | 11–10 (3.6) |
| | Full attic storage[b] plus 2 floors or roof load plus 2 floors | 2 × 4 (38 × 89) | 12 (300) | 11–10 (3.6) |
| | | 2 × 6 (38 × 140) | 16 (400) | 13–9 (4.2) |
| | Roof load, full attic storage[b] limited attic storage plus 1 floor | 2 × 4 (38 × 89) | 24 (600) | 11–10 (3.6) |
| | | 2 × 3 (38 × 64) | 16 (400) | 7–10 (2.4) |
| | Full attic storage[b] plus 3 floors or roof load plus 3 floors | 2 × 6 (38 × 140) | 12 (300) | 13–9 (4.2) |
| Exterior | Roof with or without attic storage | 2 × 3 (38 × 64) | 16 (400) | 7–10 (2.4) |
| | | 2 × 4 (38 × 89) | 24 (600) | 9–10 (3.0) |
| | Roof with or without attic storage plus 1 floor | 2 × 4 (38 × 89) | 16 (400) | 9–10 (3.0) |
| | | 2 × 6 (38 × 140) | 24 (600) | 9–10 (3.0) |
| | Roof with or without attic storage plus 2 floors | 2 × 4 (38 × 89) | 12 (300) | 9–10 (3.0) |
| | | 2 × 6 (38 × 140) | 16 (400) | 11–10 (3.6) |
| | Roof with or without attic storage plus 3 floors | 2 × 6 (38 × 140) | 12 (300) | 5–11 (1.8) |

[a] Applies to attics not accessible by a stairway.

[b] Applies to attics accessible by a stairway.

## CUTTING THE FRAME

The assembly of the frame will be made much simpler if all the pieces have been cut accurately first. Read the drawings carefully and find the length of studs. Check sole and top plate layouts for the number of full-length studs required, taking into account the extras needed at corners, partition junctions, wall openings, etc. Check the plans for the width and height of all exterior openings and for the height of the top of the openings above the subfloor. For standard wood-sash windows, the rough opening should be ¾ in. (20 mm) larger in height and width than the frame. Rough openings for wooden door frames should also be ¾ in. (20 mm) larger than the frame.

Count the number of trimmers, lintels, rough sills, and cripples required from the layout. With rough opening sizes and heights above floor, it is not difficult to calculate the length and cut these ready for assembly.

## Stud Lengths

**Regular.** The length of regular studs, corner post members, and partition junction studs will be the finished wall height plus clearance [usually 1 in. (25 mm)] less the thickness of *three* plates. For example, if the finished wall height is to be 96 in. (2400 mm), the regular stud length will be 96 in. + 1 in. − (3 × 1½) = 92½ in. [2400 + 25 − (3 × 38) = 2311 mm].

**Trimmers.** The length of a trimmer stud will be the height of the top of the opening above the floor less the thickness of *one* plate.

**Lower Cripple Studs.** The length of the lower cripple stud will be the height of the bottom of the opening above the floor less the thickness of *two* plates.

**Upper Cripple Studs.** Although it is possible to calculate the length of the upper cripple studs, it is usually more satisfactory, from a practical standpoint, to measure the distance between lintel and top plate after the remainder of the members in the wall have been assembled (see Fig. 6-8).

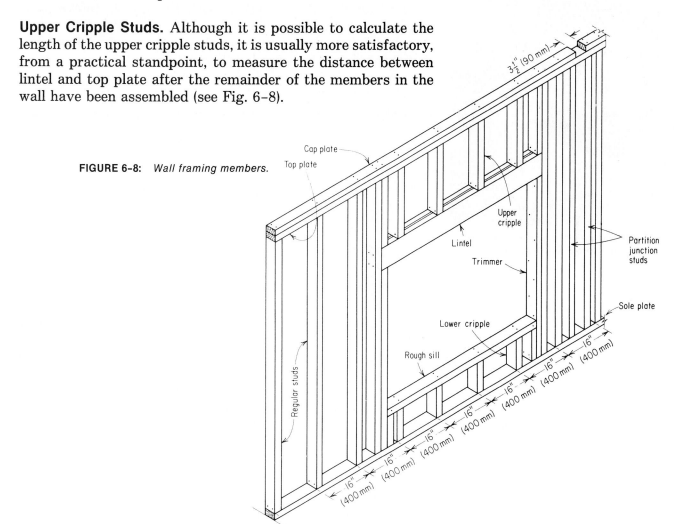

**FIGURE 6-8:** *Wall framing members.*

### Rough Sill Length

The length of the rough sill (see Fig. 6–8) will be equal to the width of the rough opening.

### Lintel

The length of the lintel will be the width of the rough opening (see Fig. 6–8) plus the thickness of two trimmers [3 in. (76 mm)], while its depth will depend on the width of the opening. Table 6–2 gives the depth of lintel required and maximum spans allowable for interior and exterior walls under a variety of loading conditions.

The thickness of the lintel will be equal to the thickness of the wall frame and must be made up accordingly. For a 2 × 4 in. (89-mm) frame, it is usually made of two pieces of 1½-in. (38-mm) material nailed together, with the proper thickness of spacer between them, as illustrated in Fig. 6–9. For a 2 × 6 (140-mm) frame, two pieces of material could be used, with a 2 × 6 nailed to the bottom edge [see Fig. 6–9(c)].

*(a) Using nailer to assemble lintel.*
*(Courtesy Bostitch Textron)*

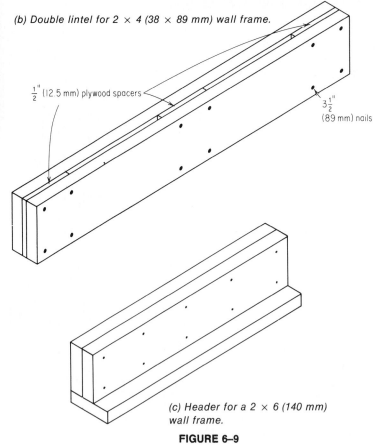

*(b) Double lintel for 2 × 4 (38 × 89 mm) wall frame.*

½" (12.5 mm) plywood spacers

3½" (89 mm) nails

*(c) Header for a 2 × 6 (140 mm) wall frame.*

**FIGURE 6–9**

**TABLE 6-2:** *Maximum spans for wood lintels*

| Location of lintels | Supported loads including dead loads and ceiling | Depth of lintel | | Maximum allowable span | |
|---|---|---|---|---|---|
| | | *in.* | *mm* | *ft-in.* | *m* |
| Interior walls | Limited attic storage | 4 | 89 | 4–0 | 1.22 |
| | | 6 | 140 | 6–0 | 1.83 |
| | | 8 | 184 | 8–0 | 2.44 |
| | | 10 | 235 | 10–0 | 3.05 |
| | | 12 | 286 | 12–6 | 3.81 |
| | Full attic storage or roof load or limited attic storage plus 1 floor | 4 | 89 | 2–0 | 0.61 |
| | | 6 | 140 | 3–0 | 0.91 |
| | | 8 | 184 | 4–0 | 1.22 |
| | | 10 | 235 | 5–0 | 1.52 |
| | | 12 | 286 | 6–0 | 1.83 |
| | Full attic storage plus 1 floor, or roof load plus 1 floor, or limited attic storage plus 2 or 3 floors | 4 | 89 | — | — |
| | | 6 | 140 | 2–6 | 0.76 |
| | | 8 | 184 | 3–0 | 0.91 |
| | | 10 | 235 | 4–0 | 1.22 |
| | | 12 | 286 | 5–0 | 1.52 |
| | Full attic storage plus 2 or 3 floors or roof load plus 2 or 3 floors | 4 | 89 | — | — |
| | | 6 | 140 | 2–0 | 0.61 |
| | | 8 | 184 | 3–0 | 0.91 |
| | | 10 | 235 | 3–6 | 1.07 |
| | | 12 | 286 | 4–0 | 1.22 |
| Exterior walls | Roof with or without attic storage | 4 | 89 | 3–8 | 1.12 |
| | | 6 | 140 | 5–6 | 1.68 |
| | | 8 | 184 | 7–4 | 2.24 |
| | | 10 | 235 | 9–2 | 2.79 |
| | | 12 | 286 | 11–0 | 3.35 |
| | Roof with or without attic storage plus 1 floor | 4 | 89 | 1–10 | 0.56 |
| | | 6 | 140 | 4–7 | 1.40 |
| | | 8 | 184 | 6–5 | 1.96 |
| | | 10 | 235 | 7–4 | 2.24 |
| | | 12 | 286 | 8–3 | 2.51 |
| | Roof with or without attic storage plus 2 or 3 floors | 4 | 89 | 1–10 | 0.56 |
| | | 6 | 140 | 3–8 | 1.12 |
| | | 8 | 184 | 5–6 | 1.68 |
| | | 10 | 235 | 6–5 | 1.96 |
| | | 12 | 286 | 7–4 | 2.24 |

Source: Courtesy National Research Council.

## ASSEMBLING THE FRAME

When the pieces have all been cut, the process of assembly can begin. The first step is to make up lintels for door and window openings. A number of types of corner and partition connections are used, as illustrated in Fig. 6–10. A multiple stud connection, made up of either two or three studs, is used at exterior corners or partition junctions to tie walls together and to provide nailing surfaces for wall board. Two stud arrangements may be used if a plasterboard clip is used for support.

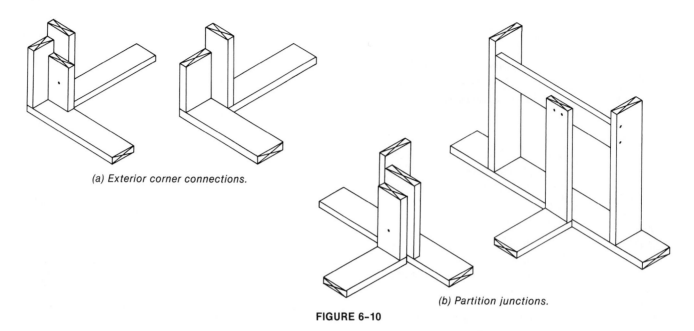

*(a) Exterior corner connections.*

*(b) Partition junctions.*

**FIGURE 6-10**

**FIGURE 6-11**

*(a) Order of wall member assembly.*

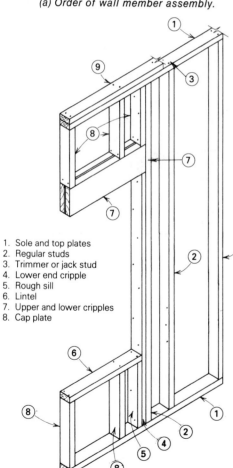

1. Sole and top plates
2. Regular studs
3. Trimmer or jack stud
4. Lower end cripple
5. Rough sill
6. Lintel
7. Upper and lower cripples
8. Cap plate

The assembly of the wall frames can now begin, starting with one of the sidewalls. If the project is a platform frame, the wall will be assembled on the subfloor and raised into position in one or more units, depending on the length. Proceed as follows:

1. Lay out the sole and top plates on edge, spaced stud length apart, with the laid-out faces toward each other. The sole plate should be near the edge of the floor frame on which it will rest.

2. Place a full-length stud at each position indicated on the layout.

3. Nail the sole and top plates to the ends of these with two 3½-in. (89-mm) nails in each end.

4. Nail the trimmers to the full-length studs on each side of openings.

5. Nail the two end lower cripple studs to the inside of the trimmers, as shown in Fig. 6–11(a).

6. Lay the rough sill on the ends of the two lower cripples and nail.

7. Set the lintels on the ends of the trimmers and endnail through the full-length studs [see Fig. 6–11(b)].

8. Set the remainder of the cripple studs, upper and lower, in position and nail. The upper cripples must be toenailed to the top edge of the lintel.

9. Nail on the cap plate. It must be kept back 3½ in. (89 mm) from the ends of the wall and a gap left open at partition junctions (see Fig. 6–12).

FIGURE 6-11    *(b) Using power nailers to assemble wall frame.*

*(b) Gap for partition connection.*

FIGURE 6-12

*(a) Gap for tying corner together.*

## WALL SHEATHING

In the case of a platform frame, it is usually advantageous to sheathe the frame before standing it in place. Begin by making sure that the frame is square. Check the diagonal distances from the bottom corners to the opposite top ones. They should be exactly the same. Tack the wall frame to the subfloor to keep it straight and square.

There are a number of materials available which may be used as sheathing. They include *shiplap, common boards, ply-*

FIGURE 6-13

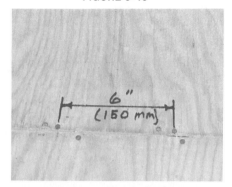

*(a) Nail spacing at edge of sheet.*

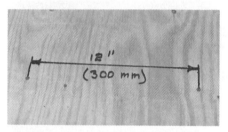

*(b) Nail spacing along intermediate supports.*

*(c) Using power nailers and routers.*

*wood, exterior fiber board, exterior gypsum board, waferboard,* and *insulating sheathing.* Sheathing-grade plywood or waferboard is probably the most widely used, but all the others do a satisfactory job, and, in an age of energy conservation, styrofoam sheathing is particularly attractive because of its high insulation value.

Common boards can be applied diagonally or horizontally [see Fig. 13(d)]. Although diagonal application is more rigid, horizontal application is more economical as it takes less material and time to complete. Use two 2¼-in. (60-mm) nails for 6-in. (140-mm) boards and three for wider material on each stud.

Plywood, minimum thickness ⁵⁄₁₆ in. (7.5 mm), should be applied with the long dimension horizontal for greater rigidity. The spacing of the end joints of the plywood should be offset two stud spaces if possible. Use 2-in. (50-mm) coated or spiral nails, spaced 6 in. along the edges of the panel and 12 in. on intermediate supports (see Fig. 6-13). A ¹⁄₁₆-in. space should be left between panels to allow for expansion (see Fig. 6-14). Some framers let the sheathing overhang past the bottom of the wall to allow for alignment (see Fig. 6-15). When the sheathing is flush with the bottom of the wall, polyethylene is used to seal the joint (see Fig. 6-16). Power nailers and routers are used to speed up the assembly of wall frames (see Fig. 6-13).

*(d) Horizontal application of boards.*

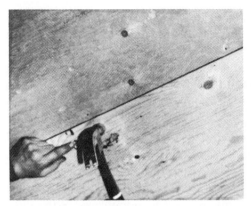

**FIGURE 6-14:** *Space between sheets.*

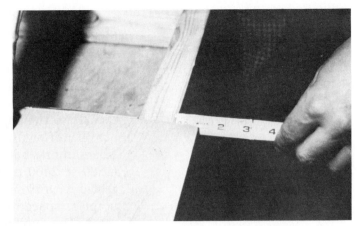

**FIGURE 6-15:** *Overhang at bottom of wall.*

**FIGURE 6-16:** *Poly for sealing joint at wall and floor.*

Waferboard sheathing is made of wood wafers or strands (narrow wafers) bonded together with heat and pressure with a waterproof resin. Wafers are of $1\frac{1}{4}$-in. (30-mm) length and uniform thickness. Waferboard comes in two types: (1) with the wafers placed randomly throughout the panel, and (2) oriented strand board (OSB) with the surface layers of wafers or strands aligned in the panel length direction. Inner layers may be cross aligned or randomly oriented. The panels range from $\frac{1}{4}$ in. to $1\frac{1}{2}$ in. (6–38 mm) in thickness, and will conform to minimums set in Table 6–3.

**TABLE 6-3:** *Thickness of structural wall sheathing*

| | Minimum thickness [in. (mm)] | |
|---|---|---|
| *Type of sheathing* | *With supports 16 in. (400 mm) o.c.* | *With supports 24 in. (600 mm) o.c.* |
| Lumber | $\frac{11}{16}$ (17) | $\frac{11}{16}$ (17) |
| Fiber board | $\frac{3}{8}$ (9.5) | $\frac{7}{16}$ (11) |
| Gypsum board | $\frac{3}{8}$ (9.5) | $\frac{1}{2}$ (12.7) |
| Plywood | $\frac{1}{4}$ (6) | $\frac{5}{16}$ (7.5) |
| Waferboard | $\frac{1}{4}$ (6.35) | $\frac{5}{16}$ (7.9) |

Waferboard is applied by the same method as plywood sheathing. Panels can be placed horizontally or vertically, and they will not be affected by the difference in strength that occurs when plywood is placed with the grain parallel to studs as opposed to perpendicular (see Fig. 6–17). Oriented strand board has more strength if placed with the length of the panel perpendicular to the supports.

Exterior fiber board, a material made from shredded wood fibers impregnated with asphalt, is commonly made in 4 × 8 ft (1200 × 2400 mm) sheets, $\frac{7}{16}$-in. (11 mm) thick. The panels are nailed with $1\frac{3}{4}$-in. (44-mm) broad-headed nails or $1\frac{1}{2}$-in. (38-mm) staples, spaced 6-in. (150 mm) along the edges and 8-in. (200 mm) along intermediate supports. Vertical joints should be offset, similar to plywood (see Fig. 6–18).

**FIGURE 6-17:** *Waferboard sheathing.*

**FIGURE 6-18:** *Fiber board sheathing.*

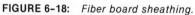

Exterior gypsum board is made with a core of gypsum encased in asphalt-impregnated paper. The sheets are 2 × 8 ft × ½-in. thick (600 × 1200 × 12.5 mm), with the long edges having a tongue and groove horizontal joint. The sheets are applied with the long dimension horizontal. Two-inch (50-mm) coated or spiral nails, spaced 6 in. (150 mm) apart on all studs, are used. All vertical joints must be staggered (see Fig. 6–19).

Insulating exterior sheathing board is applied to the outside of exterior wall studs much in the same manner as conventional sheathing. Insulating sheathing will increase the "R" values of the wall to meet today's energy-saving requirements. Insulating sheathing includes such materials as styrofoam, fiberglass, and thermax board.

Styrofoam insulating sheathing is a synthetic material made from expanded polystyrene in rigid sheets with a smooth, high-density skin. It has a thermal resistance ("R" value) of 5 per inch (25 mm). The sheets are either 2 × 8 ft (600 × 2400 mm) or 4 × 8 ft (1200 × 2400 mm), 1 to 2 in. (25 to 50 mm) thick with butt edges, and are applied like other panel sheathing. Thicknesses under 1½ in. (38 mm) must be placed over plywood or waferboard to ensure sufficient wall strength (see Fig. 6–20).

**FIGURE 6-19:** *Gypsum board exterior sheathing.*

**FIGURE 6-20:** *Styrofoam sheathing.*

Fasteners may be broad-headed (roofing) nails, staples, or screws, with a spacing of 6 in. (150 mm) for nails or staples. The length of the fasteners should be a minimum of ¾ in. (19 mm) longer than the thickness of the sheathing.

The styrofoam should be covered with exterior building paper, over which any type of exterior finish, including wood or metal siding, stucco, or brick veneer may be applied.

Styrofoam will burn, and during shipping, storage, installation, and use it must not be exposed to open flame or other ignition source.

**FIGURE 6-21:** *Glass fiber sheathing.*

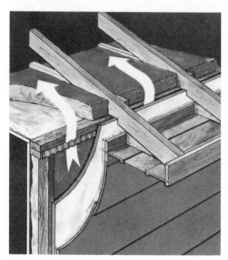

**FIGURE 6-22:** *Corrugated plastic vent strip along top plate.*

Fiberglass sheathing boards are composed of resin-bonded glass fibers faced with a durable air barrier. They will not rot even after continuous wetting and drying cycles and are not affected by fungi or insects. The glass fiber board is permeable to water vapor and will not trap moisture. The moisture-resistant facing has fair resistance to impact loads.

Glass fiber insulating board is attached to the studs with large head galvanized roofing nails. The nails should be $\frac{3}{4}$ in. (19 mm) longer than the thickness of the board. Attachment is required at spacings of 6 in. (150 mm) along edges and 12 in. (300 mm) along intermediate supports. If 1-in. (25-mm) head diameter nails or washers are used under the head, the spacing can be increased to 12 in. (300 mm) along the edges and 18 in. (450 mm) along intermediate supports.

Glass fiber sheathing is available in sheets 48 × 96 in. and 48 × 108 in. (1200 × 2400 and 1200 × 2700 mm). One-inch and $1\frac{1}{2}$-in. (25- and 38-mm) thickness sheets are available. Thermal resistance at 75°F (24°C) mean temperature is 4.4 (RSI 0.77) for 1-in. (25-mm) thickness and 6.7 (RSI 1.18) for $1\frac{1}{2}$-in. (38-mm) thickness (see Fig. 6–21).

Thermax sheathing consists of a glass-reinforced polyisocyanurate foam plastic core with aluminum foil faces. Since Thermax sheathing has a closed cell structure and aluminum faces that make an efficient barrier to moisture as well as heat flow, there is concern in colder climates for the potential of entrapped water vapor within stud spaces. A vent strip system is used for moisture relief along the top edge of the wall, allowing for the escape of water vapor (see Fig. 6–22). No special fastening is required. The boards are secured in place with galvanized roofing nails long enough to penetrate framing $\frac{3}{4}$-in. (19 mm). Thermax sheathing is not a structural panel, so wood let-ins or metal strap bracing is used for thickness under $1\frac{1}{2}$ in. (38 mm).

**FIGURE 6-23:** *Thermax sheathing.*

The panels are available in standard insulation board sizes of 4 × 8 ft (1200 × 2400 mm) and 4 × 9 ft (1200 × 2700 mm) and thicknesses varying from ½ in. (12.7 mm) to 2¼ in. (57.2 mm). Thermal resistance at 75°F (24°C) mean temperature ranges from 3.6 (RSI 0.63) for ½-in. material to 16.2 (RSI 2.85) for 2¼-in. material (see Fig. 6–23).

## ERECTING THE FRAME

Usually a one-story wall frame can be raised by hand unless it is particularly long or heavy, in which case wall jacks may be used (see Fig. 6–24). Be sure that the bottom of the frame is close to the edge of the subfloor so that as the wall is raised the sheathing overhang does not catch on the floor (see Fig. 6–24).

**FIGURE 6-24**

*(a) Raising a section of wall by hand.*

*(b) Raising a wall with wall jacks.*

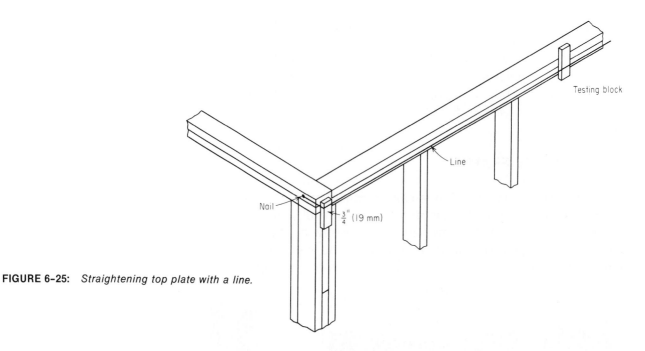

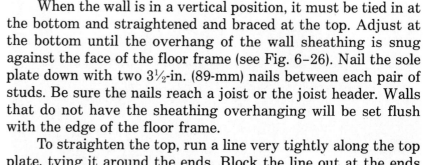

**FIGURE 6-25:** *Straightening top plate with a line.*

**FIGURE 6-26:** *Plywood overlap at exterior corner.*

When the wall is in a vertical position, it must be tied in at the bottom and straightened and braced at the top. Adjust at the bottom until the overhang of the wall sheathing is snug against the face of the floor frame (see Fig. 6–26). Nail the sole plate down with two 3½-in. (89-mm) nails between each pair of studs. Be sure the nails reach a joist or the joist header. Walls that do not have the sheathing overhanging will be set flush with the edge of the floor frame.

To straighten the top, run a line very tightly along the top plate, tying it around the ends. Block the line out at the ends with a small piece of ¾-in. (19-mm) material (see Fig. 6–25). Take another piece of ¾-in. (19-mm) material and check at various points to see if the line is the correct distance from the plate. Push the top of the wall in or out, where necessary, to correct any points not in line. Brace by nailing one end of a board to the face of a stud at the top and the other end to a block fastened to the subfloor.

When one side wall has been erected and plumbed, the opposite one may be assembled and erected in the same manner, followed by the end walls, one by one. It is impractical to sheathe the end wall frames completely on the subfloor because the end wall sheathing should extend over the corner posts, but the majority of it may be applied at this time. With the end wall erect and the sole plate nailed in position, the end studs can be nailed to the sidewall partial corner posts to make the post complete.

The remainder of the sheathing can now be applied, the wall plumbed and braced, and the end wall cap plate will overlap the sidewall top plates to tie sidewalls and end walls securely together (see Fig. 6–26).

When a balloon frame is being erected, special problems are involved. Since the studs rest on the sill plate, there is no sole plate, and they must be held properly spaced by some other means until the frame is erected or until the sheathing is applied. Because of its height, it is usually impractical to try to raise a balloon frame wall, assembled on the floor, by hand. A crane is required to do the job efficiently, and if one is available, assembly on the floor is the best method. Otherwise, the studs have to be placed in position one at a time. If the wall is sheathed on the floor, the ribbon must be put in after the wall is erected. In nearly every case, scaffolding will have to be erected during the building of balloon frame walls.

## PARTITIONS

Partitions may be *bearing* or *nonbearing*. Bearing partitions carry part of the roof load, bear one end of the ceiling joists, or both, whereas nonbearing partitions simply enclose space and carry the finishing materials (see Fig. 6–27).

**FIGURE 6–27**

*(a) Loadbearing wall.*

*(b) Non-loadbearing wall.*

*(a) Partition connection.*

Partitions may be laid out, assembled, and erected in the same way as outside walls. The position of the sole plate on the subfloor is first marked by *snapping a chalk line.* This is done by stretching a chalk line tightly along the partition position, pulling the line up in the center and letting it snap against the floor. This will mark a straight line to which the partition sole plate can be set.

Plates are laid out and studs and other members cut and assembled. Nail three blocks about 12 in. (300 mm) in length between the sidewall partition junction studs, one at the top and bottom and one in the center (see Fig. 6-28), after which the partition can be raised into place. Plumb the end studs and nail them to the partition blocks. Finally, add a cap plate, with its ends overlapping the sidewall top plate (see Fig. 6-28). Erect the longest partition first, then the cross partitions, and, finally, the partitions forming clothes closets, hallways, etc. Another method of providing backing at the junction of partition and exterior wall is to place horizontal blocking at 16 in. (400 mm) o.c. between regular studding (see Fig. 6-29).

*(b) Cap plate overlapping for tie.*
**FIGURE 6-28**

**FIGURE 6-29:**   *Partition junction.*

One partition requiring special attention will be the one for the bathroom in which the main plumbing vent stack is located. In some cases, this one will have to be made 6 in. (140 mm) wide to accommodate the size of the stack.

Broom and clothes closet partitions may sometimes be framed with 2 × 2 (38 × 38) material in order to save space, but only if the partition is short or in a protected location.

## Sliding Door Opening

Framing to provide for doors which slide into the wall also requires special consideration. The thickness of the door must first be determined. This portion of the partition frame must be wide enough to accommodate the thickness of the door plus clearance and at least ¾-in. (19 mm) framing on each side (see Fig. 6–30). The width of a pocket door opening must be twice the door width plus jamb thickness and clearance [¾ in. (20 mm)]. Height will vary depending on design of track assembly.

## Openings for Heating and Ventilating

Openings must be made in the frame to accommodate heating system stacks leading to registers, if the registers are of the wall type, as well as openings for air-conditioning and ventilating systems, where they are specified.

If the cold air return will fit between a pair of regular studs, all that is necessary is to cut the sole plate out between the studs, cut a hole in the subfloor, and put in a header between the studs at the required height [see Fig. 6–31(a)]. If a wider space is needed, a header is placed in adjacent spaces. The sole plate is cut out and a hole made in the subfloor, as above [see Fig. 6–31(b)]. Placing a piece of screen over the opening during construction will keep debris out of the heating pipes [see Fig. 6–31(c)].

**FIGURE 6-30:** *Pocket door framing.*

*(b) Wall openings for ducts and registers.*

**FIGURE 6-31**

*(a) Wall openings for registers.*

*(c) Screen over opening.*

## Wall Backing

Installations such as wall-type basins, cupboards, etc., which must be fastened to the wall must be provided with some type of solid backing. This may be done by putting a piece of 1½-in. (38-mm) material between the studs (as illustrated in Fig. 6–32).

*(a) Water line.*

*(b) Tissue holder.*

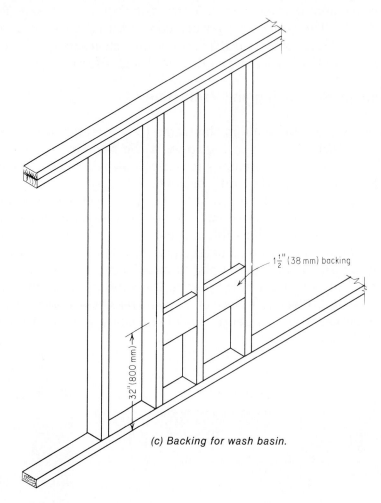

1½" (38 mm) backing

32" (800 mm)

*(c) Backing for wash basin.*

**FIGURE 6-32:**   *Wall backing.*

## LIGHT STEEL WALL FRAMING

Light steel wall framing members in several styles, depending on the manufacturer, are made from sheet steel, cold-formed, and consist basically of *studs* and *mounting channels* (see Fig. 6–33).

Studs are made in the form of channels, in two types, *loadbearing* and *non-loadbearing*. Loadbearing studs are made from several thicknesses of metal [0.036 to 0.075 in. (0.91 to 1.9 mm)], with web sizes from 3⅝ to 8 in. (92 to 203 mm) and 1⅝ to 1¾-in. (41- to 44-mm) flange. Non-loadbearing studs are made from lighter-gauge steel and in narrower widths.

(a) Prefabricated light steel wall frame. (Courtesy U.S. Steel Corp.)

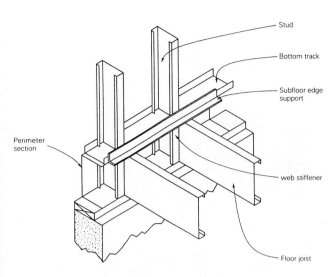

(b) Metal framing detail.

**FIGURE 6-33**

Mounting channels are made slightly wider to receive the end of the studs (see Fig. 6-33), and are used for top and bottom tracks and window sill and head track. No cap plate is required (see Fig. 6-33) since all members are fastened together.

Lintels are usually made of two wood members or metal channels or beams with their top and bottom edge enclosed by a length of mounting channel (see Fig. 6-34). Where openings do not reach to the bottom edge of the lintel, another length of mounting channel forms the top of the opening, with cripple studs between it and the lintel (see Fig. 6-34).

**FIGURE 6-34:** *Lintel framing.*

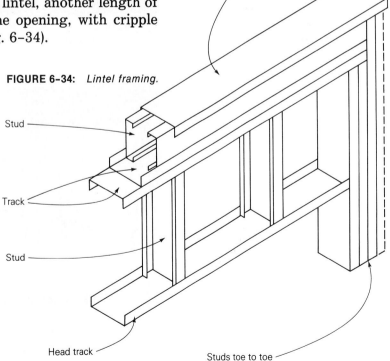

**FIGURE 6-35:** *Raising walls.*

Wall frames may be prefabricated and brought to the site ready for erection (see Fig. 6-35), assembled on the subfloor, and raised into position, as in Fig. 6-35. Usually preassembled frames are sheathed before being raised with ⅜-in. (9-mm) plywood sheathing, fastened with steel nails driven by a pneumatic hammer (see Fig. 6-13(c).

Wall frames are anchored to concrete floors with power-actuated pins, placed 24 in. (600 mm) o.c. Screws are used when fastening to wooden floors. Rafters or trusses are anchored over supports to the top plate with *U-clips*, which are welded to the frame and bolted to the roof members (see Fig. 6-36).

**FIGURE 6-36:** *U-clips for roof members. (Courtesy U.S. Steel Corp.)*

**FIGURE 6-37:** *Interior steel partitions.*

The lighter, non load-bearing framing material used for interior partitions provides a considerable saving of floor space (see Fig. 6–37). Non load-bearing studs measure $1\frac{3}{16} \times 3\frac{5}{8}$ in. (30 × 91 mm) with a metal thickness of 0.21 in. (53 mm). Studs are also available in $2\frac{1}{2}$- and $1\frac{5}{8}$-in. (64- and 40-mm) widths for further space saving. Openings in the studs are at 24-in. (600-mm) centers for easy placement of electrical wires. Electrical clips are used to protect unarmored wires (see Fig. 6–38).

Mounting channels are tapered for better grip of the studs (see Fig. 6–39) and are fastened to concrete floors with power-actuated pins and with screws to wooden floors (see Fig. 6–40).

**FIGURE 6-38:** *Placing electrical wires in metal studs.*

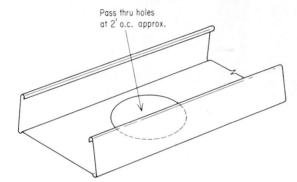

**FIGURE 6-39:** *Mounting channel.*

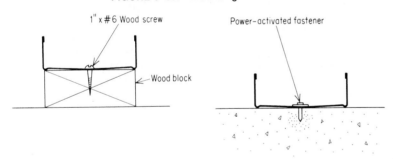

**FIGURE 6-40:** *Fastening mounting channel.*

When wood trim or base is to be fastened to metal framing, a wood runner is placed under the mounting channel. Studs are fastened to the channel with screws or a crimping tool (see Fig. 6–41). The studs are easily placed in the channel with a twisting action (see Fig. 6–41). Studs should be cut in lengths $\frac{1}{4}$ in. (6 mm) shorter than the wall height to allow for variations in height (see Fig. 6–42). Mounting channels are fastened in the desired location first, and then the studs are placed individually into the channel (see Fig. 6–41).

Wall junctions (intersections and corners) are framed as illustrated in Fig. 6–43. Studs are sometimes placed 2 in. (50 mm) away from the junctions to allow for easy access of screw guns when attaching gypsum board facing. Headers for door openings are cut 12 in. (300 mm) longer than the rough opening to allow for easy attachment (see Fig. 6–44).

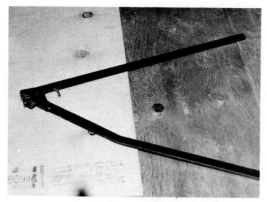

*(a) Crimping tool.*

**FIGURE 6-41**

*(b) Erecting interior wall frame. (Courtesy Steel Co. of Canada)*

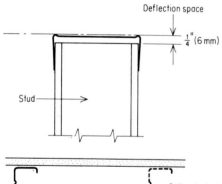

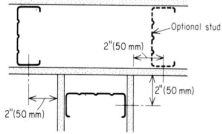

**FIGURE 6-42:** *Allowance at top of wall.*

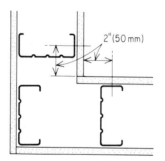

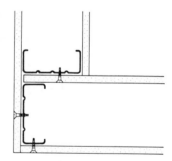

**FIGURE 6-43:** *Partition connections.*

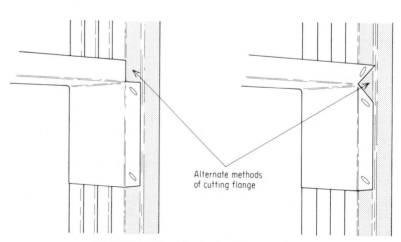

*Alternate methods of cutting flange*

**FIGURE 6-44:** *Header for door opening.*

## MASONRY WALL SYSTEMS

Masonry units may be used in walls in a number of ways in light construction. The most common one is to use brick, stone, or block units as a *veneer* over a wood frame or a concrete block backup wall. Another is to build a brick or block single wythe wall, with the masonry units as the exterior finish and in some occasions as the interior finish as well.

### Brick Veneer

**Over Wood Frame.** A single wythe of brick, $3\frac{5}{8}$ in. (90 mm) thick, is often used to face a sheathed wall, framed in wood. Both the building frame and the brick wythe must be supported on the foundation wall (see Fig. 6–45), and a 1-in. (25-mm) space should be left between brick and sheathing.

The brick must be anchored to the frame by noncorrosive metal straps, not less than 22 gauge (0.76 mm) thick and 1 in. (25 mm) wide, spaced in accordance with Table 6–4.

**FIGURE 6-45:** *Typical wall section, brick veneer on frame construction.*

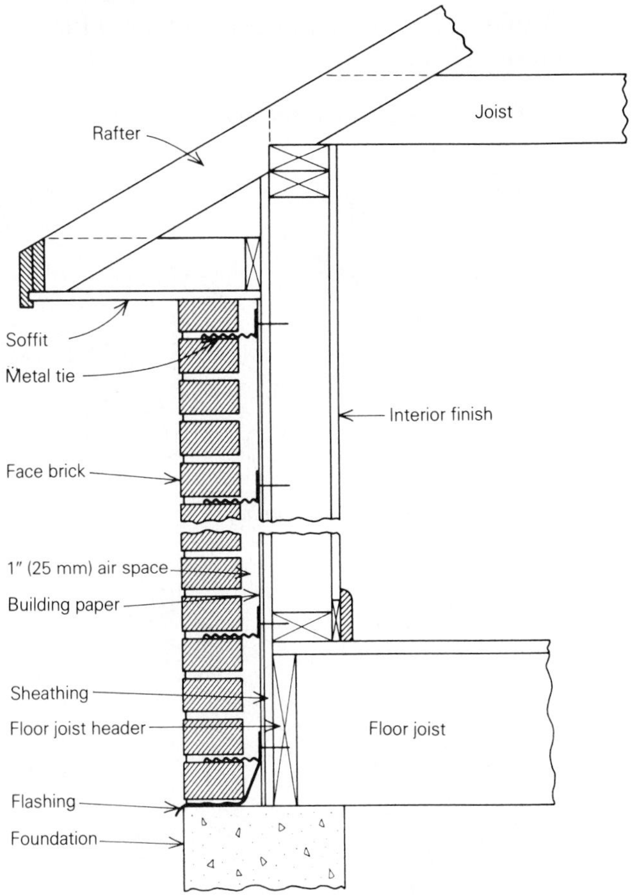

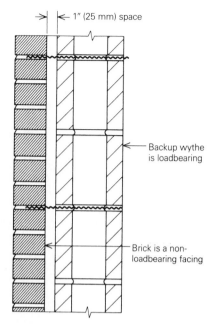

**FIGURE 6-46:** *Brick veneer.*

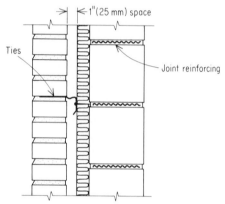

**FIGURE 6-47:** *Brick veneer with cavity insulated.*

**TABLE 6-4:** *Brick veneer tie spacing [in. (mm)]*

| Horizontal spacing | Maximum vertical spacing |
|---|---|
| 16 (400) | 24 (600) |
| 24 (600) | 20 (500) |
| 32 (800) | 16 (400) |

**Over Concrete Block.** Four-, six-, or eight-inch (100-, 150-, or 200-mm) block may be used as a backup wall for a 4-in. (100-mm) brick veneer face, depending on the height of wall. This veneer should be separated from the backup by an unfilled space of at least 1 in. (25 mm) (see Fig. 6–46). When rigid insulation is used on the outside of the block backup, the space must be increased in size so the 1-in. (25-mm) space exists between the insulation and the facing (see Fig. 6–47). The facing wythe has to carry its own weight but otherwise is not considered to contribute to the vertical or lateral load resistance of the wall. The backup is designed to resist vertical or lateral loads. The space serves as a drainage gap between the veneer and the backup wall, and any forces on the facing are transmitted across the gap to the backup by ties.

Tying to the backup wall can be accomplished by using corrugated ties embedded in the mortar joints with the tie spacing regulated by Table 6–4 or by using continuous joint reinforcing in every second or third row of the block backup (see Fig. 6–48).

**FIGURE 6-48:** *Joint reinforcing and ties.*

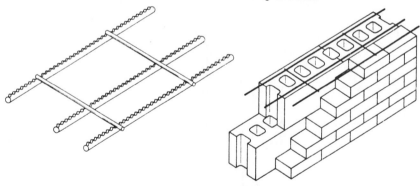

*(a) Joint reinforcing*

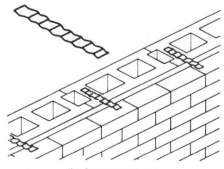

*(b) Corrugated ties*

**TABLE 6-5:** *Maximum opening span allowed for various lintel angle sizes*

| Angle size [in. (mm)] | 3-in (75-mm) brick | 3½-in. (90-mm) brick |
|---|---|---|
| 3½ × 3 × ¼ | 8 ft, 4 in. | — |
| (90 × 75 × 6) | (2.55 m) | — |
| 3½ × 3½ × ¼ | 8 ft, 6 in. | 8 ft, 1 in. |
| (90 × 90 × 6) | (2.59 m) | (2.47 m) |
| 4 × 3½ × ¼ | 9 ft, 2 in. | 8 ft, 9 in. |
| (100 × 90 × 6) | (2.79 m) | (2.66 m) |
| 5 × 3 ½ × ⁵⁄₁₆ | 11 ft, 5 in. | 10 ft, 10 in. |
| (125 × 90 × 8) | (3.47 m) | (3.31 m) |
| 5 × 3½ × ⅜ | 11 ft, 11 in. | 11 ft, 5 in. |
| (125 × 90 × 10) | (3.64 m) | (3.48 m) |

The brick veneer over openings in walls must be supported by a *lintel*, usually a steel angle with its ends supported on the brick on either side of the opening. The maximum allowable opening span depends on the size of lintel used, and Table 6–5 gives the maximum span allowed for various lintel angle sizes using both 3- and 3⅝-in. (75- and 90-mm) brick veneer.

## Single-Wythe Masonry Walls

Solid masonry walls in one-story buildings and in the top story of two-story buildings may be constructed 5½ in. (140 mm) thick provided the walls are not over 9 ft, 2 in. (2.8 m) high at the eaves and 15 ft, 1 in. (4.6 m) at the peaks of the gable ends. The exterior walls of two- and three-story buildings should not be less than 7½ in. (190 mm) thick. Solid or hollow units are normally used for this type of construction.

**FIGURE 6–49:** *5½-in. (140-mm) brick wall.*

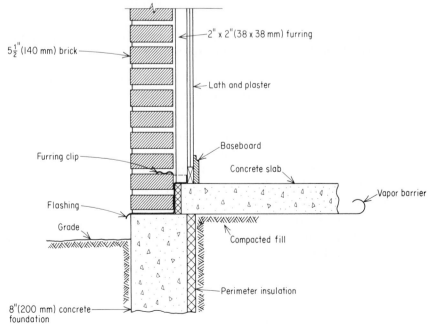

On the inside surface, the wall may be *furred out,* and the interior finish is applied to this furring. This furring allows for the application of a vapor barrier, makes for easy installation of electrical facilities, and provides space for the introduction of insulation. An 8-in. (200-mm) foundation wall is adequate, but the details of construction depend on the type of floor being used. Figure 6–49 illustrates one method of construction using a single-wythe brick wall. Single-wythe block walls were discussed in Chapter 4.

## REVIEW QUESTIONS

**6–1.** There are three basic differences between a balloon frame and a platform frame. Outline these differences briefly.

**6–2.** What is the purpose of firestops in a wall frame?

**6–3.** Explain why it is important to have wall backing at some locations in the wall frame.

**6–4.** Give two reasons for the use of cap plates in wood wall frames.

**6–5.** The frame for a given window is $62\frac{1}{2}$ in. (1560 mm) wide and $33\frac{1}{2}$ in. (835 mm) high. If $2 \times 10$s ($38 \times 235$ mm) are used for the lintel and they are placed directly below the top plate, calculate the length of each of the following members, if total wall height is 8 ft, 1 in. (2425 mm).
   (a) Window header
   (b) Rough sill
   (c) Trimmer
   (d) Bottom cripple stud

**6–6.** If board sheathing is used on the exterior of a wall frame, why should it be applied diagonally?

**6–7.** Explain why diagonal bracing may be required when glass fiber exterior sheathing is being used.

**6–8.** Using the following information, lay out a sole plate for an end wall 16 ft (4.85 m) in length:
   (a) Studs 16 in. (400 mm) o.c.
   (b) Exterior door 34 in. (910 mm) × 80 in. (2030 mm) centered 5 ft (1500 mm) from left end
   (c) Window frame $32\frac{1}{2} \times 45\frac{1}{2}$ in. (800 × 1140 mm), centered 11 ft (3300 mm) from left end
   (d) Partition junction ($2 \times 4$) centered 8 ft, 4 in. (2500 mm) from left end

# 7

# THE CEILING AND ROOF FRAME

The final step in completing the skeleton of a building is the framing of the roof system. The methods used depend on the type of roof and whether the roof assembly is built on site or premanufactured in a truss plant. If all the work is completed on the construction site, it can include the assembly of a ceiling frame as well as the roof frame. When a trussed roof system is used, the ceiling and the roof framing members are part of the same self-supporting structure.

## CEILING JOIST SIZES

The size of members used for ceiling joists depend on the span and spacing of the members, the type of material used for the ceiling, and the species and grade of lumber used. Ceiling joists supporting part of the roof load will be at least 1 in. (25 mm) greater in depth than ceiling joists not providing support. Check your local building codes to determine specific joist sizes.

## CUTTING CEILING JOISTS

The length of the joist depends on how they meet over the bearing partition. If two joists lap one another over the partition, exact lengths are not required (see Fig. 7-1).

At the outer end, the joist must be cut to conform to the slope of the roof (see Fig. 7-2). To make this cut properly, two things must be known: (1) the slope of the rafter and (2) the height of the back of the rafter above the plate (see Fig. 7-3). Having determined these, proceed as follows:

1. Check to see which is the crown edge of the stock and make sure that it becomes the *upper* edge.

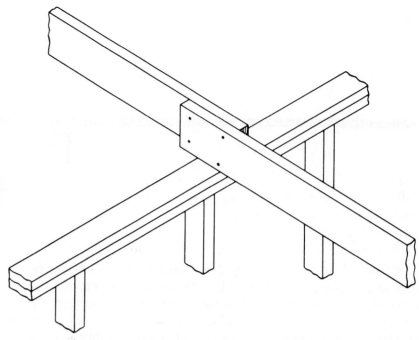

**FIGURE 7-1:**   *Ceiling joists lapped over bearing partition.*

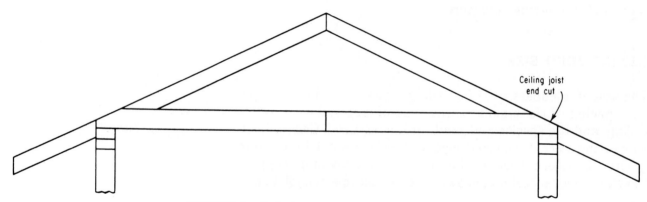

**FIGURE 7-2:**   *End of ceiling joists cut to slope of roof.*

**FIGURE 7-3:**   *Height of back of rafter above plate.*

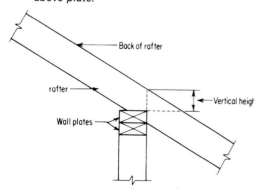

**FIGURE 7-4:**   *Layout for ceiling joist end cut.*

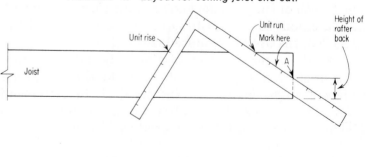

2. Measure up from the bottom edge of the joist, at the end, a distance equal to the height of the back of the rafter (see Fig. 7-4) and mark point A.

3. Lay the square on the stock with the unit rise on the tongue and 12 in. (250) (unit run) on the blade touching the top edge and the edge of the blade passing through A.

4. Mark on the blade and cut the joist end to that line.

When a hip roof is involved, ceiling joists cannot be set close to the end walls, because they would interfere with the end wall rafters. In such a case, the regular ceiling joists must be stopped back far enough for the rafters to clear them (normally one or two joist spacings, depending on the rise of the rafters), and *stub* joists are run at right angles to the end wall plate (see Fig. 7-5). In this case the joist supporting the stub joists is doubled and usually spaced the same as the regular ceiling joists.

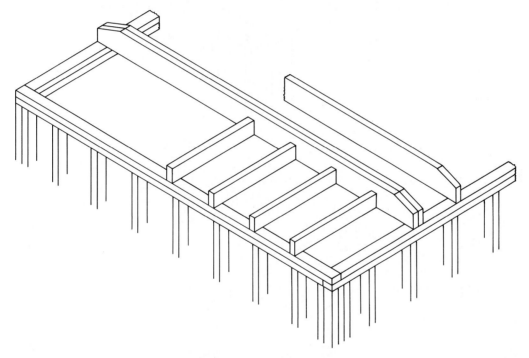

**FIGURE 7-5:** *Stub ceiling joists.*

## ASSEMBLING THE CEILING FRAME

Normally, ceiling joists run across the narrow dimension of the building, but this need not always be the case. Some joists may run in one direction and others at right angles to them. The main consideration is that there be adequate bearing and support at the ends (see Fig. 7-6).

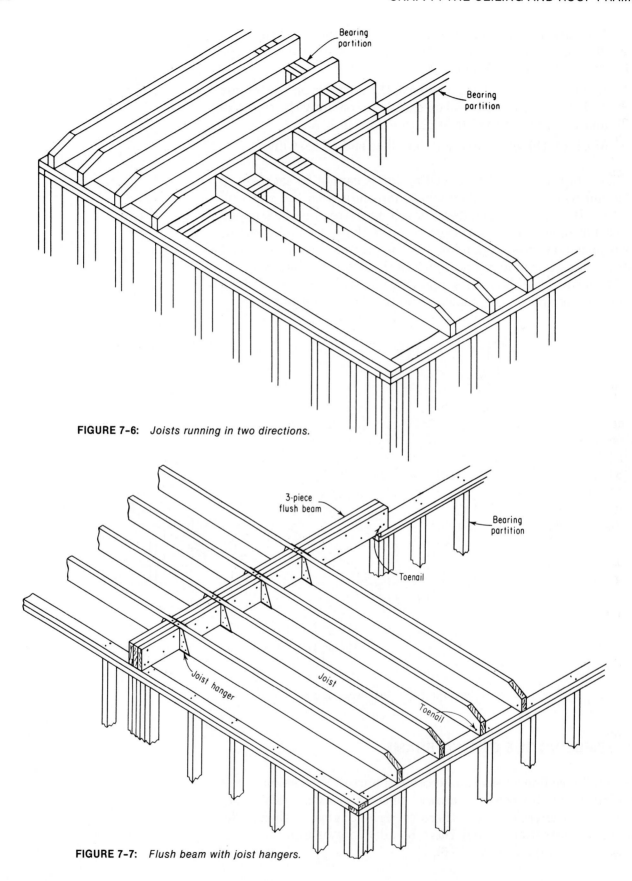

**FIGURE 7-6:** *Joists running in two directions.*

**FIGURE 7-7:** *Flush beam with joist hangers.*

Sometimes it is desired to have a *clear span ceiling* in some part of the building—a ceiling that runs unbroken from one outside wall to the other. Some means of supporting the inner ends of the joists is required, and this is done by means of a *flush beam*. A flush beam is one which has its bottom edge flush with the bottom of the ceiling joists and is supported at its ends by a bearing wall or bearing partition (see Fig. 7–7).

Ceiling joists are carried by a flush beam on *joist hangers* fastened to the face of the beam (see Fig. 7–7).

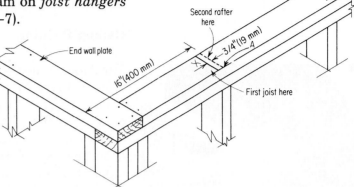

**FIGURE 7-8:** *First joist position layout.*

## Layout for Ceiling Joists

The first step in the placing of ceiling joists is the layout of their positions on the wall plate. Ceiling joists are normally spaced at 12, 16, or 24 in. (300, 400, or 600 mm) o.c. and, wherever possible, should be located to conform to the spacing of the rafters. This procedure not only facilitates the locating of the rafters but also makes it possible for ceiling joists and rafters to be nailed together.

Layout may begin either from the corners (see Fig. 7–8), from the center of the wall, or from some point along it, depending on the type of roof and the dimensions of the building. For a gable roof, the two sidewall plates must be laid out, while in the case of a hip roof, all four plates must be marked.

If the length is not evenly divisible by the joist spacing, it may be preferable to begin layout at the center of the wall and lay out both ways toward the corners.

In a hip roof, there will normally be an end common rafter (see Fig. 7–12), which will be located in the center of the end wall. There should be a stub joist position next to it, and the remainder of the stub joist positions may be laid out from it.

## Nailing of Joists

Ceiling joists must be toenailed to the plate with a minimum of two $3\frac{1}{4}$-in. (82-mm) nails at each end. In addition the joists lap at the center must be nailed with a minimum of two 3-in. (76-mm) nails at each end of the lap, as shown in Fig. 7–1.

### Joist Restraint

Roof joists supporting a finished ceiling other than plywood, waferboard, or strandboard must be restrained from twisting along their bottom edges by means of *crossbridging, blocking,* or *strapping* in a manner similar to that used for floor joists (see Chapter 5). If the ceiling is furred for application of ceiling material, the furring provides the necessary restraint.

### Ceiling Backing

Partitions which run parallel to the direction of ceiling joists or trusses must be provided with some means of carrying the edges of the ceiling material which meet the partition. This is done by nailing *ceiling backing* to the cap plate (see Fig. 7–9). A piece of 1½-in. (38-mm) material, at least 2 in. (50 mm) wider than the cap plate, is used, allowing it to project the same amount on both sides. Vapor barrier should be placed over the top of the wall and under the ceiling backing to provide a continuous barrier over the entire ceiling.

**FIGURE 7–9:** *Ceiling backing.*

### Attic Access

Building codes and fire regulations demand that there be access to the attic, and it is provided by a framed opening or *hatchway* not less than 22 × 36 in. (550 × 900 mm). When the hatchway only serves a single dwelling unit, it may be reduced to 20 × 28 in. (500 × 700 mm) (see Fig. 7–10). For appearance sake, it is usually placed in a relatively inconspicuous location in a hallway and provided with a tight fitting trapdoor or other type of cover that opens upward.

**FIGURE 7–10:** *Attic access.*

## ROOF SHAPES

The shape of the roof may be one of several common designs, which include *shed* roof, *gable* roof, *hip* roof, *gambrel* roof, *dutch hip* roof, *mansard* roof, *flat* roof and *intersecting* roof (see Fig. 7–11).

The shed roof slopes in only one direction. The gable roof has two slopes, and the continuation of the end walls up to meet the roof is known as a *gable end*. The hip roof has four slopes, which terminate at a point if the plan is square or in a ridge if the plan is rectangular (see Fig. 7–11). A gambrel roof is a modification of a gable, each side having two slopes instead of one. The Dutch hip roof is a combination of the gable and hip roof, with small gable ends and slopes on four sides. The mansard roof is a modification of the hip with two slopes on each side instead of one. The flat roof has no slope at all. An intersecting roof is formed by the meeting of two sloped roofs of one type or another.

*(a) Shed roof.*

*(b) Gable roof.*

*(c) Hip roof.*

*(d) Gambrel roof.*

**FIGURE 7–11**

*(e) Dutch hip roof.*

*(f) Modified Mansard roof.*

*(g) Flat roof.*

*(h) Intersecting roof.*

**FIGURE 7-11**

*(i) Unequal sloped gable.*

## RAFTER TERMS

To be able to understand and solve the problems involved in laying out and cutting a set of rafters, it is necessary to know the terms used in discussing the subject. By examining a plan

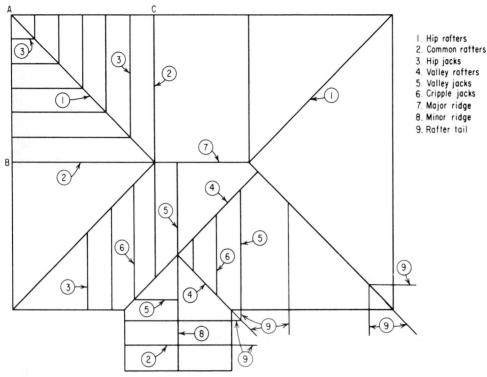

1. Hip rafters
2. Common rafters
3. Hip jacks
4. Valley rafters
5. Valley jacks
6. Cripple jacks
7. Major ridge
8. Minor ridge
9. Rafter tail

**FIGURE 7-12:**   *Roof plan.*

view of a roof frame, the different types of rafters involved in forming roofs can be easily distinguished. Figure 7–12 is a plan view of the frame of an intersecting hip roof. Here all types of rafters are involved.

The *common* rafters are those which run at right angles to the wall plate and meet the *ridge* at their top end. In a gable roof, all the rafters are *commons,* while in a hip roof, the two center end rafters and those side rafters which meet the ridge are *commons.* Hip rafters run from the corners of the wall plates to the ridge at an angle of 45° to the plates and form the intersection of two adjacent roof surfaces. *Valley* rafters occur where two roofs intersect. Jack rafters run parallel to the commons but are shorter and are named according to their position. *Hip jacks* run from plate to hip, usually meeting at the hip in pairs. *Valley jacks* run from the valley rafter to the ridge or plate. *Cripple jacks* run from hip to valley or from valley to valley, touching neither plate nor ridge. The part of any rafter that projects beyond the wall plate is known as the *rafter tail.*

## Common Rafter

One of the basic terms, which applies to all rafters, is the *span,* the dimension of a building bridged by a pair of common rafters, while that part of the span traversed by one of the pair is called the *run* of the rafter. The length of the rafter, measured on a line from the center of the ridge to the outside edge of the building, is the *line length* of the rafter (see Fig. 7–13). The *total length* of the rafter is the sum of the line length and the *tail length* (see Fig. 7–13). The vertical distance from the level of the wall plates to the line length meeting point of a pair of rafters is the *total rise* of the rafter (see Fig. 7–13).

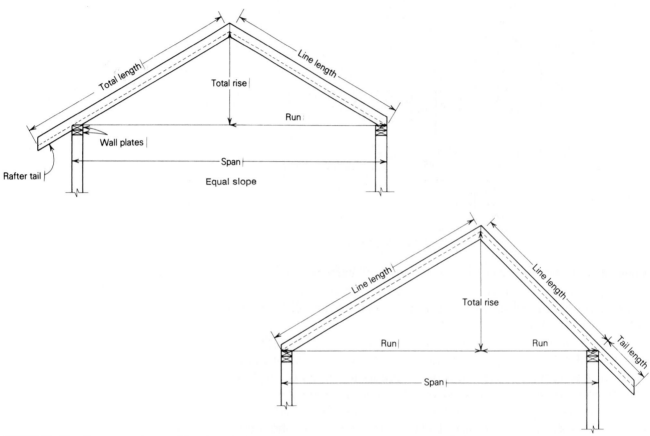

**FIGURE 7–13:**   *Span, run, rise, and line length of a rafter.*

To make rafter layout simpler, run, rise, and line length are broken down into *units*. The basic one is the *unit run*—a standard length of 12 in. (300 mm) [Fig. 7–14(a)]. The *unit rise* is the vertical distance which a rafter rises for one unit of run, while the length of rafter resulting from one unit of run is the *unit line length* [see Fig. 7–14(a)].

If a framing square is applied to a common rafter in position, as in Fig. 7–14(b), with the 12-in. (300-mm) mark on the blade coinciding with the outside edge of the wall plate, a figure on the tongue will indicate the *unit rise* of the rafter. In this case, the figure is 6 in. (100 mm) and the diagonal distance between 6 in. (100) on the tongue and 12 in. (200) on the blade is the *unit line length* for that rafter [see Fig. 7–14(b)].

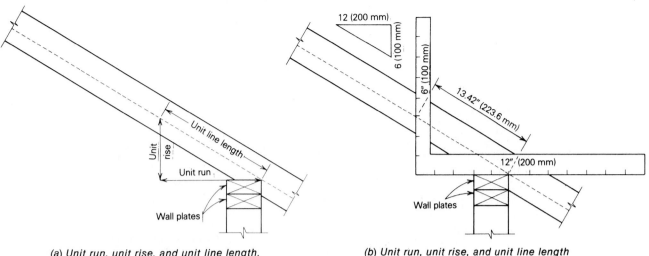

*(a) Unit run, unit rise, and unit line length.*

*(b) Unit run, unit rise, and unit line length on the framing square.*

**FIGURE 7-14**

The inclination of a rafter is called the *slope* and can be expressed as a fraction or in degrees. The slope is most commonly expressed as the unit rise per unit run. For example, in Fig. 7-14(b), the slope is $^6/_{12}$ ($^1/_2$).

In order that rafters may seat securely on the wall plate, it is common practice to cut a triangular section from the bottom edge, at the point at which it meets the wall plate, as shown in Fig. 7-15. This notch is called a *birdsmouth*, which is made by making a *seat cut*—cut horizontal when the rafter is in position—and a *plumb cut*—vertical when the rafter is in position (see Fig. 7-15). Common rafters are made to fit together at the top or fit to a ridgeboard (see Fig. 7-16) by making a *plumb cut* at the upper end of each, and the rafter tail may have a single *plumb cut* or a plumb cut and a *seat cut* at the bottom end (see Fig. 7-15). The horizontal distance from that bottom plumb cut to outside of the wall frame is known as the *overhang* (see Fig. 7-14).

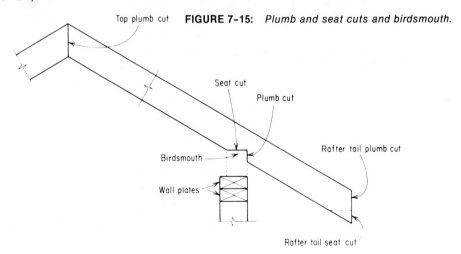

**FIGURE 7-15:** *Plumb and seat cuts and birdsmouth.*

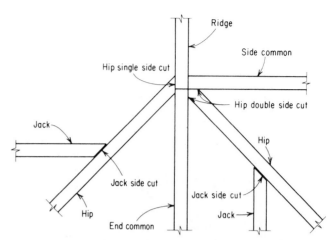

**FIGURE 7-16:** *Side cuts on hips and jacks.*

## Jack Rafter

Jack rafters run parallel to common rafters and therefore have the same unit run, rise, and line length. They have the same birdsmouth at the plate and must have a top plumb cut. But, since they meet a hip rafter at an angle, each one must also have a *side cut* or *cheek cut* at the top end.

## Hip Rafter

Hip rafters also have a birdsmouth at the plate but, since they run at an angle to the plate and the ridge, they must also have a *side cut* at the top end as well as a plumb cut. That side cut may be *single* or *double* (see Fig. 7-16), depending on how the rafter meets the ridge.

Hip rafters run at an angle of 45° to the wall plate (see Fig. 7-12), and, as a result, their unit run is different from that of a common rafter. As illustrated in Fig. 7-17(a), a hip rafter must traverse the diagonal of a square in order to span one unit of common run. Thus the unit run of a hip rafter will be the length of the diagonal of a square with sides of 12 in. (200 mm)—namely 17 in. (283 mm).

**FIGURE 7-17**

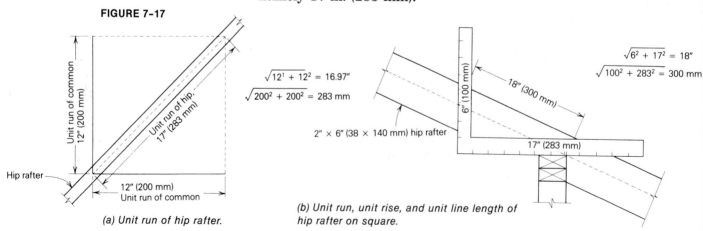

*(a) Unit run of hip rafter.*

*(b) Unit run, unit rise, and unit line length of hip rafter on square.*

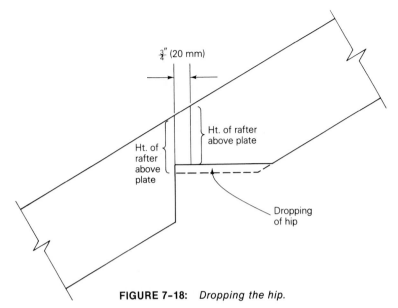

**FIGURE 7-18:** *Dropping the hip.*

(In the figure: ¾" (20 mm); Ht. of rafter above plate; Ht. of rafter above plate; Dropping of hip)

If the framing square is applied to a hip rafter in position, as shown in Fig. 7-17(b), the 17-in. (283-mm) mark on the blade must coincide with the outside edge of the wall plate to represent the *unit run,* and a figure on the tongue will indicate the *unit rise.* If the rafter has the same rise as the one shown in Fig. 7-14, then that figure will be 6 in. (100). Again, the diagonal distance between 6 in. (100) on the tongue and 17 in. (283) on the blade is the *unit line length* for the hip rafter.

Since hip rafters occur at the intersection of two surfaces of a hip roof, the *roof sheathing* on each surface must meet on a hip. To provide a flat surface on which the sheathing ends may rest, the birdsmouth must be adjusted to lower the hip rafter so that the outside edge is flush with the roof surface (see Fig. 7-18).

## Shortening

In Fig. 7-19, two common rafters have first been represented by two lines *AC* and *BC.* Then full-width rafters have been superimposed in such a way that the lines *AC* and *BC* pass through the peak of the birdsmouth. In addition, a ridgeboard is inserted between the two rafter ends.

The two lines *AC* and *BC* meet in the center of the ridge at *C,* and the distance from *A* or *B* to *C* is the line length of the rafter (see Fig. 7-13). However, the rafter actually ends at *D;* the distance from *A* or *B* to *D* is the actual length of the rafter; it has been *shortened* by a distance *CD,* which varies, depending on the rise of the rafter. However, if the *shortening* is measured at *right angles to the plumb cut,* its length will remain constant—*one-half the thickness of the ridge.* For a 1½-in. (38-mm) ridge, that distance will be ¾ in. (19 mm).

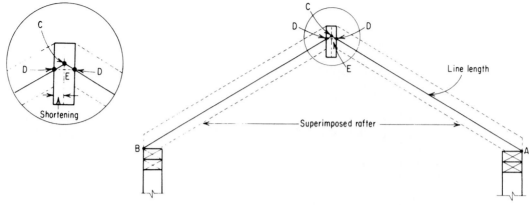

*(a) True length of common rafter.*

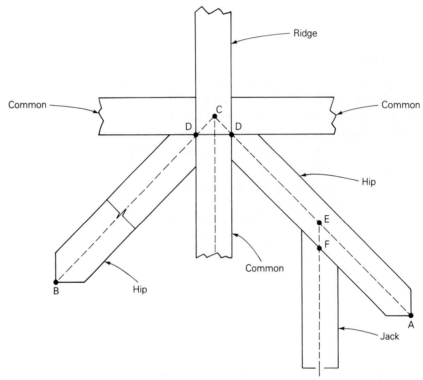

*(b) Shortening for hip or jack rafter.*

**FIGURE 7–19**

With regard to a hip rafter, it meets the ridge at an angle of 45° [see Fig. 7–19(b)] and therefore must be *shortened*, in a horizontal direction (at right angles to a plumb cut) by a distance *CD* [see Fig. 7–19(b)], *one-half the diagonal thickness of the rafter*. For a 1½-in. (38-mm) rafter, that will amount to approximately 1¹⁄₁₆ in. (27 mm).

A jack rafter meets the hip at an angle of 45° in plan [see Fig. 7–19(b)] and must be *shortened* by a distance equal to *EF*, taken at right angles to the plumb cut. For a 1½-in. (38-mm) hip, that distance will also be 1¹⁄₁₆ (27 mm).

## RIDGE

Rather than have a pair of rafters meet together at their top end, it is customary to introduce a ridgeboard between them. This ridgeboard makes it easier to keep the top line of the roof straight and provides support for the roof sheathing between rafters.

The ridge of a gable roof will have the same length as the length of the building plus roof overhang at the gable ends, if any. The length of a hip roof ridge, however, takes a little more consideration.

Turn back to Fig. 7-12 and study it a moment. In plan, the hip rafter is the diagonal of a square, the sides of which are *AB* and *AC*, *AB* being equal to half the width of the building. The top end of the hip is at a point half the width of the building *along* the length. The hip at the opposite end covers a like distance. The distance between the top ends of the two hips, then, is equal to the length of the building minus the width. In other words, the line length of the ridge is the length of building minus the width.

When a ridgeboard is introduced into the frame, the common rafters are shortened by half the ridge thickness. Consequently, the end commons would not reach the ends of the ridge if they were cut to true length. So the ridge length is increased by half its own thickness at each end. In other words, the *true length of the hip roof ridge is the length of building minus the width plus the thickness of the ridge.*

An intersecting roof contains two ridges. The ridge of the main roof is called the *major* ridge, whereas the ridge in the projection is known as the *minor* ridge.

## HOW TO USE THE RAFTER TABLE

Having considered rafter framing terminology, it is now necessary to examine the methods used to determine the lengths of various types of rafters and how to lay out and cut them.

Calculation of lengths may be done in several ways, including the use of the *rafter table and mathematics*, by *scaling on the framing square*, and by *scale drawings*. The layout of lengths may be done by *framing square step-off*. For most situations, the combination of rafter table and math, with tape measurement of lengths, is the simplest and most accurate.

### Rafter Table

Figure 7-20(a) illustrates a framing square, with a *rafter table* on the face of the blade. The numbers along the top edge of the

FIGURE 7-20

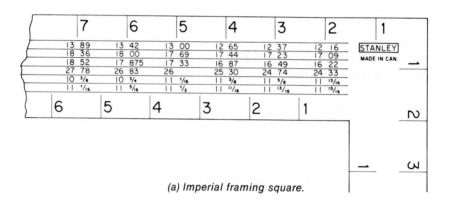

| | 18 | 17 | 16 |
|---|---|---|---|
| LENGTH COMMON RAFTERS PER FOOT RUN | 21 63 | 20 81 | 20 00 |
| LENGTH HIP OR VALLEY PER FOOT RUN | 24 74 | 24 02 | 23 32 |
| DIFFERENCE IN LENGTH OF JACKS 16" INCHES CENTRES | 28 84 | 27 74 | 26 66 |
| DIFFERENCE IN LENGTH OF JACKS 2' FEET CENTRES | 43 27 | 41 62 | 40 |
| SIDE CUT OF JACKS USE | 6 11/16 | 6 15/16 | 7 3/16 |
| SIDE CUT HIP OR VALLEY USE | 8 1/4 | 8 1/2 | 8 3/4 |

(top edge numbers: 23 22 21 20 19 18 17 16; bottom edge numbers: 22 21 20 19 18 17 16 15 14)

| | 15 | 14 | 13 | 12 | 11 | 10 | 9 | 8 |
|---|---|---|---|---|---|---|---|---|
| | 19 21 | 18 44 | 17 69 | 16 97 | 16 28 | 15 62 | 15 00 | 14 42 |
| | 22 65 | 22 00 | 21 38 | 20 78 | 20 22 | 19 70 | 19 21 | 18 76 |
| | 25 61 | 24 585 | 23 588 | 22 625 | 21 704 | 20 83 | 20 | 19 23 |
| | 38 42 | 36 08 | 35 38 | 33 94 | 32 56 | 31 24 | 30 | 28 84 |
| | 7 1/2 | 7 13/16 | 8 1/8 | 8 1/2 | 8 7/8 | 9 1/4 | 9 5/8 | 10 |
| | 9 1/16 | 9 3/8 | 9 5/8 | 9 7/8 | 10 1/8 | 10 3/8 | 10 5/8 | 10 7/8 |

(bottom edge numbers: 14 13 12 11 10 9 8 7 6)

| | 7 | 6 | 5 | 4 | 3 | 2 | 1 |
|---|---|---|---|---|---|---|---|
| | 13 89 | 13 42 | 13 00 | 12 65 | 12 37 | 12 16 | STANLEY |
| | 18 36 | 18 00 | 17 69 | 17 44 | 17 23 | 17 09 | MADE IN CAN. |
| | 18 52 | 17 875 | 17 33 | 16 87 | 16 49 | 16 22 | |
| | 27 78 | 26 83 | 26 | 25 30 | 24 74 | 24 33 | |
| | 10 3/8 | 10 3/4 | 11 1/16 | 11 3/8 | 11 5/8 | 11 13/16 | |
| | 11 1/16 | 11 5/16 | 11 1/2 | 11 11/16 | 11 13/16 | 11 15/16 | |

(bottom edge numbers: 6 5 4 3 2 1; side arm numbers: 1 2 3)

(a) Imperial framing square.

| MM RISE | PER METRE | OF RUN | 250 | 300 | 400 | 500 | 600 | 700 | 750 | HIP |
|---|---|---|---|---|---|---|---|---|---|---|
| MM LENGTH | COMMON RAFTERS PER METRE RUN | | 1031 | 1044 | 1077 | 1118 | 1166 | 1221 | 1250 | VALLEY |
| " | HIP OR VALLEY " " " | | 1436 | 1446 | 1470 | 1500 | 1536 | 1578 | 1601 | RAFTER |
| MM DIFF. IN LENGTH OF JACKS 400 MM O.C. | | | 412 | 418 | 431 | 447 | 466 | 488 | 500 | SET |
| " " " " " 600 MM | | | 618 | 626 | 646 | 671 | 700 | 732 | 750 | POINT |
| SIDE CUT OF | JACKS | USE OPP. 200MM LINE | 206 | 209 | 215 | 224 | 233 | 244 | 250 | |
| " " " | HIPS OR VALLEYS " " " " | | 203 | 204 | 208 | 212 | 217 | 223 | 226 | |

(scale numbers above: 90 80 70 60 50 40 30 20 10 ... 500 400 300; below: 500 400 300)

| | | | | | COMMON | | | | | |
|---|---|---|---|---|---|---|---|---|---|---|
| HIP | 800 | 900 | 1000 | 1100 | COMMON | 1200 | 1300 | 1400 | 1500 | 2MM |
| VALLEY | 1281 | 1345 | 1414 | 1487 | RAFTER | 1562 | 1640 | 1720 | 1803 | GRADUATIONS |
| RAFTER | 1625 | 1676 | 1732 | 1792 | SET | 1855 | 1921 | 1990 | 2061 | |
| SET | 512 | 538 | 566 | 595 | POINT | 625 | 656 | 688 | 721 | |
| POINT | 768 | 807 | 848 | 892 | | 937 | 984 | 1032 | 1082 | |
| | 256 | 269 | 283 | 297 | | 312 | 328 | 344 | 361 | |
| | 230 | 237 | 245 | 253 | | 262 | 272 | 281 | 292 | |

(scale numbers: 300 200 100; below: 200 100)

(b) Metric framing square.

blade represent *unit rises,* with calculations for 17 rises ranging from 2 to 18. Figure 7–20(b) illustrates a metric framing square, with calculations for 14 rises ranging from 200 to 1500 mm, in increments of 100 mm. The first step in using the rafter table, then, is to locate the number which corresponds to the unit rise of the roof in question.

To find the *unit line length* of a common rafter, look on the first line of the table under the unit rise concerned; the figure found there is the line length for one ft (1000 mm) of common run. Multiply that figure by the number of units of run for that rafter to obtain the line length of the common rafter in in. (mm). The number of units of run for the rafter may be calculated by dividing the *total run* of the rafter in in. by 12 (mm by 1000).

The second line gives the *unit line length* of a hip or valley rafter per unit of common run. The line length of the hip or valley rafter will be that figure, multiplied by the number of units of common run in the building.

The third line gives the difference in length of successive jack rafters spaced 16 in. (400 mm) o.c. and is also the line length of the first jack rafter from the corner, spaced 16 in. (400 mm) o.c. Thus, having found the *true* (shortened) length of the first jack rafter from the corner, the length of the next one is found by adding that "difference in length" figure to the shortened length.

The fourth line on the square gives the difference in length of jack rafters spaced 2 ft (600 mm) o.c.

The fifth line indicates the figure to use on the tongue for the side cut of jack rafters. Again, 12 in. (200) is the blade figure, and the cut is marked on the blade.

The sixth line on the square indicates the figure to use on the tongue of the square in laying out the side cuts for hip and valley rafters. The blade figure is always 12 in. (200 mm), and the cut is always marked on the blade.

## Framing Calculations and Layout

Figure 7–21 is a plan view of a hip roof with an intersecting gable roof, with dimensions as indicated. On it are marked a number of typical roof framing members whose length and layout will be demonstrated.

## Length of Major Ridge (A)

The length of the ridge for a hip roof is the length of the building minus the width plus the thickness of the rafter. In this example the length is 32 ft − 24 ft + 1½ in. = 8 ft, 1½ in. (10,000 mm − 8000 mm + 38 mm + 2038 mm). The size of the material for the ridge will normally be 2 × 6 in. (38 × 140 mm).

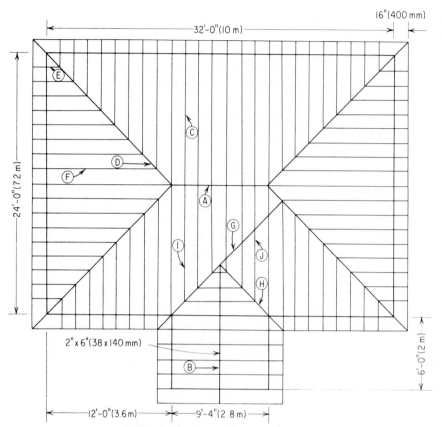

**FIGURE 7-21:**  *Plan view, intersecting roof.*

## Length of Minor Ridge (B)

The length of the minor ridge will be the length of the projection (see Fig. 7–21) plus one-half of its width plus the overhang minus one-half the diagonal thickness of the supporting valley rafter. In this case the length will be 6 ft + 4 ft + 16 in. − $1\frac{1}{16}$ in. = 11 ft, $2\frac{15}{16}$ in. (2000 mm + 1200 mm + 400 mm − 27 mm = 3573 mm).

## Length and Layout of Common Rafter (C)

The unit line length for a common rafter with a slope of 6 to 12 as shown under 6 [see Fig. 7–20(a)] is 13.42. The line length of the rafter is equal to the number of units of run (feet) times the unit line length: 12 × 13.42 = 161.04 in. or 13 ft, $5\frac{1}{16}$ in. The corresponding metric slope of $\frac{1}{2}$ will result in a unit line length of 1118 as shown under 500. The number of units of run for the common rafter with a run of 3600 mm will be 3600 ÷ 1000 = 3.6. The line length of the rafter will be 1118 × 3.6 = 4024.8 ≈ 4025 mm.

The line length of the rafter tail will be $\frac{16}{12}$ × 13.42 = 17.89 in. ( $\frac{400}{1000}$ × $\frac{1118}{447.2}$ ≈ 447 mm).

A typical common rafter (C) may now be laid out, cut, and used as a pattern for all the common rafters. Proceed as follows:

1. Pick out a piece of straight 2 × 4 (38 × 89 mm) stock of sufficient length and lay out a plumb cut at the top end. This is done by laying the square on the stock with the rise—6 in. (100 mm)—on the tongue and the unit run—12 in. (200 mm)—on the blade. Mark along the tongue, making sure the square is setting so the crown is on the topside of the rafter [see Fig. 7–22(a)].

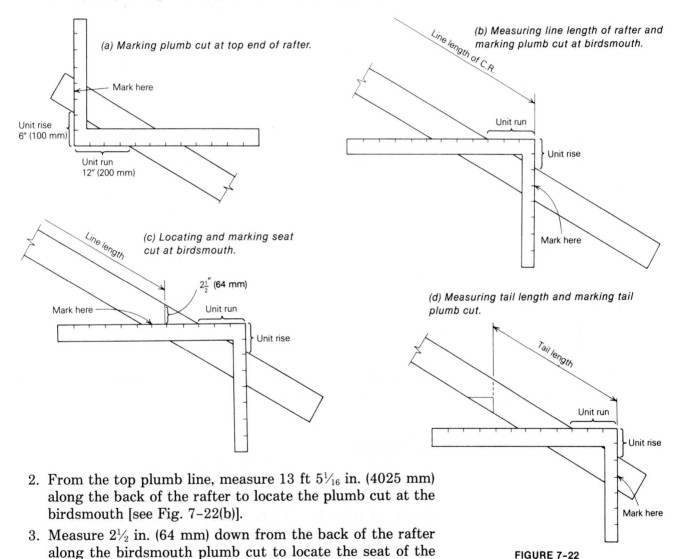

(a) Marking plumb cut at top end of rafter.

Mark here

Unit rise
6″ (100 mm)

Unit run
12″ (200 mm)

(b) Measuring line length of rafter and marking plumb cut at birdsmouth.

Line length of C.R.

Unit run

Unit rise

Mark here

(c) Locating and marking seat cut at birdsmouth.

Line length

2½″ (64 mm)

Mark here

Unit run

Unit rise

(d) Measuring tail length and marking tail plumb cut.

Tail length

Unit run

Unit rise

Mark here

**FIGURE 7-22**

2. From the top plumb line, measure 13 ft 5$\frac{1}{16}$ in. (4025 mm) along the back of the rafter to locate the plumb cut at the birdsmouth [see Fig. 7–22(b)].

3. Measure 2$\frac{1}{2}$ in. (64 mm) down from the back of the rafter along the birdsmouth plumb cut to locate the seat of the birdsmouth; draw a line perpendicular to the plumb cut at this point to establish the seat cut [see Fig. 7–22(c)].

4. From the birdsmouth plumb cut, measure 17$\frac{7}{8}$ in. (447 mm) along the back of the rafter to the tail plumb cut. Draw a plumb line through this point parallel to the other plumb lines [see Fig. 7–22(d)].

5. Measure a distance equal to the thickness of the rough fascia perpendicular to the tail plumb cut for the shortening at the tail end. Cut the tail end at this point [see Fig. 7–22(e)].

6. At the top end of the rafter, shorten the rafter a distance equal to half the thickness of the ridge. This measurement is made at right angles to the plumb line at the top end of the rafter. Cut the top end at this point [see Fig. 7–22(f)].

7. Use this cut rafter as the pattern for other rafters. Make sure that the crown (bow) is always placed on the top edge of the rafter [see Fig. 7–22(g)].

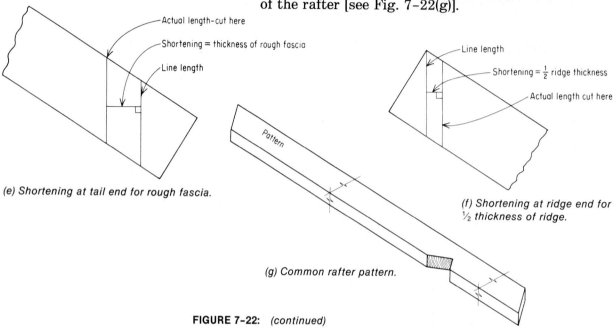

(e) Shortening at tail end for rough fascia.

(f) Shortening at ridge end for ½ thickness of ridge.

(g) Common rafter pattern.

**FIGURE 7–22:**   *(continued)*

### Length and Layout of Hip Rafter (D)

The unit line length for a hip rafter with a unit rise of 6 in. is 18 in. [as shown under 6 on the second line of the rafter table in Fig. 7–20(a)]. Since the number of units of run is 12, the line length of the rafter will be $12 \times 18 = 216$ in. $= 18$ ft. The line length of the rafter tail will be $^{16}/_{12} \times 18 = 24$ in.

The corresponding metric slope of 1 to 2 will result in a unit line length of 1500 mm [as shown under 500 on the second line of the rafter table in Fig. 7–20(b)]. The line length is equal to the number of units of run for the common rafter (3.6) times the unit line length ($3.6 \times 1500 = 5400$ mm). the line length of the rafter tail is $^{400}/_{1000} \times 1500 = 600$ mm.

A typical hip rafter (D) may now be laid out using the following procedure:

1. Pick out a straight piece of $2 \times 6$ ($38 \times 140$ mm) stock of sufficient length; lay out the plumb line as near the top as possible. This is done by using the unit rise (6 in. or 100

mm) on the tongue and the unit run (17 in. or 283 mm) on the blade and marking the plumb along the tongue. Make sure the crown of the 2 × 6 corresponds with the topside of the rafter [see Fig. 7–23(a)].

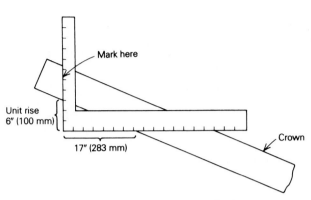

*(a) Marking plumb cut at top of rafter.*

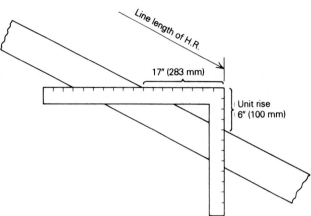

*(b) Marking plumb cut at birdsmouth.*

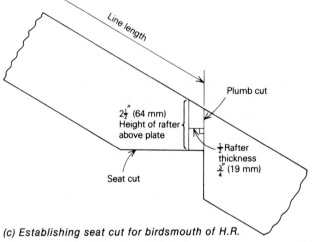

*(c) Establishing seat cut for birdsmouth of H.R.*

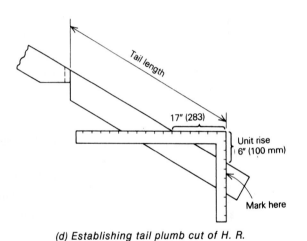

*(d) Establishing tail plumb cut of H. R.*

**FIGURE 7-23**

2. From the top end plumb line, measure 18 ft (5531 mm) along the back of the rafter to the plumb line at the birdsmouth [see Fig. 7–23(b)].

3. Measure 2½ in. (64 mm) down from the back of the rafter along a parallel line ¾ in. (19 mm) from the birdsmouth plumb line to locate the seat of the birdsmouth. Draw a line perpendicular to the plumb line at this point to establish the seat cut [see Fig. 7–23(c)].

4. From the birdsmouth plumb line, measure 24 in. (600 mm) along the back of the rafter to establish the tail plumb line [see Fig. 7–23(d)].

5. Measure a distance equal to the diagonal thickness of the rough fascia perpendicular to the tail plumb cut for the shortening at the tail end. This would be 2⅛ in. for a 2 × 6

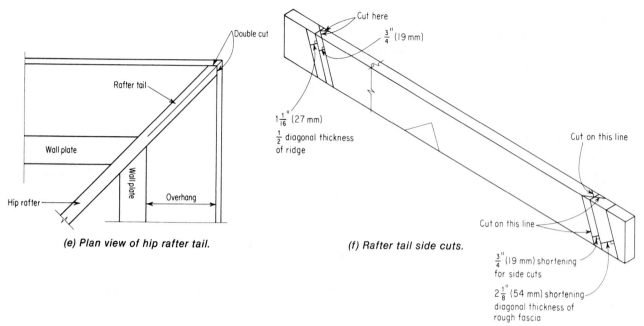

*(e) Plan view of hip rafter tail.*          *(f) Rafter tail side cuts.*

**FIGURE 7–23:**  *(continued)*

(54 mm for a 38 × 140) fascia. The end of the rafter tail must fit into the apex of an external angle and therefore must have a *double cut* at the end [see Fig. 7–23(e)]. Lay out the two side cuts by drawing a line parallel to the shortened plumb cut a perpendicular distance of one-half the thickness of the rafter from the plumb cut. Join this line to the midpoint of the top of the plumb cut squared across the edge [see Fig. 7–23(f)].

6. From the top plumb cut line, measure back at right angles a distance equal to one-half the diagonal thickness of the ridge ($1\frac{1}{16}$ in. or 27 mm) and through this point draw a second plumb line. The rafter is now properly *shortened* for the ridge. Square across the top edge of the rafter from this line and mark the center point. Single or double side cut lines will be drawn through this point to a point established by measuring back at right angles a distance equal to one-half the thickness of the rafter [see Fig. 7–23(f)].

### Length and Layout of Jack Rafter (F)

The rafter tail and the birdsmouth layout of this rafter are identical to the common rafter. The third line of the rafter table indicates that, for a 6-in. (500 mm) rise, the difference in length of jack rafters 16 in. (400) o.c. is 17.875 in. (447 mm). That is also the amount the longest jack rafter is shorter than the common rafter. To lay out this rafter, proceed as follows:

1. Pick out a piece of stock (2 × 4) and mark a plumb cut as near the top end as possible. This is done by using the unit rise—6 in. (100 mm)—on the tongue and the unit run—12 in. (200 mm)—on the blade. Mark along the tongue, making sure the crown of the rafter is on the top edge [see Fig. 7-22(a)].

2. From the plumb cut, measure the jack rafter line length to locate the birdsmouth. The longest jack rafter line length is equal to the common rafter line length minus the difference in length of adjacent jack rafters: 161.04 in. − 17.875 = 143.165 in. = 11 ft. 11³⁄₁₆ in. (4025 − 447 mm = 3578 mm) [see Fig. 7-22(b)].

3. The layout of the birdsmouth and the rafter tail are exactly the same as for the common rafter.

4. From the top plumb cut line, measure back at right angles a distance equal to half the diagonal thickness of the hip rafter—1¹⁄₁₆ in. (27 mm)—and through it draw a second plumb line parallel to the first plumb line. With the electric handsaw set at 45° cut along this line. Remember that these rafters are cut in pairs to be placed on opposite sides of the hip rafter (see Fig. 7-24).

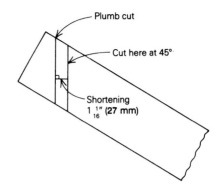

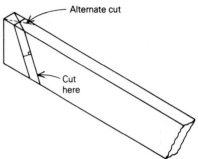

**FIGURE 7-24:** *Shortening at top of jack rafter.*

## Line Length and Layout of Jack Rafter (E)

The jack rafter (E) is the eighth and shortest rafter in the series, and therefore its length will be eight times the difference in length of jack rafters shorter than the common rafter.

## Length and Layout of Valley Rafter (G)

The total run of the valley rafter (G) is 16 in. (400) less than that of a common rafter, namely 10 ft, 8 in. (3200 mm). Its line length will be 10.67 × 18 = 192.06 in. or 16 ft, ¹⁄₁₆ in. ($^{3200}/_{1000}$ × 1500 = 4800 mm).

The layout for the rafter tail plumb line and top plumb line is the same as for a hip rafter of the same rise. The layout for the birdsmouth differs, as the rafter must fit in an inside corner as opposed to the outside. Figure 7-25 illustrates the layout of the birdsmouth.

The valley meets the hip at right angles in the plan view, and therefore the *shortening* will be one-half the thickness of the hip, ³⁄₄ in. (19 mm), measured at right angles to the plumb line (see Fig. 7-26).

The end of the valley rafter tail must fit into an internal angle, as illustrated in Fig. 7-27. Figure 7-25 illustrates the layout of the double cut needed.

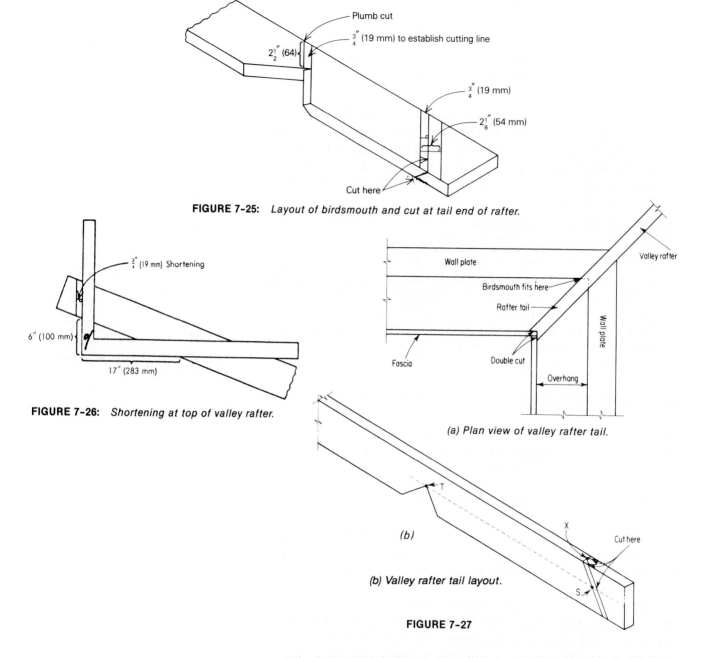

**FIGURE 7-25:** *Layout of birdsmouth and cut at tail end of rafter.*

**FIGURE 7-26:** *Shortening at top of valley rafter.*

*(a) Plan view of valley rafter tail.*

*(b) Valley rafter tail layout.*

**FIGURE 7-27**

The layout of valley rafter (H) is exactly the same as valley rafter (G); the only difference is that the run is shorter so it will affect the line length.

### Length and Layout of Valley Jack (I)

The run of valley jack (I) is 16 in. (400 mm) less than the run of the common rafter without a rafter tail. The line length of the rafter will be 161.04 in. − 17.875 = 143.165 in. = 11 ft, $11\frac{3}{16}$ in. (4025 − 447 = 3578 mm).

The plumb line and shortening at the top end are the same as for a common rafter, while the plumb line, shortening (one-half the diagonal thickness of the valley rafter), and the side cut at the bottom end are identical to the top end of a hip jack.

### Line Length and Layout of Cripple Jack (J)

The run of cripple jack (J) is 3 ft, 4 in. (1000 mm). The line length of the rafter will be $3.33 \times 13.42 = 44.69$ in. or 3 ft, $8\frac{11}{16}$ in. ($\frac{1000}{1000} \times 1118 = 1118$ mm). Shortening and side cuts, top and bottom, are the same as for other jack rafters.

## ROOF FRAME ASSEMBLY

When all the rafters have been cut, they can then be assembled into a roof frame. In a gable roof, the end rafters are positioned first, at the ends of the wall plates (see Fig. 7–28) and nailed to the plate and to the ridge. The remainder of the rafters are then raised and positioned against the ceiling joists, properly spaced at the top and then nailed to the plate, ridge, and the ceiling joists.

In a hip roof, the common rafters at the ends of the ridge (see Fig. 7–12) will be erected first, with their bottom end against a ceiling joist and nailed, bottom and top, as above. The end commons are raised next, followed by the hip rafters and finally, the jacks, in pairs. End commons and all jacks will be located against a regular or stub joist (see Fig. 7–5) and nailed, top and bottom.

**FIGURE 7-28:** *Gable studs.*

## GABLE FRAME

In a building with a gable roof, that triangular portion of the end wall which extends from the top of the wall plate to the rafters is known as the *gable*.

The method used to frame the gables will depend on the type of framing system employed. If a *balloon frame* is being used, the end wall studs extend from sill plate to rafters. If *platform framing* is used, the gable is framed separately; those short studs extending from top plate to rafters are *gable studs* (see Fig. 7–28). In either case, the cuts at the top ends of the studs will be the same.

Each gable stud will be laid out in exactly the same way and each will be longer than the preceding one by the line length of the first. Those on the opposite side of center will be marked and cut with the opposite slope. Openings for ventilating louvres are framed as illustrated in Fig. 7–29 and should be as near the ridge as possible.

**FIGURE 7-29:**  *Opening for a louvre.*

## RAFTER BRACING

As is the case with other load-bearing members, the free span
of rafters is limited, depending on width of rafter, spacing, and
species of timber used. Local building codes give maximum free
spans for a number of species, with varying widths and spacings. The free span is expressed in terms of the horizontal projection of the rafter.

When the free span of rafters exceeds the maximum allowable, they must be provided with a support. The support is
given, where possible, by braces resting on a bearing partition
(see Fig. 7-30). First, a *purlin* is nailed to the underside of the

**FIGURE 7-30:**  *Rafters supported on bearing partition.*

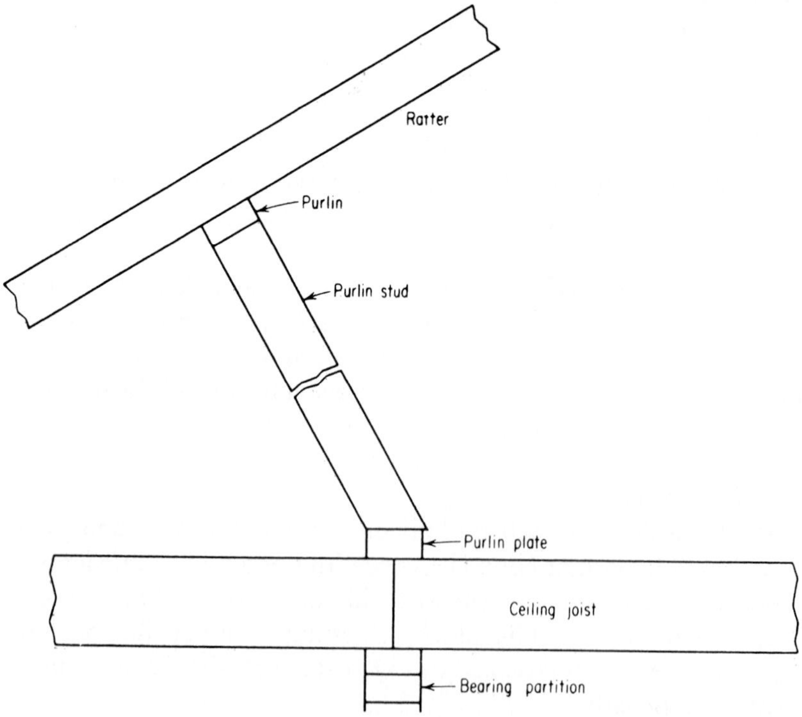

Ratter

Purlin

Purlin stud

Purlin plate

Ceiling joist

Bearing partition

rafters, as shown in Fig. 7–30, and a purlin plate to the ceiling joists over the partition. Purlin studs are cut to fit between these, preferably at right angles to the rafters. If they are so placed, the cut at the bottom of the stud will be the same as that on gable studs. If the purlin studs are vertical, this same cut will apply to the top end (see Fig. 7–31).

When no bearing partition is available to carry the load, a strongback must be used (see Fig. 7–32). A strongback is a straight timber, either solid or laminated, rigid enough to carry the imposed roof load. This member runs over the ceiling joists, blocked up so that it will clear the joist by ¾ in. (19 mm). Another method is to have the dwarf wall set on the ceiling joists. When this occurs, the size of the ceiling joists must be increased to carry the load.

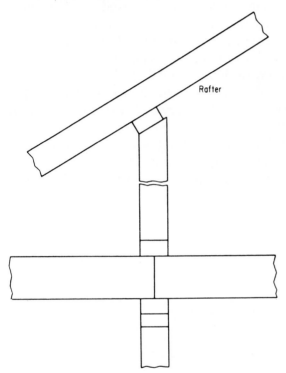

**FIGURE 7–31:** *Vertical purlin stud.*

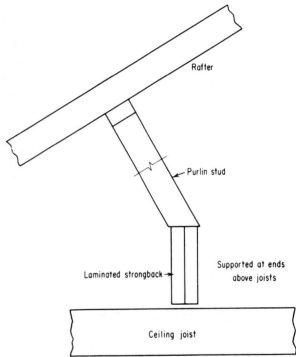

**FIGURE 7–32:** *Rafters supported by strongback.*

## Collar Ties

Rafters are tied together and stiffened by means of *collar ties*. These are horizontal supports nailed to the rafters, as illustrated in Fig. 7–33, and should be located in the middle third of the rafter length. For rafters on roof slopes of 4 in 12 (1 in 3) or more, intermediate support is generally provided by 2 × 4s (38 × 89 mm). When the length of the ties is over 8 ft (2400 mm), the ties are stiffened by nailing a 1 × 4 (19 × 89 mm) member across the center of their span, from end to end of the roof.

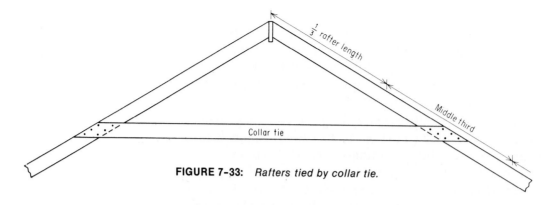

**FIGURE 7-33:**  *Rafters tied by collar tie.*

## Gable End Projection

Construction of roof projections commonly used at gable ends is shown in Fig. 7–34. Roof overhang projections less than 16 in. (400 mm) over the gable end face will usually terminate with a framing member called a *rake rafter*. When plywood soffit is used, a ladder-type construction is nailed to the rafter located above the gable end wall. Blocking usually spaced 24 in. (600 mm) o.c. will act as backing for the plywood soffit. When metal or vinyl is used for soffit material, no special framing is needed for fastening of the soffit. The overhang is finished with a 2 × 6 (38 × 140 mm) rake rafter, supported at the top by the ridge and at the bottom by the rough fascia with the roof sheathing providing the intermediate support.

**FIGURE 7-34**

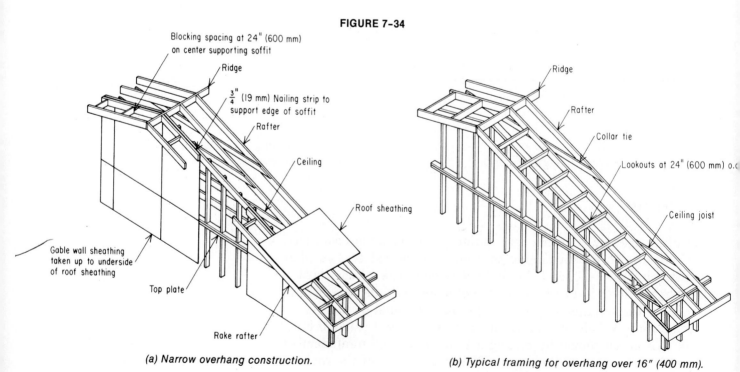

*(a) Narrow overhang construction.*

*(b) Typical framing for overhang over 16" (400 mm).*

Roof overhang projections over 16 in. (400 mm) beyond the gable end wall are supported by members called *lookouts*. These will extend back into the roof system a distance equal to the overhang. When the lookouts are placed with their narrow dimension parallel to the roof sheathing, the gable end is built lower to allow room for the lookouts. When the lookouts are placed with the wider dimension parallel to the roof sheathing, the gable end rafter is notched to allow room for the lookouts (see Fig. 7–35).

FIGURE 7-35: *Overhang framing using lookouts on flat.*

## DORMER FRAMING

Sometimes it is desirable to let light into the building through the roof, and this may be done by means of vertical windows. The house-like structure containing such windows is called *dormer* (see Fig. 7–36). In addition to letting in light, a dormer may increase the usable floor space in the attic.

The roof frame must be reinforced to support the dormer. This is done by doubling the rafters on which the sides of the dormer rest and by putting in double headers at the upper and

FIGURE 7-36: *Dormer.*

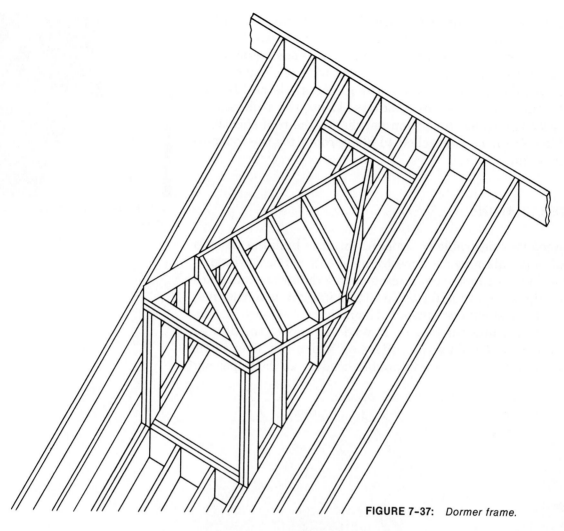

**FIGURE 7-37:** *Dormer frame.*

lower ends of the opening. On this reinforced frame the dormer is built, as illustrated in Fig. 7-37. Framing procedure is the same as for any other wall and roof frame. Cuts on the bottom end of the dormer studs will be the same as for gable studs. If the studs are spaced 16 in. (400 mm) o.c., each will be longer or shorter than the preceding one by the amount of rise for 16 in. (400 mm) of common run.

The rough opening for the dormer window is framed in the same way as the opening for a window in a wall frame. Window headers usually need not be as large, since they carry very little load.

## TRUSSED ROOF SYSTEMS

Trussed rafters are rafters which have been tied together in pairs, along with the bottom chord, to form an individual unit. In addition to the two rafters and the bottom chord, compression and tension webs are incorporated into the unit, making it a truss—a self-supporting structure. Roof trusses are now much more commonly used for roof framing than standard rafters and ceiling joists. They save material and can be put into place much quicker than standard framing. Trusses are usually designed to span from exterior wall to exterior wall, so a great deal of flexibility is available in size and shape of rooms. The entire living area can be designed as a single living area.

A wide variety of roof shapes and types can be framed with trusses. Numerous sloped truss types are available including King post, Fink, Howe, mono, and scissor, as illustrated in Fig. 7-38. Flat or parallel chord trusses are widely used for floor systems and flat roof systems, and are often more economical than open web steel joist systems. Some types of parallel chord (flat) trusses utilize steel tension members and can be supported either by the top or bottom chord (see Fig. 7-39). Flat trusses may be ordered with built-in camber to offset deflection and to provide drainage when used as a flat roof system. Special

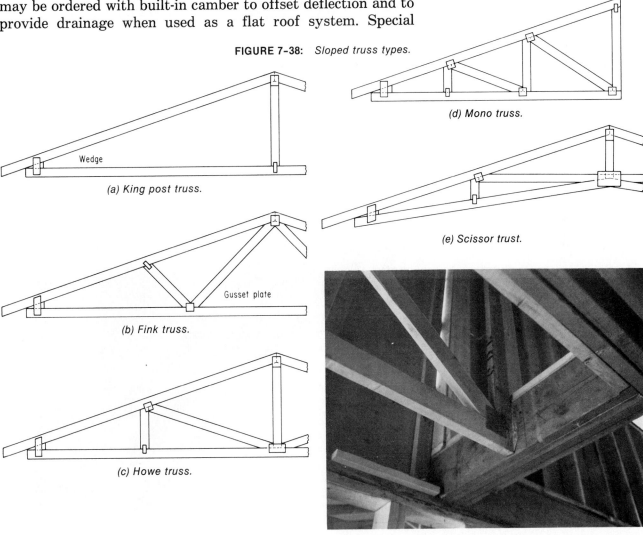

**FIGURE 7-38:** *Sloped truss types.*

*(a) King post truss.*

*(b) Fink truss.*

*(c) Howe truss.*

*(d) Mono truss.*

*(e) Scissor trust.*

**FIGURE 7-38:** *(f) Joist hangers used to support mono truss.*

**FIGURE 7-39**

Wood truss

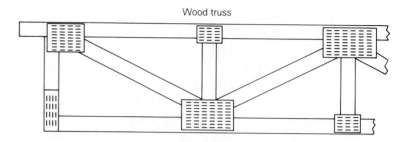

Tension web truss

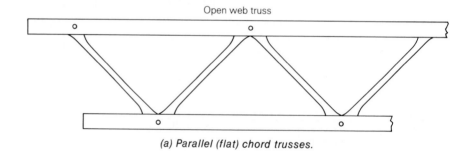

Open web truss

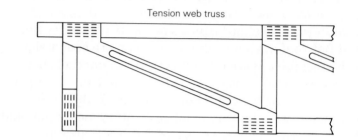

*(a) Parallel (flat) chord trusses.*

*(b) Flat truss.*

trusses such as gable end trusses, hip trusses, and girder trusses are used to meet special needs (see Fig. 7–40). Trusses are most adaptable to rectangular houses because of the constant width requiring only one type of truss. This quick erection of the roof frame results in the fast enclosing of the house. Trusses can also be used for L-shaped houses with the use of some special trusses (See Fig. 7–41). For hip roofs, hip trusses are provided for each end, and valley areas require valley trusses (see Figs. 7–40 and 7–41).

**FIGURE 7-40:**  *Special trusses.*

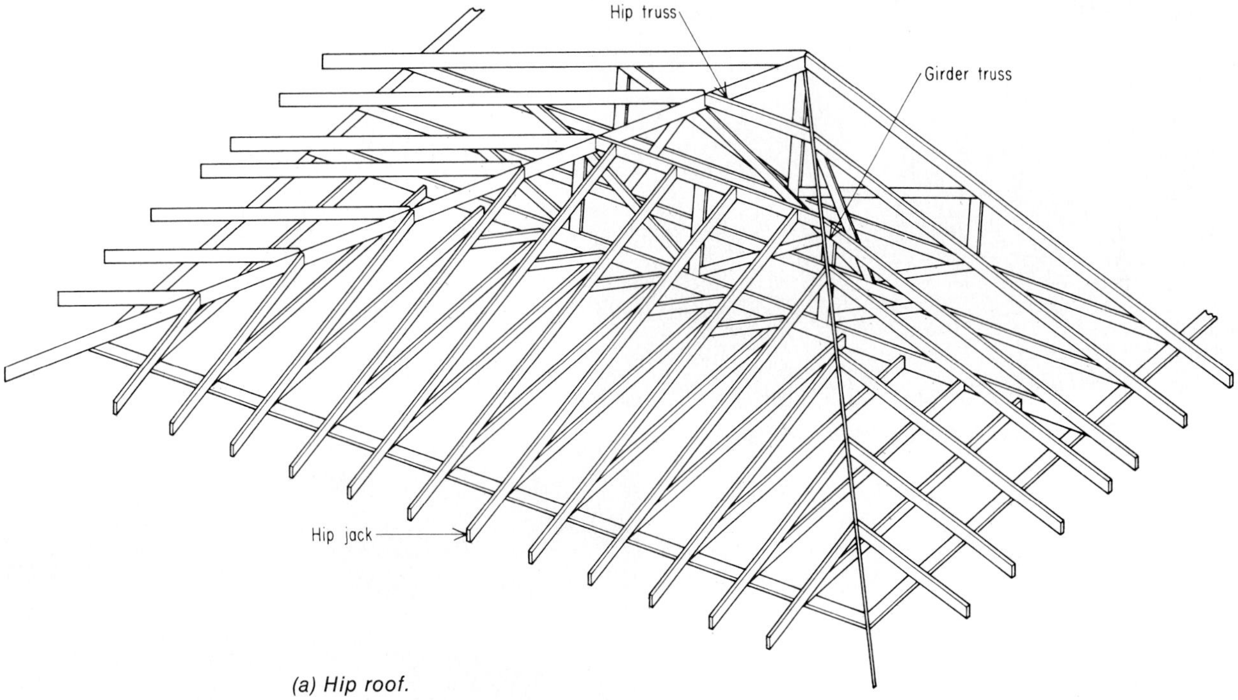

*(a) Hip roof.*

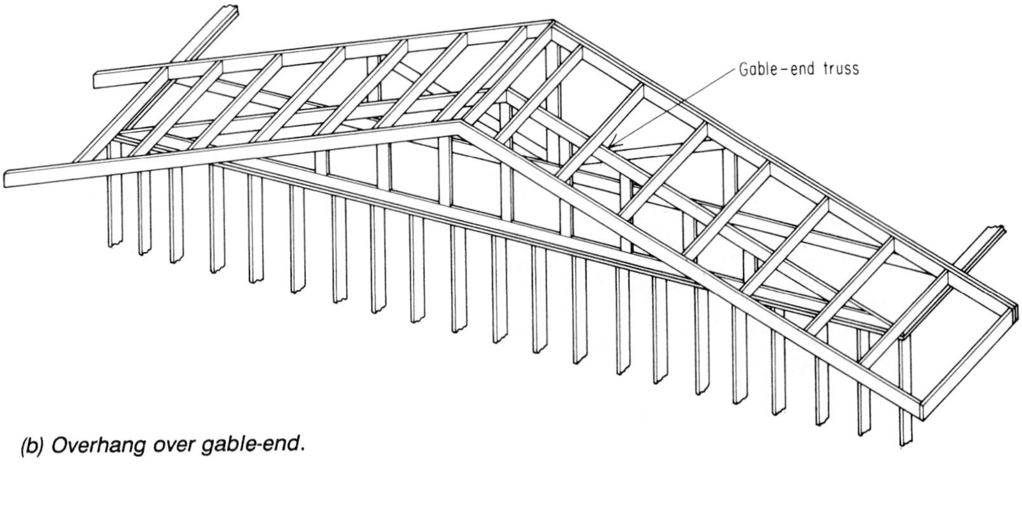

*(b) Overhang over gable-end.*

Trusses are commonly spaced at 24 in. (600 mm) o.c., allowing efficient use of exterior sheathing or interior finish. Roof trusses must be designed, however, in accordance with accepted engineering practice for the particular details being used. Suppliers of pressed-on metal truss plates have developed an economical design service to fill this need. Trusses for smaller sections of roofs can be prefabricated on the ground and then lifted into place with a crane (see Fig. 7-40(c)].

**FIGURE 7-40**

*(c) Girder truss used in L-shaped building.*

*(d) Prefabricated roof section.*

**FIGURE 7-41:** *Framing for an intersecting roof.*

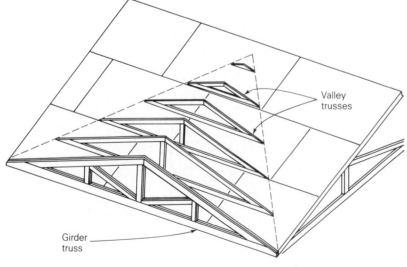

Valley trusses

Girder truss

## Standard Gable Roof

A standard gable roof consists of a number of common trusses set at 24-in. (600-mm) spacings and finished at either end with gable-end trusses (see Fig. 7-40). Eave overhangs may be formed in two ways. One is with the type of truss illustrated in Fig. 7-42(a). Here the overhang will be exactly the same as that formed by an ordinary rafter with a rafter tail. The back of the rafter can be raised further above the wall plate to allow extra room for insulation [see Fig. 7-42(b)]. If the truss is made so that its bottom chord extends to the ends of the rafters, then the truss overhang will be formed by part of the truss end extending beyond the plate line [see Fig. 7-42(c)]. Figure 7-43 illustrates two methods of supporting overhang over the gable end.

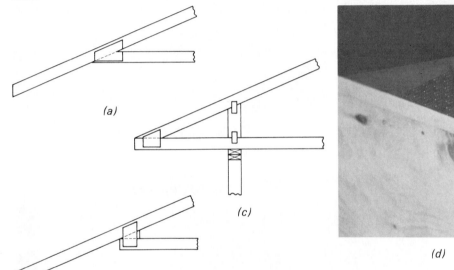

*(a)*

*(c)*

*(b)*

*(d)   Truss at exterior wall.*

**FIGURE 7-42:**  *Framing eave overhangs.*

**FIGURE 7-43:**  *Overhang support at gable-end.*

Erection of trusses will usually begin at one end with the gable end and then continue by adding common trusses and nailing them at prescribed spacing. Bracing is added to keep the gable end plumb (see Fig. 7–44), as well as a strip nailed to chords or web members to keep members straight and at correct spacing (see Fig. 7–45). Trusses are delivered to the job site banded and ready for placement (see Fig. 7–46). Cover if left over five days.

**FIGURE 7-44:**  *Bracing gable-end.*

**FIGURE 7-45:**  *Bracing web members.*

**FIGURE 7-46:**  *Trusses delivered to job-site.*

### The L-Shaped Roof

The L-shaped roof requires common trusses as well as some specialty trusses (see Fig. 7–41). The girder truss is placed first and braced in a plumb position. Truss hangers are fastened to the lower chord of the girder to support the ends of the common trusses (see Fig. 7–47). If the overhangs of the trusses to be supported by the girder are still in place, cut them off prior to placement in hangers. After all common trusses are nailed into position, valley trusses are nailed in position on the sloped roof (see Fig. 7–48). Care must be taken to keep the peaks of the valley trusses in line with the common trusses. Blocking is nailed between the trusses at the peak to set spacing and provide support for sheathing (see Fig. 7–49).

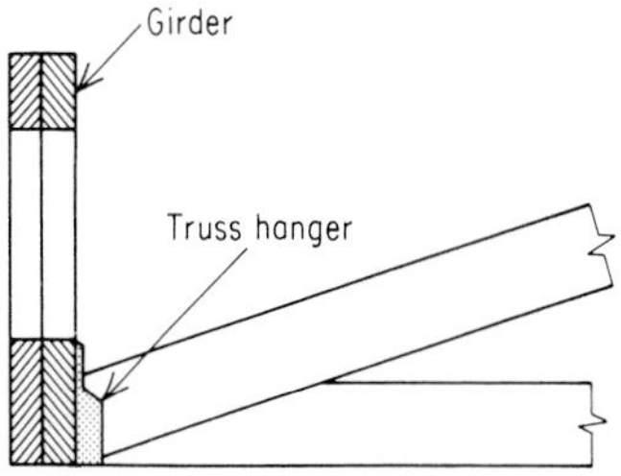

**FIGURE 7–47:** *Truss hangers supporting trusses.*

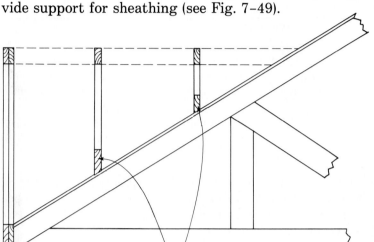

**FIGURE 7–48:** *Valley trusses nailed in position.*

**FIGURE 7–49:** *Blocking at peak of roof.*

## Hip Roof

Hip roof construction starts with the placement of the hip girder in location as specified on the drawings. Hip jacks are then fastened to the girder and nailed to the end wall plate. Hip trusses are then positioned, followed by the common trusses [see Fig. 7–40(a)]. The other end of the roof is finished in the same way as the first end. Apply all permanent bracing as per the structural truss drawing, and the roof is ready for sheathing.

## ROOF SHEATHING

Sheathing for the roof frame may be plywood, particle board, shiplap, or common boards. Minimum thicknesses for roof sheathing materials, based on the rafter spacing, are given in Table 7–1.

**TABLE 7-1:**  *Minimum thickness of roof sheathing [inches (mm)]*

| Joist or rafter spacing | Plywood and 0-2 grade waferboard and strandboard | | Waferboard and strandboard | Lumber |
|---|---|---|---|---|
| | Edges supported | Edges unsupported | | |
| 12 (300) | $\frac{5}{16}$ (7.5) | $\frac{5}{16}$ (7.5) | $\frac{3}{8}$ (9.5) | $\frac{11}{16}$ (17) |
| 16 (400) | $\frac{5}{16}$ (7.5) | $\frac{3}{8}$ (9.5) | $\frac{3}{8}$ (9.5) | $\frac{11}{16}$ (17) |
| 24 (600) | $\frac{3}{8}$ (9.5) | $\frac{1}{2}$ (12.5) | $\frac{7}{16}$ (11.1) | $\frac{3}{4}$ (19) |

Shiplap or common boards must be applied solid if composition roofing is to be used, but boards may be spaced if wood shingles or tile roofing are applied in areas not subjected to wind-driven snow (see Fig. 7–50).

When plywood is used for roof sheathing, it should be placed with the face grain perpendicular to the roof framing. The end joints of the panels are staggered to provide a good tie and spaced at least $\frac{1}{8}$ in. (2–3 mm) to prevent buckling when expansion occurs. The thickness of plywood or particle board depends on the spacing of the framing members. To prevent damage to the roof covering when thinner material is used, the joints running at right angle to the rafters should be supported by blocking nailed between framing members or by using H-clips (see Fig. 7–51).

**FIGURE 7-50:**  *Spaced roof sheathing.*

Sheathing on roof joists requires special consideration so that condensation doesn't build up in the roof system. Two by fours (38 × 89 mm) are nailed at right angles to the joists to allow a good movement of air between the joist spaces (see Fig. 7-52). The sheathing is then laid with the grain parallel to the roof joists (see Fig. 7-53).

Using roof joists can also require a change in the method used to frame the end walls. As the interior room will have a sloping ceiling, the wall must be framed with a corresponding slope at the top (see Fig. 7-54).

**FIGURE 7-51:** *Using H-clips.*

**FIGURE 7-52:** *Members nailed at right angles to roof joists.*

**FIGURE 7-53:** *Sheathing laid parallel to roof joists.*

**FIGURE 7-54:** *Wall framing for roof joist system.*

## ALTERNATE ROOF SYSTEMS

When one thinks of a roof on a building in the category of light construction, particularly a house roof, the same picture usually appears. It is the picture of a sloped roof, either gable or hip, made with the conventional roof-framing materials. And, indeed, a great percentage of the roofs, on dwelling houses especially, are made in just that way.

There are alternatives to this roof, and more and more in modern light construction one of these alternatives is being used. Among them are (1) a *flat roof* in which the ceiling joists are also the roof joists, (2) a flat roof carried by laminated beams resting on the top of the walls, (3) a *stressed-skin panel roof*, and (4) an *arched roof.*

The roof to be used in a particular situation is a matter of some architectural importance. A number of factors are involved in the choosing of a roof type, and they must all be weighed carefully before making the final choice.

One of the important factors is the overall appearance desired. If the long, low look is being sought, the flat or low-pitched roof will probably do most to enhance it. On the other hand, flat roofs may tend to be troublesome in wet climates or where the snowfall is heavy or wet.

Special effects are obtained by using roof beams with either a flat or a sloped roof, but the cost of the roof may be increased, because of the quality of roof decking usually required.

From the foregoing it is evident that there are a number of alternatives possible in the selection of a roof type. However, that choice should not be made lightly. Once the choice is made, every effort should be made to see that it is properly executed. The following pages will outline the general appearance and steps in construction of each of the roof types mentioned above.

## FLAT ROOF WITH REGULAR JOISTS

We have already seen the procedure for framing a ceiling when a regular sloped roof is to be used on the building. If a flat roof is to be used instead, the same general ceiling framing scheme may be used with some important alterations.

In the first place, the size of the ceiling joists will have to be increased. In general, 2 × 6 (38 × 140 mm) members are commonly used for ceiling joists. If the ceiling joists are also to be the roof joists, the size must be increased, because of the additional loads of roofing materials, snow, and live loads. Size 2 × 8, 2 × 10, and 2 × 12 (38 × 184 mm, 38 × 325, and 38 × 286 mm) members are commonly used, the choice in a particular case depending on the above-mentioned factors.

It was also noted in Fig. 7–2 that the outer ends of ceiling joists are cut off flush with the outside of the plate and that the top edge at the end is cut in the plane of the roof. If they are acting as roof joists, the ends will be cut off square, and the joist ends will extend beyond the wall plate if the building is to have a cornice (see Fig. 7–55).

The overhang on the end walls will be formed by stub joists

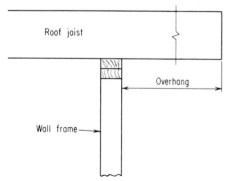

**FIGURE 7-55:** *Roof joist overhang.*

Roof joist

Overhang

Wall frame

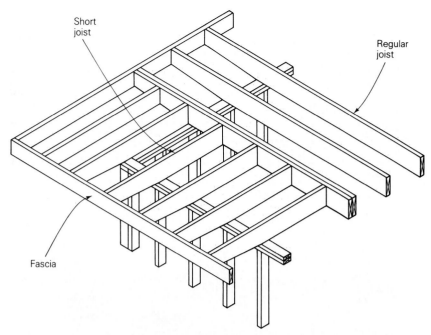

Short joist

Regular joist

Fascia

**FIGURE 7-56:** *Framing a flat roof.*

extending over the end wall plates and anchored at their inner ends to a double regular joist. Remember that these stub joists should extend at least as far inside the wall plate as they project beyond it. For example, if the joists are on 16-in. (400-mm) centers, the last regular joist should be kept back two spaces or 32 in. (800 mm) wide (see Fig. 7-56).

## Sloped Roof Joists

It is sometimes desirable to have enough slope to a flat roof so that the water will drain in one direction. It is generally considered that a slope of 1:25 is sufficient. This will allow the water to run but will not be noticeable as a slope on the roof. One method to provide for roof drainage is to slope each joist. This can be achieved by building the supporting walls of different heights or by tapering each joist or by adding a tapered strip to the top of each joist. Where insulation for the roof is placed between the roof joists, a ventilated space of at least $3\frac{1}{2}$ in. (89 mm) must be provided between the top of the joists and the underside of the roof sheathing. This can be achieved by placing 2 × 4 stringers on edge at right angles over the top of the joists (see Fig. 7-57).

An easier way to build a roof that has good ventilation capability is to use flat trusses as the roof system. Cross ventilation is easily achieved through the web openings (see Fig. 7-58(c)).

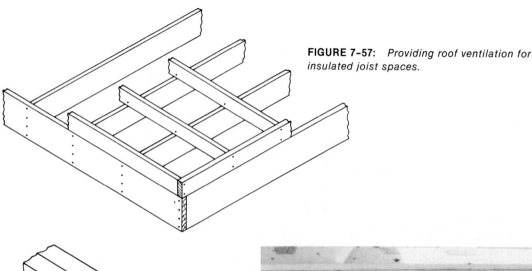

**FIGURE 7-57:** *Providing roof ventilation for insulated joist spaces.*

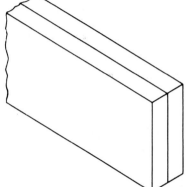

*(a) On edge.*

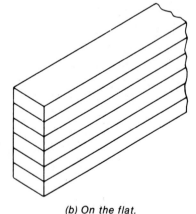

*(b) On the flat.*

**FIGURE 7-58:** *Laminated roof beams.*

*(c) Flat trusses.*

## FLAT ROOF WITH LAMINATED BEAMS

An open *style* ceiling may be produced in a flat roof by using heavy roof beams to carry the roof decking and leaving the underside of the decking and the beams exposed to view. It is necessary, therefore, that both decking and beams be of such a grade of material as to make that exposure practical.

The roof beams are normally laminated members—that is, they are made up of several pieces glued together to form a solid unit. The lamination may be of two or more pieces on edge or of several pieces laminated on the flat [see Fig. 7-58(a) and (b)]. Material to be used will usually have to be clear or nearly clear stock, since the finished beam will form part of the interior finish. In some cases, regular stock may be used and the two sides and the bottom of the beam covered with a thin veneer of the required type or texture. Laminated veneer lumber and parallel strand lumber have been recently substituted for laminated beams (see Fig. 5-2).

The sizes of the beams to be used will depend on their span and their spacing. The size required for a particular job should never be decided arbitrarily. Consult an engineer or other building authority to determine the width and depth best suited to the case.

Laminated beams are made to order by manufacturers specializing in this type of construction. Facilities for applying great pressure are required, since the parts of the beam are glued together, no nails or other fasteners being used. In addition, suitable means of planing and sanding the beams must be available, since they represent a finished product.

The sizes of the beams required must be calculated for each job. Size will depend, as stated previously, on span and spacing as well as on the type of roofing used. The longer the span, of course, the greater the load imposed on the beam for any given type of roofing. And the farther apart the beams are spaced, the more of the roof must be carried by each beam. Nothing can be said, therefore, about the size of beam that should be used. Generally, however, they will be relatively narrow in width in comparison to their depth. Remember that the strength of a beam varies directly as its width. In other words, if you double the width of a beam, you double the strength. On the other hand, the strength of a beam varies as the square of its depth. That means that if you double the depth, you then increase the strength four times.

The number of beams used for the roof, or, in other words, the spacing of the beams, will depend on the span, the weight of the roofing material, and the type of roof decking used. The maximum spacing allowed by most codes is about 84 in. (2100 mm) if 2 in. (38-mm) decking is to be used. Check the local building code for greater detail.

## Roof Decking

Roof decking over roof beams usually consists of 1½-in. (38-mm) single tongue-and-grooved or 2½- and 3½-in. (64- and 89-mm) double tongue-and-grooved (depending on load and span) cedar, douglas fir, or hemlock 5 or 7 in. (127 or 178 mm) wide. The underside of this decking will probably be exposed, so that certain precautions must be taken in selecting and laying it.

First, the material must be dry so that shrinkage and cracking are eliminated or kept at a minimum. Second, the appearance of the decking must be such that it harmonizes the rest of the interior finish. Third, the pieces must be drawn tightly together by edge nailing through predrilled holes with 8-in. (200-mm) spiral nails, spaced about 30 in. (750 mm) o.c. and then face-nailed to the beams (see Fig. 7–59). In some cases, clear material may be required, while in others a knotty appearance may be specified.

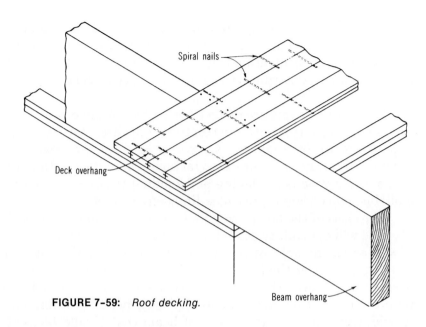

**FIGURE 7-59:**   *Roof decking.*

## Stressed-Skin Roof Panels

A *stressed-skin* panel consists of a frame of dimensional material covered on both sides with oriented strand board or plywood (see Fig. 7-60). The internal structure consists of spacer studs made of strand board or dimension lumber and, when insulation is required, injected with polyurethane insulation. The panel parts are glued and stapled together to form a structural panel of great strength and dimensional stability. To tie the panels together effectively, the skin projects over the frame at the edge to overlap the adjoining panel.

**FIGURE 7-60:**   *Stressed skin panels.*

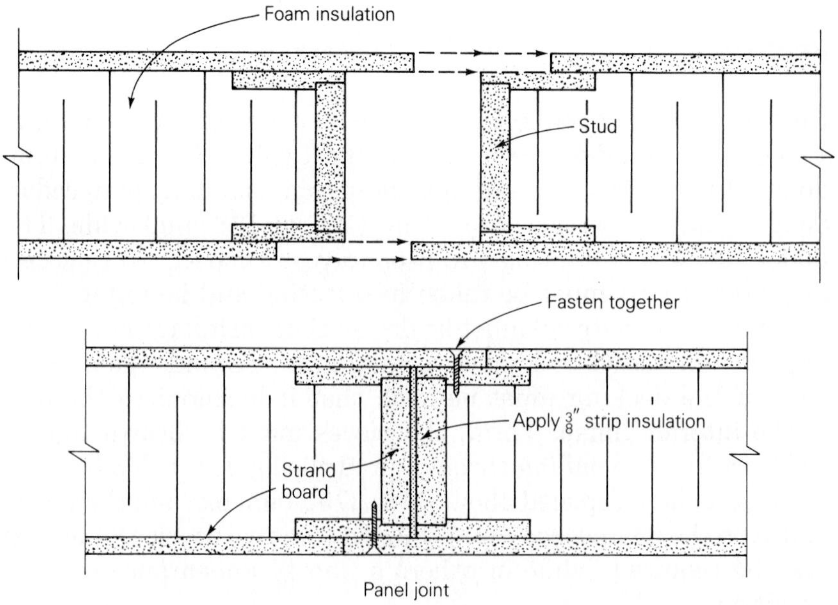

Panels may be of various shapes but are most often either *rectangular* or *triangular.* The spacing of framing members for stressed-skin panels depends on the thickness of the skin and the direction the face grain in relation to the long dimension of the framing member. Sizes can range up to 8 × 24 ft (2.4 × 7.2 m) and 4 in. to 6 in. (100 mm to 150 mm) in thickness.

Large panels result in a saving on construction time. Even larger time savings are possible with factory-applied wall and ceiling coverings such as gypsum board. A variety of modern coatings can be applied directly to the panels ranging from spray on fiber reinforced acrylic stuccos to torch-on modified bitumen roof membranes.

## GLUE-LAMINATED ARCHES

Glue-laminated arches are structural components made by gluing together thin pieces of lumber of any required width. In this way a member of any desired thickness and shape may be produced. Because of the wide scope in shape, size, and span, buildings using laminated arches for their frames are becoming increasingly popular. A great many are made commercially, some very large, with spans of 180 ft (60 m) or more. Great care is taken in the selection of lumber and the cutting of splices so that pieces fit perfectly, end to end, in the manufacture of these large arches. Large bandsaws and planers are used to cut and dress them to size. They are finally sanded, treated, and wrapped so that when they arrive on the job they are unmarked and, when in place, produce a finished appearance.

Smaller, lighter arches, in two or three standard shapes, with spans up to about 54 ft (18 m), are made with less sophisticated equipment for use in buildings such as that illustrated in Fig. 7–61.

**FIGURE 7-61:** *Arched rafter building.*

Although many shapes are possible, probably the most often used ones are the semicircular arched, the parabolic arch and the gothic arch (see Fig. 7–62). The semicircular and sometimes the parabolic arch are made in one piece, but in most other cases two separate halves of the complete arch are formed. The two halves are put together on the site, being secured together at the top by bolts or with steel plates acting as gussets.

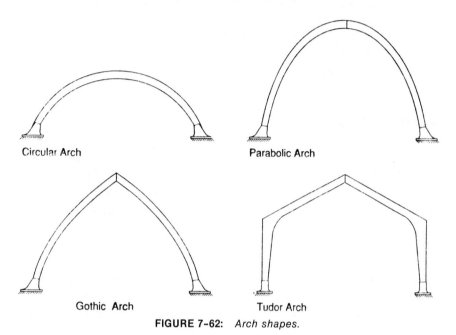

Circular Arch                     Parabolic Arch

Gothic Arch                       Tudor Arch

**FIGURE 7–62:** *Arch shapes.*

Spacing of the arches varies greatly, depending on the design, the span, and the type of roof deck to be applied. In some instances the roof decking will be carried on purlins running across the arches or hung in between them. With other designs, the decking will be $2\frac{1}{2}$- or $3\frac{1}{2}$-in. (64- or 89-mm) tongue-and-grooved material, usually cedar, spanning directly from arch to arch.

## REVIEW QUESTIONS

7–1. List three main factors that influence the size of ceiling joists to be used in any particular situation.

7–2. What figures would you use on the framing square to lay out the cut on the outer end of ceiling joists used in conjunction with a 7-in. (600-mm) rise roof. Mark on _____.

7–3. When is it necessary to use *stub* ceiling joists?

7–4. When can joist restraint be eliminated under the ceiling finish on the bottom edge of roof joists?

7-5. (a) What is the purpose of ceiling backing?
   (b) What width of ceiling backing should be used on a 2 × 4 (38 × 89 mm) partition?

7-6. (a) What is the main reason for providing access to the attic through the ceiling?
   (b) What minimum size of opening is required?
   (c) In what area of the ceiling would you suggest that the opening be placed?

7-7. On a simple diagram, illustrate each of the following rafter terms: (a) span, (b) run, (c) unit run, (d) unit rise, (e) total rise, (f) overhang, (g) rafter tail, (h) line length, (i) plumb cut, (j) seat cut.

7-8. What do you understand by "a rafter with a 12-in. (1000-mm) rise?"

7-9. By how much do line length and total length of a rafter differ?

7-10. What is the reason for "dropping" a hip rafter?

7-11. Give the length of the ridgeboard in each of the following cases:
   (a) Hip roof, plan dimensions 22 ft (6600 mm) × 26 ft (7800 mm) 1½-in. (38 × 89 mm) ridgeboard
   (b) Hip roof, plan dimensions 26 ft, 10 in. (7850 mm) × 32 ft, 8 in. (9675 mm), ¾-in. (19 × 140 mm) ridgeboard

7-12. Give the unit length of the common rafter for each of the following rises:
   (a) 6 in. (500 mm)
   (b) 8 in. (650 mm)
   (c) 10 in. (800 mm)

7-13. Calculate the total length of the common rafter in each of the following:
   (a) Span—24 ft; overhang—12 in.; rise—8 in.
   (b) Span—8000 mm; overhang—400 mm; rise—500 mm
   (c) Span—29 ft; overhang—16 in.; rise—4 in.
   (d) Span—9600 mm; overhang—700 mm; rise—400 mm

7-14. Find the unit line length of the hip rafter for each of the rafter rises listed in Question 7-12.

7-15. Calculate the total line length of the hip rafter in each of the cases listed in Question 7-13.

7-16. Explain the difference in the truss framing of a gable roof and a hip roof.

7-17. Explain the difference between a trussed rafter and a standard common rafter.

7-18. List three advantages of open web joists over conventional wood joists.

# 8

# STAIR BUILDING

Stair building is virtually a trade in itself, and it would be impossible to cover the subject in all its facets in a single chapter. Nevertheless, a stair of one kind or another is still a necessity in many types of light construction, and we shall look into the basic elements of the subject to find out how to construct some of the most commonly required kinds of stairs. Stairs are often prefabricated in a shop and then transported to and installed at the job site.

## TERMS USED IN STAIR BUILDING

Stairs lead from one floor level to another through a *stairwell opening*. It must be framed during the floor-framing stage of construction, so the length and width of the opening must be known. Stairs consist primarily of *risers* and *treads* carried on *stringers* (see Fig. 8-1). The height of each riser is called the *rise,* and the width of the tread (exclusive of nosing) is called the *run* (see Fig. 8-2). The sum of all the individual rises gives the *total rise,* and the sum of the runs gives the *total run* (see Fig. 8-1).

Two important terms used in stair work are *line of flight* and *headroom clearance*. The line of flight is a line drawn through the extremities of the nosings (see Fig. 8-3). Headroom clearance is the vertical distance from the underside of the end of the stairwell opening to the line of flight (see Fig. 8-1).

## STAIR DIMENSIONS

Most building codes provide guidelines for dimensions of stair parts. For example, interior stairs in residences and exterior stairs serving residences are allowed a maximum riser height of 8 in. (200 mm), a minimum run of 8¼ in. (210 mm), and a minimum tread width of 9 ¼ in. (235 mm). Interior stairs in buildings

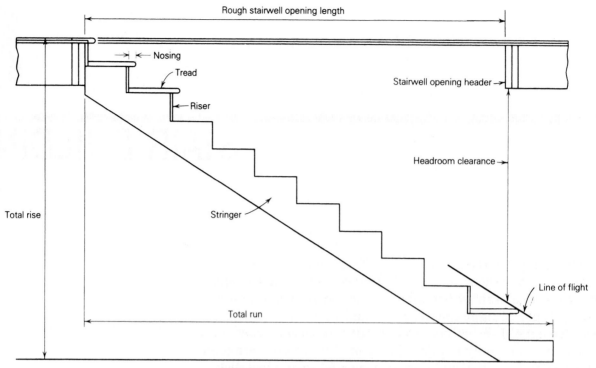

**FIGURE 8-1:** *Stair elevation.*

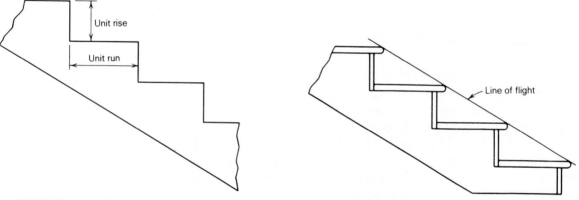

**FIGURE 8-2:** *Stair unit rise and unit run.*

**FIGURE 8-3:** *Line of flight.*

other than residences and exterior stairs, except those serving single residences, are restricted to a maximum riser height of 8 in. (200 mm), a minimum riser height of 5 in. (125 mm), a run not less than 9 in. (230 mm) or more than 14 in. (355 mm), and a minimum tread width of 10 in. (250 mm).

If the run of a stair is less than 10 in. (250 mm), it is necessary to provide a *nosing* which will project at least 1 in. (25 mm) beyond the face of the riser (see Fig. 8-1) or to provide at least as much backslope to the risers (see Fig. 8-4).

Stairs should have a minimum width of 2 ft, 10 in. (860 mm) and a minimum headroom clearance of 6 ft, 4 in. (1.95 m) in residences (see Fig. 8-1). In other types of buildings, the mini-

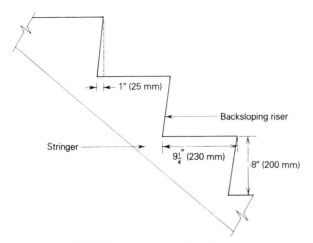

**FIGURE 8-4:** *Backslope on risers.*

mum width should be 3 ft, 0 in. (900 mm) and the headroom clearance should be 6 ft, 8 in. (2.05 m). The stairwell opening length will depend on the steepness of the stair and must be calculated accordingly.

Handrails run parallel to the stairs and are designed to be grasped while ascending or descending the stairs. All interior stairways of two or more risers should have a handrail. It should be installed on both sides if the stair is over 43 in. (1.1 m) wide. Handrail height should be between 32 and 36 in. (800 and 920 mm) above a line drawn through the outside edge of the stair nosing.

## TYPES OF STAIRS

Stairs are classified by the *kind of stringer* used in their construction, by the way the complete *stair is fitted into the building,* and by the *shape* of the complete stair.

### Stringer Types

One type of stringer used is the *open stringer* (see Fig. 8–5), in which pieces are cut from the stringer and risers and treads attached so that their ends are exposed. Another type is the *semi-housed stringer,* in which a piece of ³⁄₄-in. (19-mm) material is cut out, as in Fig. 8–5, and then fastened to the face of a solid 1½-in. (38-mm) stringer, which has as illustrated in Fig. 8–6. The ends of the risers and treads are thus concealed in the finished stair. A third type is the *housed stringer,* which has *dadoes,* ½ in. (12 mm) deep, cut on its inner face to receive the ends of the risers and treads (see Fig. 8–7). The dadoes are tapered so that wedges can be driven below the tread and behind the riser to hold each tightly in place.

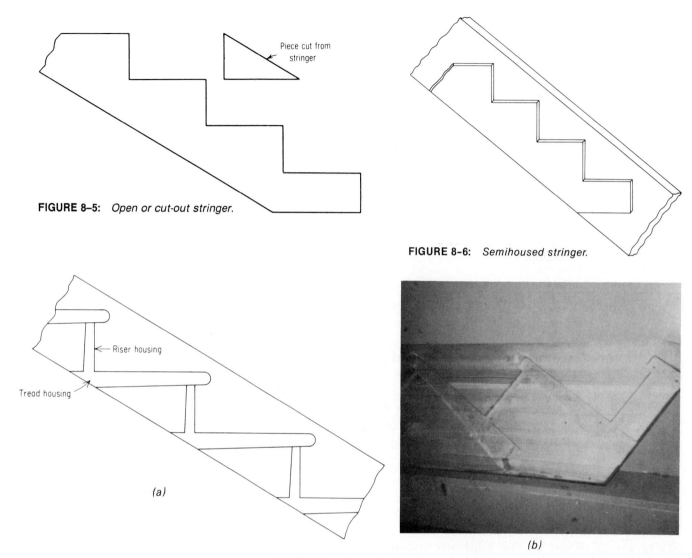

**FIGURE 8–5:** *Open or cut-out stringer.*

**FIGURE 8-6:** *Semihoused stringer.*

**FIGURE 8-7:** *Housed stringer.*

## Stair Types

A complete stair that has no wall on either side is called an *open stair.* If it has a wall on one side only, it is a *semihoused stair;* if it is built between two walls, it is a *housed stair.*

## Stair Shapes

A stair that rises with uninterrupted steps from floor to floor is known as a *straight flight;* if it has a break between top and bottom, it is a *straight flight with landing.* A stair that makes a right-angle turn by means of a landing is called an *L stair,* and a stair that makes a right-angle turn step by step is called a *winder.* A stair that makes a 180° turn is called a *U stair* (see Fig. 8–8).

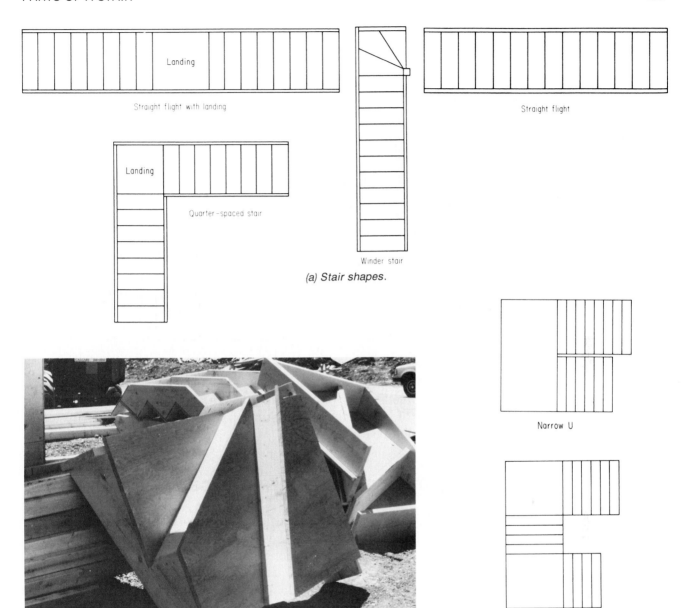

(a) Stair shapes.

Straight flight with landing

Landing

Straight flight

Landing

Quarter-spaced stair

Winder stair

Narrow U

Wide U

(b) Prefab winders.

(c) U-stairs.

**FIGURE 8-8**

## PARTS OF A STAIR

The parts of a stair include some already mentioned. The first is the *stringer*, the purpose of which is to carry the other members of the stair and to support the live load. Next is the *tread*, the surface on which to walk and then the *riser*, which covers the vertical spacings. A *nosing piece* is attached at the upper floor level, and a *molding* may cover the joint between riser and tread. *Wedges* hold the risers and treads tight in a housed stair.

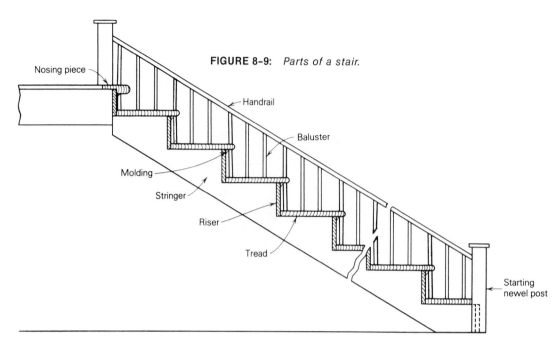

**FIGURE 8-9:** *Parts of a stair.*

A semihoused or open stair will have a *newel post* or newel posts at the bottom, which carries the bottom end of the *handrail.* Between handrail and treads there are *balusters;* the complete unit of handrail and balusters, with newel post, makes up a *balustrade* (see Fig. 8–9).

## HOW TO BUILD AN OPEN STRINGER STAIR

The first calculation necessary in connection with a stair is that of finding the length of the stairwell opening. This actually must be done during the floor-framing stage, because the opening must be framed at that time.

### Calculation of Stairwell Opening Length

A simple method of calculating the stairwell opening length is by comparison of two similar triangles involved in the stair layout. One contains unit rise and unit run as two sides of a triangle and the other the stairwell opening as one side and the headroom clearance plus thickness of ceiling finish, floor frame, subfloor, and finish floor as another. A portion of the line of flight is the third side of both.

As a specific example, suppose the finish floor to finish floor height is 108 in. (2.7 m), the headroom clearance required is 6 ft, 4 in. (1.95 m), and the floor assembly thickness is 11½ in. (240 mm). The unit rise is to be between 7 and 7½ in. (175 and 190 mm). The product of the unit rise and the unit run should be 70–75 in. (45,000–48,500 mm). What length of stairwell opening is required?

Use the following procedure to determine stairwell opening length:

1. Determine the number of risers required by dividing the rise by 7 (175):

$$^{108}\!/_7 = 15.4 = 15 \text{ risers} \qquad (^{2700}\!/_{175} = 15.4 = 15 \text{ risers})$$

2. Determine the size of each riser by dividing the rise by the number of risers:

$$^{108}\!/_{15} = 7.2 \text{ in.} \qquad (^{2700}\!/_{15} = 180 \text{ mm})$$

3. Determine the unit run by dividing 72 (45,000) by the individual riser size:

$$^{72}\!/_{7.2} = 10 \text{ in.} \qquad (^{45000}\!/_{180} = 250 \text{ mm})$$

4. Determine the drop to line of flight by adding the floor assembly thickness to the headroom (see Fig. 8-10):

6 ft, 4 in. + 11½ in. = 7 ft, 3½ in.  or  87.5 in.
(1950 mm + 240 mm = 2190 mm)

5. Determine the finished stairwell opening by setting up a ratio with the common sides of the two triangles:

$$\frac{\text{unit rise}}{\text{unit run}} = \frac{\text{total drop}}{\text{finish stairwell opening}}$$

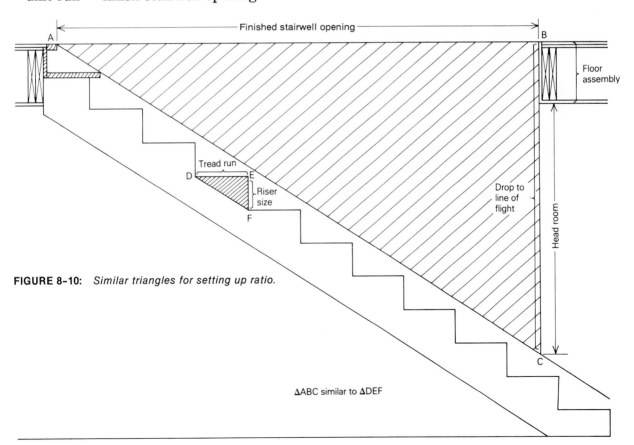

**FIGURE 8-10:** *Similar triangles for setting up ratio.*

ΔABC similar to ΔDEF

$$\frac{7.2}{10} = \frac{87.5}{\text{F.S.O.}}, \text{F.S.O.} = \frac{87.5 \times 10}{7.2} = 121.5 \text{ in.} \left( \frac{180}{250} = \frac{2190}{\text{F.S.O.}}, \text{F.S.O.} = \frac{2190 \times 250}{180} = 3042 \text{ mm} \right)$$

$$= 10 \text{ ft, } 1\frac{1}{2} \text{ in.}$$

6. The rough stairwell opening is equal to the stairwell opening plus the riser thickness plus the nosing and finish on the stairwell header. Usually adding $2\frac{1}{2}$ to 3 in. (65 to 75 mm) to the opening will allow for these items.

rough stairwell opening = 10 ft, $1\frac{1}{2}$ in. + $\frac{3}{4}$ + $1\frac{1}{4}$ + $\frac{1}{2}$ in. ← finish on stairwell header

= 10 ft, $4\frac{1}{2}$ in.

↑ nosing

riser thickness

= (3042 + 75 = 3117mm)

## Layout of Stair Stringer

Take the unit rise on the tongue of a framing square and the unit run on the blade and clamp a pair of stair gauges to the square at these points (see Fig. 8-11). Lay the square on the stringer stock, close to one end, as illustrated in Fig. 8-12, and carefully draw on the stock the rise and run. Slide the square along to the end of the run line and repeat. Continue until the required num-

**FIGURE 8-11:** *Square with stair gauges attached.*

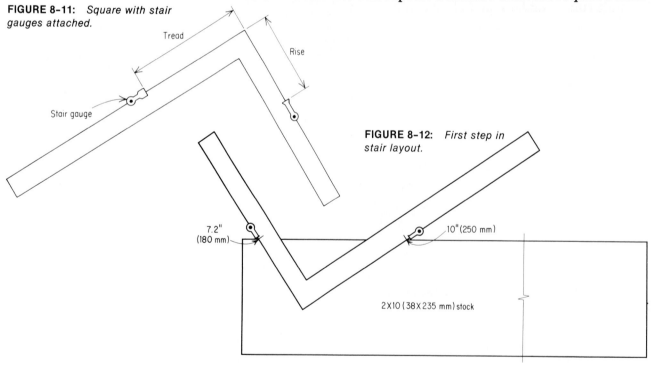

**FIGURE 8-12:** *First step in stair layout.*

**FIGURE 8-13:** *Stringer laid out.*

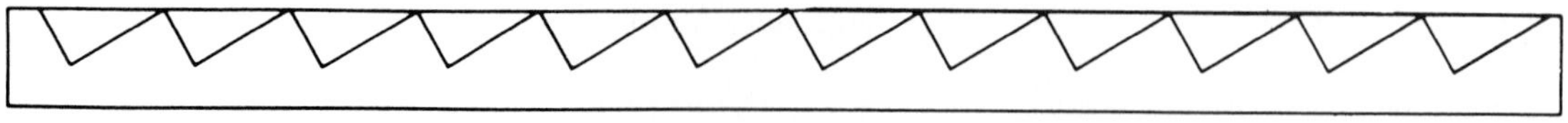

ber of risers and treads have been laid out. The stock will now look like the illustration in Fig. 8–13.

Since the stair begins with a riser at the bottom, extend the last riser and tread lines to the back edge of the stock, as shown in Fig. 8–14. Cut the stringer off along these lines.

At the top end, extend the last riser and tread lines to the back edge of the stock and cut as shown in Fig. 8–14. Cut very carefully along all the rise and tread lines to produce a cutout stringer (see Fig. 8–15).

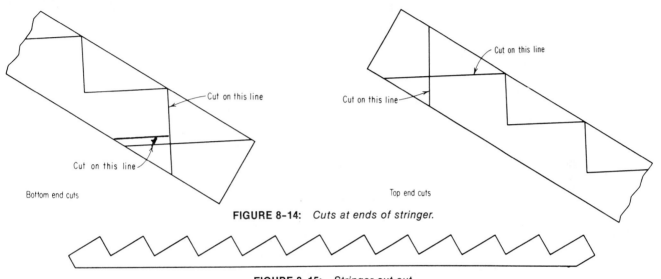

Bottom end cuts

Top end cuts

**FIGURE 8–14:** *Cuts at ends of stringer.*

**FIGURE 8–15:** *Stringer cut out.*

**FIGURE 8–16:** *Stringer set up.*

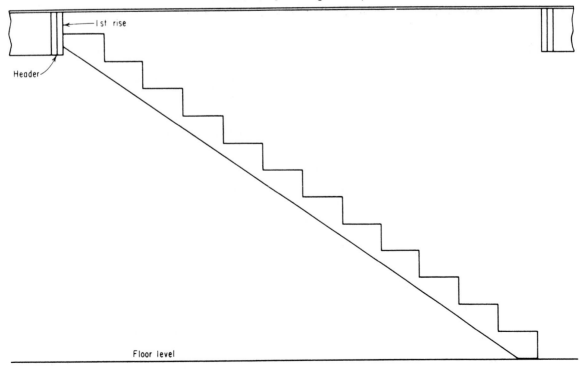

When this stringer is set up in place (see Fig. 8–16), it is seen that the face of the header becomes the first riser. But when the treads are set in place (see Fig. 8–17), the bottom step becomes higher than the rest, and the top step becomes shorter than the others, each by the thickness of the tread. To remedy this discrepancy, cut off from the bottom an amount equal to the thickness of the tread (see Fig. 8–18). Now when the stringer is set in place, the bottom rise is less than the rest, and the top is greater, but when the treads are in place, all the rises will be equal.

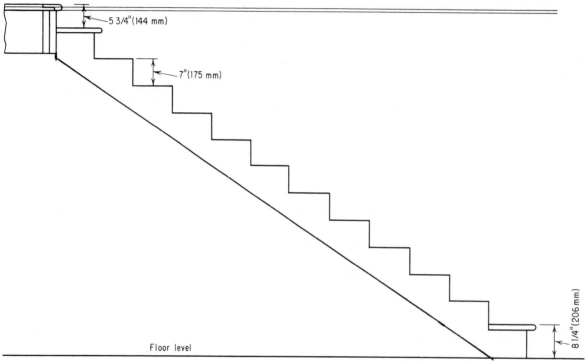

FIGURE 8–17:  *Unequal risers.*

FIGURE 8–18:  *Bottom riser reduced.*

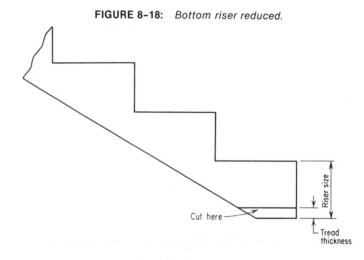

## Stair Assembly

At the top of the stair, a nosing with the same projection as the rest of the steps should be provided. The method used will depend on the material used for the finish floor and stair finish (see Fig. 8–19).

Tread material should be clear, dry, edge grain (if treads are exposed), or plywood (if covered) as illustrated in Fig. 8–19. The nosing is usually half-round, and the overhang should extend a distance equal to the thickness of the tread (see Fig. 8–19). If the tread nosing is to be capped with a metal molding, it should be shaped to fit that molding rather than being made half-round.

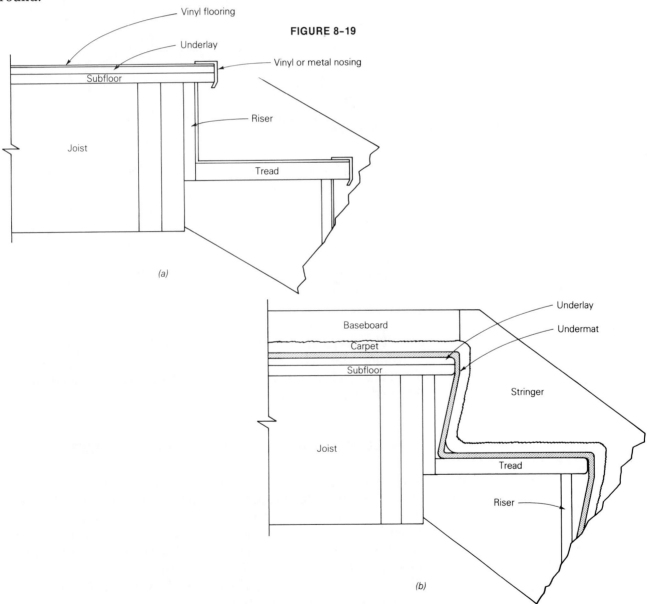

**FIGURE 8-19**

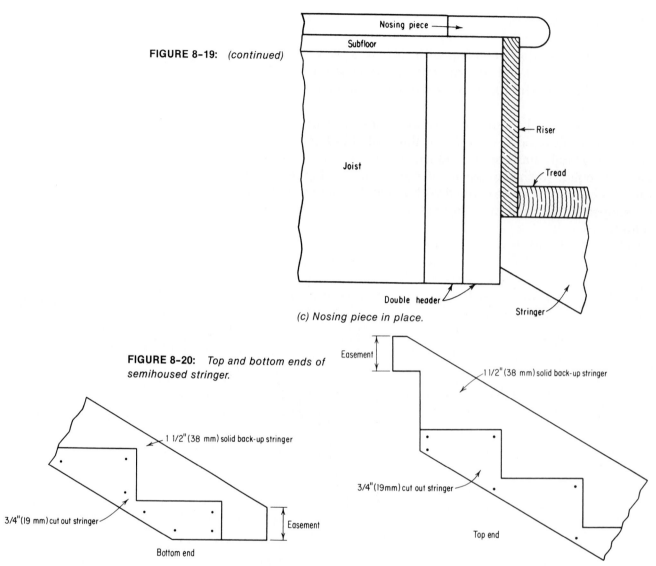

FIGURE 8–19: *(continued)*

*(c) Nosing piece in place.*

FIGURE 8–20: *Top and bottom ends of semihoused stringer.*

The risers are put in place first, nailed with 2½ in. 65-mm finishing nails. The treads are then put on, nailed in place, and from the back the bottom edges of the risers are nailed to the back edge of the treads.

## HOW TO BUILD A SEMIHOUSED STRINGER STAIR

When this type of stair is to be built, the ¾-in. (19-mm) cutout stringers are made in exactly the same way as described above. The ends of the solid, backup stringers will, however, be cut differently. At the bottom, the stringer will be allowed to run past the riser until the vertical cut is equal to the height of the baseboard, if any (see Fig. 8–20). At the top end, it will be cut as illustrated in Fig. 8–20, again so that the vertical cut will be the same height as the baseboard.

Glue and nail ¾-in. (19-mm) cutout pieces to the solid stringers so that the tread nosings will be the required distance from the upper edge of the stringer. Set the stringers in place, and set in the risers and treads. Care must be taken so that the ends fit snugly against the face of the stringer.

## HOW TO LAY OUT AND CUT A HOUSED STRINGER

Calculations for riser heights are the same as for other types of stairs, but the method of layout is considerably different.

Tapered dadoes are cut in the stringer to receive the treads and risers; these can be drawn with a template but are more commonly cut out with the aid of a router. Adjustable templates are available that make the cutting of the dadoes a simple chore. These templates can be set to the required riser and tread size making a 1 in 16 taper to allow for installation of wedges to hold pieces in place (see Fig. 8-21). A simple template can be made from hardboard to be used with a router equipped with a collar (see Fig. 8-22). To lay out and cut the stringer, proceed as follows:

1. Joint the top edge of the stringer so that it is perfectly straight.

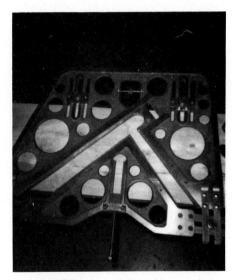

**FIGURE 8-21:** *Adjustable metal template.*

**FIGURE 8-22**

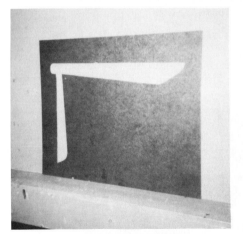

*(a) Masonite template.*

*(b) Router, collar, and bit.*

2. Using the required run and rise figures, draw the slope of the tread across the face of the stringer (see Fig. 8–23).

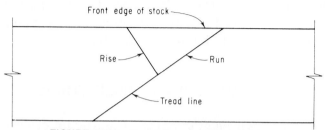

**FIGURE 8-23:**   *Tread line drawn on stringer.*

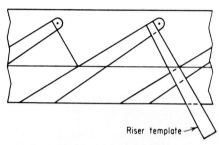

**FIGURE 8-24:**   *Nosing line.*

3. Lay the template to this line, making sure the nosing is the required distance from the top edge of the stringer. Draw a line through this point parallel to the top edge. This distance is usually at least 1 in. (25 mm), as shown in Fig. 8–24.

4. Mark on the tread line the width of the tread, and through this point draw a line parallel to the front edge. This is the baseline from which the layout is made (see Fig. 8–25).

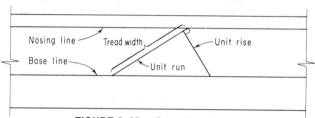

**FIGURE 8-25:**   *Base line drawn.*

5. Fasten the template to the stringer in the correct location and cut out the dadoes for each step using the router (see Fig. 8–26).

**FIGURE 8-26:**   *Template ready for routing.*

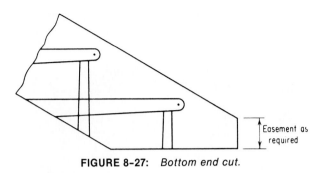

FIGURE 8-27: Bottom end cut.

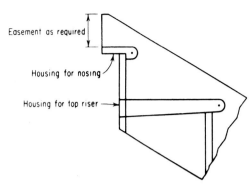

FIGURE 8-28: Top end cut.

6. At the bottom end, cut the stringer as illustrated in Fig. 8-27.

7. At the top end, cut the stringer as shown in Fig. 8-28, making sure to cut the dado for the nosing piece.

8. Chamfer the top inner edge of the stringer as required and sand the surface clean.

## ASSEMBLING THE STAIR

Lay the stringers top edge down on the floor, far enough apart to take the treads and risers. Set all the treads in place first and hold the assembly together with bar clamps placed to ensure that the stair is square. Check to see that the front edge of the groove in each tread lines up with the front edge of the riser dado. Set the nosing piece in place.

Now set all the risers in place. Check to see that the back edge of each tread fits snugly against the front face of its riser. The top riser cannot be wedged, since its dado is open at the back. Apply glue to the ends and nail it in place from the back.

The next step is to wedge the treads in place. Apply glue to the wedges and drive each firmly into place. The tread should thus be brought into a tight fit against the upper edge of the housing. Be sure that the wedges do not project beyond the back edge of the treads.

Now wedge the risers in place. Cut off the thin end of each wedge so that, when driven, it will not interfere with the tread above. Nail the bottom of each riser to the back edge of the tread, as illustrated in Fig. 8-29.

FIGURE 8-29: Riser and tread nailed.

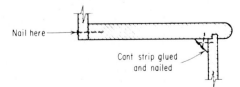

**FIGURE 8-30:**  *Glued and nailed strip at junction of step.*

Nail and glue a cant strip into the junctions between risers and treads (see Fig. 8-30). The stair is now complete and ready to install.

**FIGURE 8-31:**  *Brackets supporting handrail.*

## ASSEMBLING THE HANDRAIL

Once the stair assembly has been installed and fastened into place, the handrail must be assembled. Handrails for housed stairs are easily fastened to the studs in the wall supported by wooden or metal brackets, as illustrated in Fig. 8-31. Handrails for semihoused or open stairs that do not have walls nearby are supported by newel posts at either end with balusters evenly placed along the length to support the handrail (see Fig. 8-32).

**FIGURE 8-32:**  *Wooden railing.*

The newel posts are generally placed first, with the bottom end extending into and fastened to the floor frame to provide lateral support or fastened directly to the top of the joists with double pointed lag screws where lateral support is provided by the handrail (see Fig. 8–33). If the handrail should run into a wall at either end, a ½ newel post is fastened to the wall to provide support for the end of the handrail (see Fig. 8–34). The baluster shoe is placed next, fitted between the newel posts and fastened to the floor with screws. The handrail is usually placed next, fastened with screws to the newel posts at either end, as shown in Fig. 8–35.

**FIGURE 8-33:** *Newel post fastened to floor frame.*

**FIGURE 8-34:** *Railing fastened to wall.*

**FIGURE 8-35:** *Handrail fastened to newel post.*

Balusters are then placed and held in place with blocks fitted and glued into the slot in the shoe and under the handrail (see Fig. 8–36). Recessed screws are used to hold the top of balusters to handrails with designs that do not have the slot to allow for the placement of blocks between the balusters.

**FIGURE 8-36:** *Fastening balusters.*

**FIGURE 8-37:** *Camouflage plug.*

Wooden plugs are then used to cover the screws (see Fig. 8-37). Handrail parts are then finish sanded prior to painting or staining to match the decor of the room.

## REVIEW QUESTIONS

8-1. Fill in the blank or blanks in each sentence with the correct word or phrase:
   (a) A stair begins at the bottom with a _____.
   (b) A stair leads to an upper floor through a _____.
   (c) A line drawn through the extremities of the nosings of stair treads is the _____.
   (d) Stair risers and treads are carried on _____.
   (e) The vertical distance from the underside of the stairwell opening header to the line of flight is the _____.
   (f) The vertical distance from one floor level to the next is the _____ of a stair.
   (g) A stair tread is the width of the _____ wider than the run.
   (h) Stairs should have a slope of from _____ to _____ degrees.
   (i) Minimum stair width should be _____.
   (j) Run multiplied by rise should equal approximately _____.

8-2. Name three types of stringers used in stair building and indicate the differences between them.

8-3. Explain briefly the difference between an open, a semi-housed, and a housed stair.

8-4. What is the purpose of
   (a) Wedges in a stair?
   (b) A newel post?
   (c) A baluster?
   (d) A stringer?
   (e) A tread and riser template?

8-5. If the headroom clearance is to be 6 ft, 4 in. (1.95 m), the floor frame 2 × 10 (38 × 235 mm) material, the subfloor ⅝-in. (15-mm) plywood, the finish floor ⅛-in. (3-mm) inlaid, the underlay ⅜-in. (10-mm) particle board, the ceiling and header finish ½-in. (12-mm) gypsum wallboard, the risers ¾ in.(19 mm) thick, and the nosing projection 1 ¼ in. (32 mm),
   (a) What should the length of the stairwell opening be if the tread run is 10 in. (250 mm)?

(b) How many risers will there be in the stair if the rise is to be kept as close to 7 in. (175 mm) as possible and the total rise between floors is 9 ft, 4½ in. (2858 mm)?

(c) How many treads will there be in the stair?

8-6. By means of a diagram, illustrate how a nosing piece fits at the top of an open stair stringer.

8-7. Explain why no extra cutoff of the stringers at the bottom is necessary when a housed stringer stair is being built.

# 9

# EXTERIOR FINISHING

Once the frame of the building has been completed, the next step is to apply the exterior finish. This involves installing window and door frames and outside casings, roofing, exterior paper, cornice work, and the application of whatever is to be used to cover the exterior.

The usual order in which these operations are carried out is as follows: (1) cornice work, (2) roofing, (3) fitting of door and window frames, (4) application of exterior paper, (5) application of exterior finish.

## CORNICE WORK

The *cornice*, or eave, is formed by the overhang of the rafters and may be *open* or *boxed.* In either case, the work of finishing the eave should be done as soon as the rafters are in place.

### Open Eaves

With open eaves, the rafter tails and the underside of the roof sheathing are exposed from below, and consequently the roof sheathing over that section of the roof may be replaced by a better quality of material.

In addition, it is necessary to block off the openings between the rafters above the cap plate, and this is done by the use of *windblocks.* These are pieces of $1\frac{1}{2}$-in. (38-mm) material cut to fit snugly between each pair of rafters (see Fig. 9-1).

With this type of eave, a single fascia may be used over the ends of the rafter tails, as shown in Fig. 9-1.

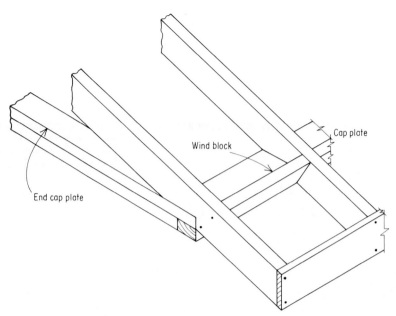

**FIGURE 9-1:**   *Open eave with wind block in place.*

## Boxed Eaves

With boxed eaves, the underside of the roof overhang is enclosed. This may be done by applying a *soffit* to the bottom edge of the rafter tails, as illustrated in Fig. 9-2. In such a case, the *rough fascia*, which supports the outer edge of the soffit between rafters, has both top and bottom edges beveled to the slope of the roof.

An alternative and more common method is to build a frame to which a horizontal soffit may be attached to enclose the eave (see Fig. 9-3). Such a frame is made up of a *lookout ledger*, nailed to the wall, a *rough fascia* over the ends of the

**FIGURE 9-2:**   *Eave boxed on slope of roof.*

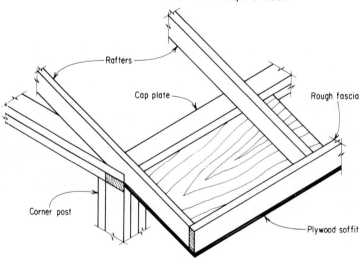

FIGURE 9-3: *Boxed eave frame.*

(a)

(b)

rafter tails, and *lookouts,* which span between the two and lie alongside each rafter tail (see Fig. 9–4). It may be fabricated on the ground and raised into place as a unit.

At the gable-end additional framing is required to support the 2 × 6 (38 × 140 mm) verge rafter. Lookouts are installed and are extended over the gable-end back to the next truss to give sufficient support (see Fig. 9–5). In a hip roof building, the horizontal soffit is framed the same way on all sides of the building.

FIGURE 9-4: *Boxed eave framing.*

Insulation stop

Roof sheathing

Rafter

Wall plates

Building paper

Stud

Finish fascia

Lookout ledger

Rough fascia

Lookout

Sheathing

Soffit

Ventilation screen

**FIGURE 9-5:** *Overhang support.*

The introduction of metal and vinyl soffit material onto the market has almost eliminated the use of wood finished soffits as the amount of labor required is reduced. The only framing required for a metal or vinyl soffit is a rough fascia at the edge of the roof overhang as the soffit material is supported by a molding where it meets the building (see Fig. 9-6). The outer end of the soffit is stapled to the underside of the rough fascia and is then covered with a preformed finish fascia. The use of metal or vinyl soffit material not only reduces the labor required for installation, but also provides a prefinished surface that needs little maintenance.

With a gable roof, the horizontal eaves on the side walls can either stop at the corner of the building, as illustrated in Fig. 9-7(a), or it can extend flush with the edge of the roof, as shown in Fig. 9-7(b). The ends of the eave are then finished, as shown in Fig. 9-8. The gable-end soffit is finished the same way as the soffits on the side walls.

**FIGURE 9-6:** *Finished metal soffit.*

*(a) Eave stopped at corner of the building.*

*(b) Eave flush with the edge of the roof.*

**FIGURE 9-7**

Another method of finishing the boxed eave at the gable end is illustrated in Fig. 9-9. This is known as *returning the cornice*. A set of truss overhangs are nailed to the gable wall, producing the same overhang as the regular eave. The tops of the returns are shingled like the roof, and the soffit is carried around, finishing the underside.

**FIGURE 9-8:** *Finishing end of eave.*

**FIGURE 9-9:** *Cornice returns.*

If there is no gable overhang (see Fig. 9-10), a rough fascia is nailed to the outside of the gable-end, covering the edge of the roof sheathing. A preformed finish fascia is then nailed to the rough fascia with colored nails to finish the edge of the roof.

Also, before the roofing is applied, provision must be made at the lower edges of the roof for the proper direction of rainwater into the eaves trough. One method is to fasten eave flashing, like that illustrated in Fig. 9-11, to the edge of the roof, under the roofing.

**FIGURE 9-10:** *Gable-end with no roof overhang.*

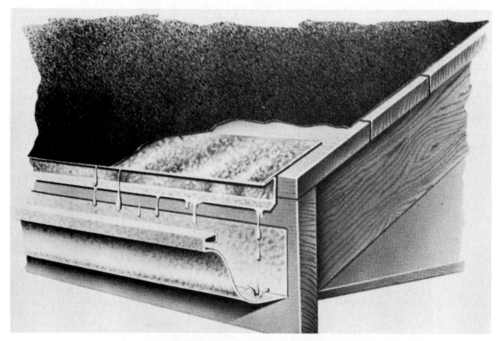

**FIGURE 9-11:** *Eave flashing.*

## ROOF COVERINGS

Roof covering is installed as soon as the roof framing and sheathing have been completed. This will provide a weatherproof working space in the building so that the other construction trades can begin. The most common type of roofing used on sloped roofs are shingles of one sort or another. These include wood (usually cedar or pine), asphalt, and hardboard. Roofing tile, sheet metal, and roll roofing are also used on sloped roofs. Roofing tile is commonly made of concrete, clay, or metal. Sheet metal roofing is made of galvanized steel or aluminum and is effective in areas subjected to heavy snowfall. Built-up roofing with a gravel topping or a cap sheet is commonly used on a flat or low slope roof.

## Wood Shingles

Wood shingles are generally made from cedar, because it changes very little with atmospheric changes and withstands weathering better than most woods. Machine-cut wood shingles are made in a number of grades, but the commonly used grades for residential roofing are No. 1 and No. 2. The widths of these shingles vary from a minimum of 3 in. (75 mm) to a maximum of 14 in. (350 mm), and lengths vary from16 to 24 in. (400 to 600 mm).

The portion of shingle that should be exposed to the weather will depend on the steepness of the roof slope and the grade and length of shingles used. Table 9–1 gives recommended maximum exposure, depending on the slopes.

The area of roof covered by one bundle of shingles will depend on the shingle exposure, and Tables 9–2(a) and (b) give the approximate area covered by one bundle of shingles for various exposures.

**TABLE 9-1:** *Shingle exposure*

|  | Maximum shingle exposure [in. (mm)] | | |
|---|---|---|---|
|  | No. 1 grade, length of shingle | | |
| Roof slope | 16 in. (400 mm) | 18 in. (450 mm) | 24 in. (600 mm) |
| 1 in 3 or less | 3¾ (95) | 4⅛ (105) | 5¾ (145) |
| Over 1 in 3 | 4⅞ (125) | 5½ (140) | 7½ (190) |

Source: Courtesy Council of Forest Industries of B.C.

**TABLE 9-2: (a)** *Shingle coverage*

| Length and thickness | Approximate coverage in ft² of one bundle based on the following weather exposures | | | | | | | | |
|---|---|---|---|---|---|---|---|---|---|
|  | 3½ in. | 4 in. | 4½ in. | 5 in. | 5½ in. | 6 in. | 6½ in. | 7 in. | 7½ in. |
| 16 × ⅜ | 18.2 | 20.2 | 23.2 | 25.3* | 28.3 | 30.3 | 33.4 | 36.4 | 38.4‡ |
| 18 × ⁷⁄₁₆ | 16.4 | 18.2 | 21.0 | 22.7 | 25.5* | 27.3 | 30.0 | 32.7 | 34.5 |
| 24 × ½ | 12.3 | 13.7 | 15.7 | 17.1 | 19.2 | 20.4 | 22.5 | 24.5 | 25.9* |

*Notes:* *Maximum exposure recommended for roofs.
‡Maximum exposure recommended for single-coursing No. 1 and No. 2 grades on sidewalls.

**TABLE 9-2: (b)** *Shingle coverage*

| Length and thickness | Approximate coverage in m² of one bundle based on the following weather exposures | | | | | | | | | | | |
|---|---|---|---|---|---|---|---|---|---|---|---|---|
|  | 90 mm | 100 mm | 115 mm | 125 mm | 140 mm | 150 mm | 165 mm | 180 mm | 190 mm | 200 mm | 215 mm | 225 mm |
| 400 mm × 10 mm | 1.69 | 1.88 | 2.16 | 2.35* | 2.63 | 2.82 | 3.10 | 3.38 | 3.57† | 3.76 | 4.04 | 4.23 |
| 450 mm × 11 mm | 1.52 | 1.69 | 1.95 | 2.11 | 2.37* | 2.54 | 2.79 | 3.04 | 3.21 | 3.38 | 2.64† | 3.81 |
| 600 mm × 13 mm | 1.14 | 1.27 | 1.46 | 1.59 | 1.78 | 1.90 | 2.09 | 2.28 | 2.41* | 2.54 | 2.73 | 2.85 |

*Notes:* *Maximum exposure recommended for roofs.
†Maximum exposure recommended for single-coursing No. 1 and No. 2 grades on sidewalls.

## Decking for Cedar Shingles

Roof decking for wood shingles may be solid or spaced. If the deck is solid, it is usually made of oriented strandboard or plywood. The thickness should be ⅜ in. (9.5 mm) when trusses are spaced 24 in. (600 mm) o.c.

Spaced sheathing is usually 1 × 6 or 1 × 8 (19 × 140 or 19 × 184) boards, spaced on centers equal to the exposure of the shingles (see Fig. 9–12).

**FIGURE 9-12:** *Spaced sheathing deck.*

## Paper for Cedar Shingles

Asphalt-impregnated paper is not usually used under cedar shingles. It prevents the completed roof from "breathing, " that is, from allowing the moisture vapor under the roof to escape. If paper is required, plain or breather type paper is recommended.

## Application of Wood Shingles

Shingles should extend beyond the finish fascia about 1 in. (25 mm) to provide sufficient watershed (see Fig. 9–13). Tack a narrow piece of board 1 in. (25 mm) thick lightly to the fascia as a guide.

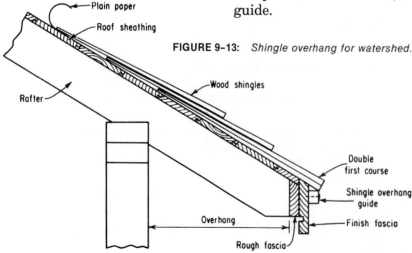

**FIGURE 9-13:** *Shingle overhang for watershed.*

**FIGURE 9-14:** *Doubled first course.*

The first course of shingles at the eave must be doubled (see Fig. 9-14). Lay the first row with shingles ¼ in (6 mm) apart, butts to the guide strip. Use *two nails only* for each shingle, regardless of its width; nails should not be more than ¾ in. (20 mm) from the edge of the shingle. The second layer of the first course is laid directly over the first, shingles also spaced ¼ in. (6 mm) apart. Be sure that a joint between shingles does not come closer than 1½ in. (38 mm) to a joint in the layer below (see Fig. 9–15). If a third layer is used, it too must have joints offset 1½ in. (40 mm) from those underneath.

**FIGURE 9-15:** *Side lap with wood shingles.*

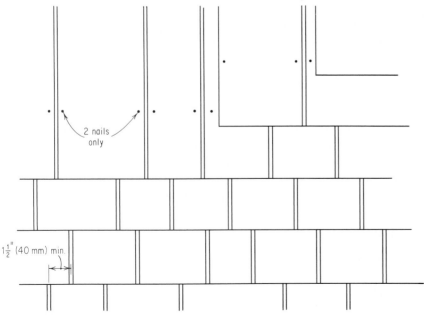

The second and succeeding courses are laid, with the specified exposure, measured from the butts of the course below. A strip of lumber may be used as a straightedge against which to lay the shingles; a chalk line may also be used as a guide, or a shingling hatchet is sometimes used by expert shinglers to keep the shingles in a straight course. Nails should be placed ¾ to 1½ in. (19 to 38 mm) above the butt line of the next course.

### Shingling Ridges and Hips

When ridges and hips are being shingled, the so-called modified *Boston lap* is used for best results. Use edge grain shingles at least 1 in. (25 mm) wider than the exposure used and select them all the same width. For hips, cut the butts at an angle so that they will be parallel to the butt lines of the regular courses (see Fig. 9–16).

(a) Shingling a hip.

(b) Preassembled ridge and hip caps.

**FIGURE 9–16**

Run a chalk line up the roof on each side of the hip centerline at a distance from the centerline equal to the exposure. Lay the first shingle to one of the chalk lines and bevel the top edge parallel to the plane of the adjacent roof surface. Now apply a shingle on the opposite side in the same way, beveling its top edge, as shown in Fig. 9–16(a). Place the nails so that they will be covered by the course above. The next pair of shingles is applied in *reverse order*, and each pair is alternated up the hip.

Ridges are done in much the same way. Start at the ends and work toward the center of the ridge, the last pair of shingles being cut to the exposure length. In recent years the shingles caps for the ridges and hips are delivered to the job site preassembled, as illustrated in Fig. 9–16(b), reducing the onsite cutting and fitting time.

### Shingling Valleys

Valleys have to be *flashed* before they are shingled. The method of shingling the valley will determine if the valley is referred to as "open" or "closed."

FIGURE 9-17

*(a) Valley flashing.*

*(b) Valley open. (Courtesy Masonite Canada Inc.)*

*Open valleys* are usually flashed with a strip of sheet metal at least 24 in. (600 mm) wide or with two layers of roll roofing (see Fig. 9–17). When two layers of roll roofing are used to flash the valley, the bottom layer will be an 18 in. (457 mm) strip of type S smooth surface roll roofing or type M mineral surface roll roofing applied with the mineral surface down. A 36-in. (900-mm) strip of type M roll roofing is placed over the first strip with the mineral side up. The top layer is applied over a 4-in. (100-mm) wide strip of cement along each edge of the bottom layer, and fastened with enough nails to hold the roofing in place until shingles are applied. The open part of the valley is usually 4 in. (100 mm) wide and will increase in size towards the lower end at a rate of 1:100.

*Closed valleys* are flashed with one layer of sheet metal or type S roll roofing at least 24 in. (600 mm) wide. Each course of asphalt shingles is continued across the valley ensuring that shingle nails are not placed within 3 in. (75 mm) of the valley center line. The courses are alternated to ensure a watertight valley. Another method of finishing the valley is to cut the shingles from the second roof slope along the valley center line and set them in a strip of cement (see Fig. 9–18). Closed valleys should not be used with rigid shingles.

FIGURE 9-18: *Closed valley.*

### Roof Flashing

Flashing has to be placed around chimneys, dormers, or other structures projecting above the roof surface. Along the sides which are perpendicular to the shingle courses, individual flashings must be used, one for each course of shingles. Each is bent at a right angle, so that part of the flashing lies flat on the roof, on top of the shingle, while the other half rests against the side of the chimney or dormer, with the upper edge embedded in a mortar joint or covered by dormer finish (see Fig. 9–19).

The upper and lower sides are flashed and counterflashed—one flashing running under the shingles and the other lying on top of them (see Fig. 9–20).

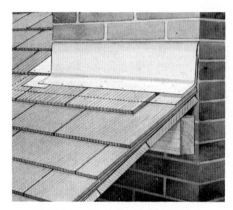

**FIGURE 9-20:** *Chimney flashing.*

**FIGURE 9-19:** *Shake roof.*

### Chimney Saddle

To prevent water from collecting on the *up-roof* side of a chimney which projects through the roof, a *saddle* should be built behind it to shed the water. It should be the same width as the chimney, built like a miniature gable roof (see Fig. 9–21) with flashing at the chimney and in the valleys.

### Wood Shakes

Wood shakes are commonly made of cedar and more recently from pine (see Fig. 9–22). Shakes, however, are longer and thicker, and they have a textured finish due to the splitting action used in the manufacture (see Fig. 9–24). There are three types of wood shakes generally available: handsplit and resawn,

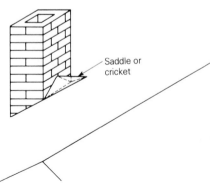

**FIGURE 9-21:** *Chimney saddle.*

FIGURE 9-22: *Pine shakes.*

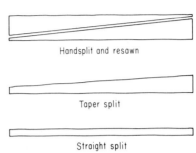

Handsplit and resawn

Taper split

Straight split

FIGURE 9-23: *Wood shake types.*

FIGURE 9-24: *Wood shake roof.*

taper split, and straight split (see Fig. 9-23). Shakes are generally produced in 18- or 24-in. (450- or 600-mm) lengths with butt thicknesses varying from ⅜ to 1¼ in. (9–32 mm). The maximum exposure recommended for double coverage on a roof is 10 in. (250 mm) for 24-in. (600-mm) shakes and 7½ in. (190 mm) for 18-in. (450-mm) shakes. Shakes are recommended on slopes of 1 in 3 or steeper, and spacing should conform to limits set for wood shingles in areas where wind-driven snow conditions prevail, solid roof sheathing is recommended.

### Application of Shakes

Apply a starter strip of No. 15 asphalt-saturated felt underlayment 36 in. (900 mm) wide along the eaves and 12 in. (300 mm) along hips and ridges. The first course is doubled, just like regu-

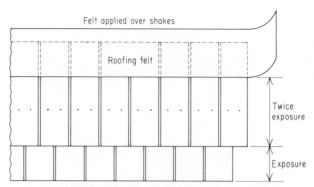

**FIGURE 9–25:** *Positioning of felt.*

lar wood shingles. After each course of shakes is applied, an 18-in. (450-mm) strip of No. 15 asphalt-saturated felt is applied over the top portion of the shakes, extending onto the sheathing (see Fig. 9–24). The bottom edge of the underlayment should be positioned above the butt a distance equal to twice the exposure (see Fig. 9–25). Individual shakes should be spaced from $\frac{1}{4}$ to $\frac{3}{8}$ in. (6–10 mm) to allow for expansion. The joints in each row should be offset $1\frac{1}{2}$ in. (40 mm) from the joints in the previous row.

Two nails are used in each shake, regardless of width. The nails used are rust resistant, normally 2 in. (50 mm) long placed approximately 1 in. (25 mm) from each edge and 1 to 2 in. (25–50 mm) above the butt line of the following course. Staples are commonly used to fasten shingles and shakes with the advent of air- and electric-powered staples (see Fig. 9–26).

**FIGURE 9–26:** *Stapling shakes.*

## Eave Protection

Eave protection shall be provided on all shingle and shake roofs, extending from the edge of the roof to a line up the roof slope not less than 12 in. (300 mm) inside the inner face of the wall.

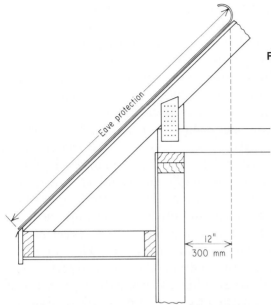

**FIGURE 9-27:**  *Eave protection.*

This protection is not necessary when the building is not likely to have ice forming along the eaves, causing a backup of water (see Fig. 9–27). Eave protection is not required over unheated garages, carports, and porches, or where the roof overhang exceeds 36 in. (900 mm) measured along the roof slope, or where low-slope shingles are used. A solid decking is typically used under the portion of the roof covered by the eave protection.

## Application of Asphalt Shingles

So-called *asphalt shingles* are made by impregnating heavy felt paper with hot asphalt and covering the upper surface with finely crushed, colored slate. Many types are available, one of the most common being what is known as a *triple-tab* shingle, actually three shingles in one [see Fig. 9–28(a)]. Interlocking asphalt shingles are also available, and they are very good for re-roofing jobs [see Fig. 9–28(b)].

**FIGURE 9–28**

*(a) Roof shingled with triple-tab shingles.*

*(b) Roof shingled with interlocking shingles.*

Laying starts at the bottom edge of the roof, and on some occasions a chalk line is snapped down the center of the roof to act as a guide for vertical alignment. Eave flashing is usually placed before the eave protection to protect the edge of the roof sheathing from upward moisture migration (see Fig. 9–11).

The starter course along the lower edge of the roof is applied over the eave protection. The first course is doubled, with the first layer being placed with the tabs pointing up the roof slope (see Fig. 9–29). This row extends over the edge of the roof to provide a watershed. A strip of shingles is also nailed up the rake to provide a straight edge and to divert moisture away from this edge (see Fig. 9–29). The first layer should be nailed near the eave edge, making sure the nails are not exposed in the slots in the next layer. The second layer of the first row is staggered so the joints do not line up with the joints in the first layer, and each succeeding row is either offset one-half or one-third of a tab to provide a watertight roof (see Fig. 9–30). The shingles are fastened by nailing or stapling about ½ in. (12 mm) above the top of the slot. To ensure straight vertical alignment of slots (see Fig. 9–31), some shinglers will build a pyramid up the roof slope rather than in horizontal rows [see Fig. 9–28(b)].

**FIGURE 9-29**

*(a) Starter strip.*

*(b) Strip along rake.*

**FIGURE 9-30:** *Staggering slots.*

**FIGURE 9-31:** *Alignment of slots.*

They will also use all of the shingles from one bundle before opening another, as shingle lengths between bundles can vary, causing crooked slot lines.

Most triple-tab shingles have a strip of adhesive along the face of the shingle to cement the tabs down. Interlocking shingles are manufactured so the bottom edge hooks in and is very good in windy regions [see Fig. 9–28(b)]. A starter strip is needed on the bottom edge to provide a double layer over the entire roof slope. Individual shingles with the bottom portion cut off are commonly used to provide the starter strip. Open valleys are formed (see Fig. 9–32) using a double layer of roll roofing with a matching granular finish showing or a metal flashing, as discussed under wood shingles. A closed valley is also often used, as illustrated in Fig. 9–18. The shingles from one side are placed over a valley liner of roll roofing and up the opposite slope at least 12 in. (300 mm). The shingles on the other slope will be cut along the valley line and embedded in a continuous strip of roofing cement.

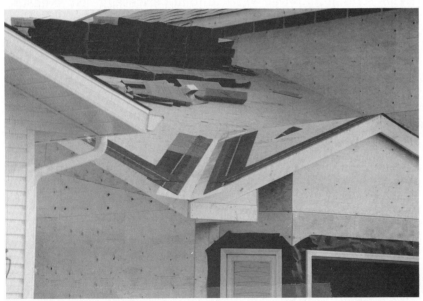

**FIGURE 9-32:** *Open valley—metal flashing.*

**FIGURE 9-33:** *Ridge cap.*

Individual shingles are used to cap hips and ridges (see Fig. 9–33). Fold the shingle over the ridge or the hip and nail so that the nails will be covered by the succeeding shingles. On the ridge they are placed in a direction so that the prevailing winds do not lift the edges of the tab.

Low-slope shingles are larger and are placed so that there are three layers over the entire roof surface. The shingles have two tabs instead of three. A continuous band of roofing cement is applied on each row equal to the width of the shingle exposure plus 2 in. (50 mm) located 2 in. (50 mm) above the butt line of the overlying shingle. Low-slope shingles can be used on a minimum slope of 1 in 6, while normal asphalt shingles can only be placed on a minimum slope of 1 in 3.

Architectural asphalt shingles are becoming increasingly popular in residential construction. These decorative shingles are a particular kind of premium shingle with a decorative cut or finish, giving it a more upscale appearance and allowing it to compete aesthetically with wood shakes and roofing tiles at a more affordable rate. This architectural appeal is achieved by laminating and texturing the tabs of the shingle.

## Hardboard Shingles

Hardboard shingles are made of wood fibers, are resin treated, and are pressed into a dense mat. The mat has a cedar shake pattern embossed into the fibers (see Fig. 9–34). The individual shingles are 12 × 48 in. (300 × 1200 mm) and are manufactured with a self-aligning exposure line and a nailing line (see Fig. 9–35). On the job, conventional tools are used in the application of this roofing material. Vertical joints are staggered to ensure a watertight roof. Precut or field-cut hip and ridge caps are available, and valley treatment follows the conventional open valley practice [see Fig. 9–17(b)].

**FIGURE 9–34:**  *Hardboard shingled roof.*

**FIGURE 9–35:**  *Hardboard shingle.*

Nailing line  →
Alignment line  →
Embossed pattern  →

## Built-Up Roofing

There are two methods for preventing external water from entering a building through a roof. One is to use watershed units like various types of shingles, and the other is to use continuous membranes. Shingles rely on the principle of gravity and overcoming capillary action to prevent water entry through a roof, where the continuous membranes rely on the membrane preventing water penetration through it. A conventional built-up roof—so called because it is built up from several layers of material—is commonly used on flat or low-sloped decks. The materials consist of a primary membrane composed of several layers of #15 organic felts mopped, a separator sheet of two plies of #15 organic mechanically fastened to the deck. The primary membrane is covered with a flood coat of asphalt bitumen with sufficient gravel embedded to protect and hold down the roofing membrane.

The amount of material used determines the approximate life of the roof. The example in Fig. 9–36 illustrates a common procedure for laying a conventional flat roof system. Here are the steps in this procedure:

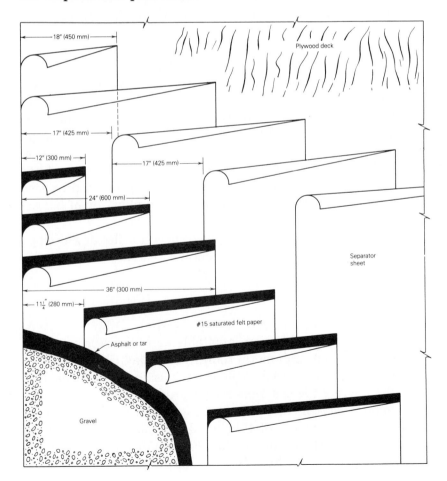

**FIGURE 9-36:** *Built-up roof.*

1. Lay down two layers of #15 organic felt, starting with a half roll and then lapping each sheet 19 in. (480 mm) over the preceding one, and nailing or stapling it well enough to hold it in place.

2. Lay down three additional layers of the same felt as above, securing each by a layer of hot asphalt or tar bitumen (0.2 lb/ft (1 kg/m), mopped full width. This step is begun by cutting a roll of felt into a 12 in. and 24 in. (300 mm and a 600 mm) width. Lay down the 12 in. (300 mm) strip first, as illustrated in Fig. 9-36, then the 24 in. (600 mm) strip over it, and then the full width roll. Notice that these three layers all start from the same edge, resulting in three layers of mopped felt over the entire roof.

3. Cover the entire surface with a uniform coat of hot asphalt at the rate of 0.6 lb/ft (3 kg/m), with sufficient gravel embedded to allow minimal bitumen to show through. The weight of the gravel is approximately 3 lb/ft (15 kg/m) and should be rolled while the flood coat is hot to ensure that it is well embedded.

4. Check to make sure that the roofing is well up over the flashing and that there is a good seal where the flashing and roofing meet.

If the roof has insulation on top of the deck, the procedure must, of necessity, be somewhat different. A vapor retardant must be placed on the deck prior to the placement of the rigid insulation. If the insulation does not have a minimum compressive strength of 25 psi (172 kPa) a ½ in. (12.5 mm), layer of wood fiberboard or fiberboard sheathing is placed over the insulation prior to the placement of the primary membrane. If the roof has a slope of over 1:4 the primary membrane is protected by two plies of wide selvage roofing with interply application of hot asphalt.

Single-ply membranes may also be used for flat or low-slope roofs, but are not often used on small roofs that are typically part of wood frame construction.

### Roofing Tile

A number of types of tile are available as roof covering. They include concrete tile and metal roofing tile. Clay tile has been in use for a long time and is still used in some areas [see Fig. 9-37(a)]. Concrete tile is a more recent product, and for the most part, shapes resemble clay tiles [see Fig. 9-37(b)]. Concrete roof tiles have a nominal size of 16½ × 13 in. (420 × 330 mm) with an interlocking side lap of 1³⁄₁₆ in. (30 mm). Metal roofing tiles are made of a lightweight galvanized steel, shaped to resemble

*(a) Clay tile.*

**FIGURE 9-37**

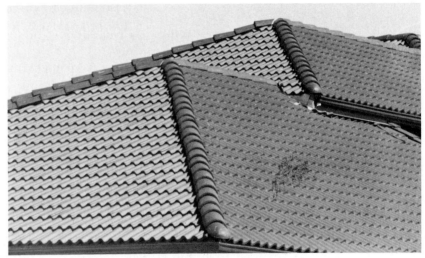

*(b) Concrete roofing tiles.*

clay or concrete tiles. The surface has a coating of stone particles to give good protection from weather.

## Roofing Tile Application

Concrete and clay tiles are applied over solid sheathing such as
plywood. Spaced sheathing may be used with thermo-ply underlayment. A series of counter battens are fastened through the
deck into the supporting roof members. These counter battens
run from the eave to the ridge elevating the horizontal tile battens, allowing a natural flow of air to pass beneath the tiles.
The raising of the batten eliminates the build-up of moisture
absorbing debris which could lead to rotting and premature failure of the support system. A heavy duty, quality underlayment
is applied over the counter battens prior to the application of
the tile battens. Standard roofing felt should not be used for this
application, as the material will not provide the life expectancy
required for tile applications. The size of batten will be deter-

FIGURE 9-38:    *Roofing felt and strapping application.*

mined by the spacing of roof trusses and whether a solid roof deck is used.

Tiles are predrilled to allow nailing near the top edge with corrosion-resistant roofing or shingle nails. Fascia is raised 1 in. (25 mm) above sheathing when rake tiles are used along a roof edge (see Fig. 9–38).

Strapping is built up under ridges and hips to provide support under caps (see Fig. 9–38 and 9–40). Joints should be sealed with caulking or a putty made with masonry mortar [see Fig. 9–40(b)]. Open valleys are used and installed with metal flashing, using the method discussed under wood shingles [see Fig. 9–40(c)].

Metal roofing tiles are available in classic or Spanish roofing styles. The tiles are interlocking with a natural stone finish on the galvanized tiles (see Fig. 9–41). Strapping and asphalt-saturated paper are used under the tiles similar to method used with concrete tiles (see Fig. 9–38). Strapping must also be built up under hips and ridges, as illustrated in Fig. 9–40(a). The main difference is that these tiles are started at the top of the roof working down the slope using rust-resistant screws along the

**FIGURE 9-39**

*(a) Roof ready for shingling—note raised barge boards.*

*(b) Rake tiles installed.*

(a) Strapping built up for hip.

(b) Hip completed including sealing.

(c) Valley construction—tiled roof.

FIGURE 9-40

bottom edge to fasten the tiles to the strapping (see Fig. 9–41). Open valleys are used, similar to the style used with wooden shingles (see Fig. 9–41).

(a) Metal roofing tiles.

(c) Forming a valley.

FIGURE 9-41

(b) Metal rake in place.

(d) Applying metal roofing tiles.

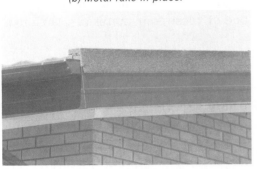

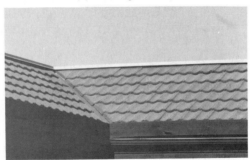

## Sheet Metal Roofing

Sheet metal roofing is more commonly used in areas that are subject to heavy snow loads. Many colors and profiles are available meeting a large range of aesthetic needs. Sheet metal roofing is manufactured in 30 to 45 in. (762 to 1143 mm) widths, depending on the profile of the corrugation and in any lengths specified by the designer. Panels are available in full lengths, reaching from the eaves to the ridge. Accessories are available for hips, valleys, eave starter, and roof edges. Galvanized steel and aluminum are the most common metals used and the minimum metal thickness [0.02 in. (0.5mm)] will vary depending on local snow loads.

Sheet metal panels may be installed directly over continuous sheathing or over horizontal wooden battens (see Fig. 9–42).

**FIGURE 9-42:**  *Sheet metal roofing application.*

The profile and the metal thickness will determine the required spacing for the horizontal battens, usually around 16 in. (400 mm) o.c. Battens shall be 1 × 3 in. (19 × 70 mm) for 16 in. o.c. truss spacing and 1 × 4 in. (19 × 89 mm) for 24 in. o.c. truss spacing; however, if better attachment and support is needed 2 × 4 in. (38 × 89 mm) material is used.

## WINDOWS

Windows form an important part of a building exterior, and a great variety of styles and sizes is manufactured to suit every conceivable purpose. Basically, they consist of one or more panes of *glass* surrounded by a *sash,* which is set into a *frame.* The sash may be wood, aluminum, PVC, or steel, and the frame also may be made of any one of these four materials, the most common one being wood.

### Window Styles

Common window styles include *gliding* windows, in which the sash slide horizontally past one another (see Fig. 9–43), and *double hung,* in which the sash slide vertically (see Fig. 9–44).

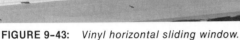

**FIGURE 9-43:** *Vinyl horizontal sliding window.*

**FIGURE 9-44:** *Vertical sliders.*

Another style is the *swinging* window, in which the sash are hinged at either top or bottom (see Fig. 9-45). If the sash swings inward, it is called a *hopper* type; if it swings outward, it is an *awning* type. *Casement* windows have the sash hinged at the side (see Fig. 9-46), and in *fixed* windows, the sash does not move in the frame. Glass blocks are also becoming very popular (see Fig. 9-47).

**FIGURE 9-45:** *Awning window.*

**FIGURE 9-46:** *One- and two-sash casement.*

Many windows are made with no sash and consist of a single sheet of glass or two sheets sealed together, set directly into a window frame. When a large glass unit is fixed in a frame, it is commonly known as a *picture* window (see Fig. 9-47). Windows that project out from the wall to create an extra interior space give a nice effect to the building exterior. These bay or curved bow windows are often found in residential living or bedrooms, but are effective in any room (see Fig. 9-48).

*(a) Glass block windows.*

*(b) Picture windows.*

FIGURE 9-47

*(a) Bay window.*

*(b) Bow window.*

FIGURE 9-48

## Window Manufacture

Modern windows are made in a factory—a millwork plant—and shipped to the construction site, either ready for assembly or, in most cases, already assembled and ready for installation in the openings. Windows will usually have the outside casing in place and be provided with braces or battens to keep them square.

Windows may be made with a variety of combinations of panes in a sash. For example, Fig. 9-49 illustrates various combinations available in single- and two-sash casement window styles.

Large, multipaned windows may be assembled by *stacking* sash made for this purpose in a large frame. Figure 9-49 illustrates the installation of a number of such units to make a large window.

Considerable attention has been given to improving window design and performance because of their importance in the building envelope. The drive for energy conservation and com-

*(a) Horizontal combination of casement and fixed units.*

**FIGURE 9–49**

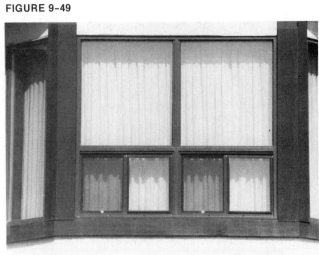

*(b)Vertical and horizontal combination of units.*

fort led to improvements in thermal performance, installation, operation, and maintenance. One way of improving the thermal performance is to control thermal radiation losses. The use of transparent low emissivity coatings provides a significant reduction in heat loss. Adding a low-E coating to the third surface of a clear insulating unit can increase insulating value by 50% [from R2 to R3 (RSI 0.35 to 0.53)]. Increasing the space between panes of glass and increasing the number of panes to three will also increase thermal performance. The introduction of argon gas into the space between panes in a sealed window also has a positive effect.

In sunny climates, where you want a dramatic view but do not want the heat gain and faded upholstery, the installation of low-E coating on the second surface of an insulating unit is especially effective in reducing heat gain and glare from the outside. Heat mirror, a transparent coated film that is suspended between the panes of glass, is often chosen since it is very effective in keeping solar heat out of the building. The installation of narrow slat blinds or pleated shades between the panes of double insulating glass or on the inside of the window will also help reduce heat gain.

Windows are manufactured in a variety of materials including wood, either natural or clad, metal, or solid PVC construction. Most windows are made with a wood sash set in a wood frame (see Fig. 9–50). The application of a colored metal cladding or a vinyl coating to the outside reduces the need for frequent painting. Metal windows, in either wooden or metal frames, have been used for years, and solid PVC windows have made extensive inroads into the residential market (see Fig.

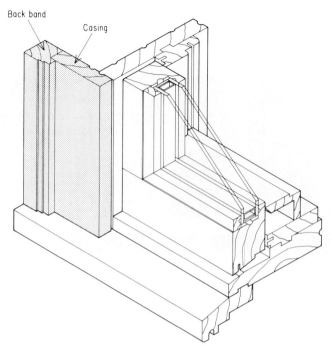

**FIGURE 9-50:** *Sealed unit in wood sash.*

9–43). These windows are available in many colors and are not susceptible to decay, making them popular in humid climates.

## Window Openings

The openings in the wall frame for the installation of windows must be large enough that the frame can be leveled and plumbed. It is therefore necessary to ascertain from the manufacturer either the size of rough opening that is required for the particular style, the size and combination of window chosen, or the dimensions of the frame (see Fig. 9-51). If the frame dimensions are given, it is common practice to allow at least $\frac{3}{8}$ in. (10 mm) *on each side* of the frame and $\frac{3}{8}$ in. (10 mm) *above and below* the frame for this purpose.

In residential construction, it is standard practice to frame the top of the rough opening so that the height of window and door openings will normally be the same. The height of the bottom of the opening above the floor will depend on the location of the window. In a living room, for example, a common distance of 12 to 24 in. (300 to 600 mm) above the floor, while in a dining room, it will normally be 30 to 36 in. (500 to 600 mm). Kitchen windows are usually over a counter, and the standard height for the bottom of the opening for such windows is 44 in. (1100 mm). In other rooms the height is optional and will depend on the size of windows to be used.

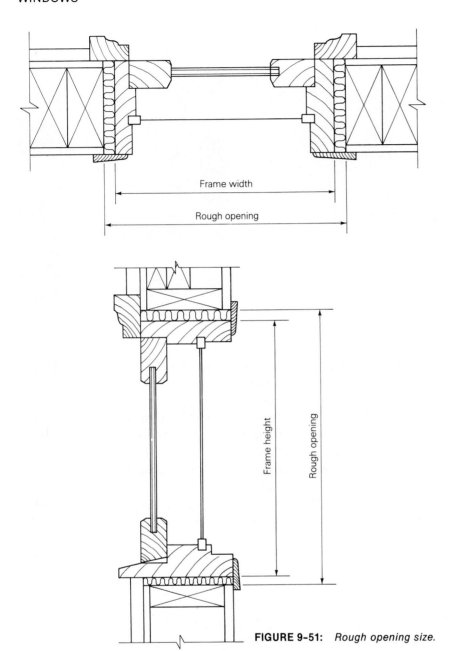

Frame width

Rough opening

Frame height

Rough opening

**FIGURE 9-51:** *Rough opening size.*

## Window Installation

If the rough opening is the proper size and is level and plumb, it is a relatively easy matter to install windows. The first step is to tack a 12-in. (300-mm) wide strip of exterior sheathing paper around the opening on the outside (see Fig. 9–52). Then place the window, with the outside casing attached, into the opening from the outside and secure it temporarily, after having closed the sash and locked them in place.

FIGURE 9-52:   *Building paper around opening.*

FIGURE 9-53:   *Fastening window in place.*

FIGURE 9-54:   *Exterior door with sidelights.*

Wedge blocks are placed under the sill and can also be adjusted so that the sill is perfectly level. Long sills should have three or more wedges under them to prevent them from sagging in the middle. Nail the lower end of the side casings or flanges to secure the bottom of the frame in place (see Fig. 9-53).

Nail the top end of the side casings temporarily and check to see that the sash slides properly and that the window hardware operates as it should.

Finally, nail the window permanently in place with noncorrosive nails, long enough so that they will reach well into the building frame.

## EXTERIOR DOORS

Exterior doors may be made of wood, glass, metal, or combinations of these, such as wood and glass or metal and glass.

Wooden doors vary from a plain slab to ornate paneled doors, either of which may have glass inserts or a full glass panel. In some cases, *sidelights* may be introduced on one or both sides of the door (see Fig. 9-54).

Wooden doors and their frames are made in a millwork plant and may come to the construction site as a complete unit, with the door hinged in the frame and the outside casing attached.

Glass doors are usually sliding doors, mounted in an aluminum track, top and bottom, and traveling on rollers. They are frequently used in a living or family room, as illustrated in Fig. 9-55.

(a) Patio doors.

FIGURE 9-55

(b) Sliding patio doors.

Metal doors have become very popular in residential construction. The door is made with two steel faces, separated by wooden stiles and a polyurethane foam core. This makes the door more energy efficient and resistant to warping. The door surface is usually embossed with a series of patterns, and often glass panels are included in the design (see Fig. 9-56).

**FIGURE 9-56:** *Insulated metal door detail: (1) Galvanized steel treated with rust inhibitive prime finish; (2) Polyurethane foam core; (3) Wood stiles and rails act as a thermal break; (4) Adjustable sill.*

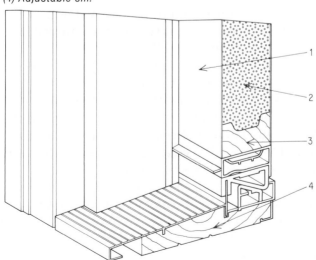

## Door Sizes

The standard size of exterior doors used in residential construction is 2 ft, 8 in. (810 mm) wide by 6 ft, 8 in. (2030 mm) high by 1¾ in. (45 mm) thick. Door widths of 2 ft, 10 in. and 3 ft (860 and 910 mm) are used when larger openings are required.

## Door Frame Installation

If the sole plate is still in the opening, it must be cut out, flush with the trimmers. A filler piece may be required under the door sill to raise the top of the sill a sufficient distance above the finish floor to allow for a mat in wet weather.

If a prehung door unit is being used, the door is left in the frame during installation. Staple a strip of paper around the outside of the opening, as was done with windows. Then apply two or three beads of caulking along the bottom of the opening to seal the crack under the sill. Place the frame into the opening from the outside, center it, and fasten it temporarily. Check the hinge side of the frame for plumbness and shim it to hold it in the correct position and then nail the bottom ends of the side casings to secure the bottom of the frame. Place additional wedges between the trimmer and the jamb at the hinge locations to make sure the jamb is straight. Secure the wedges by driving a nail through the jamb and the wedges into the trimmer, as illustrated in Fig. 9-57. Check to ensure that the bottom of the door is parallel to the sill to allow proper swing of the door. Finally, nail the rest of the casing and shim the other side jamb to secure the frame. A temporary cover should be placed over the sill during construction to protect it from damage.

## Lock Installation

Locks for exterior doors are often more elaborate than interior locks, and the installation instructions, contained in the package with the lock, should be followed carefully.

Open the door to any convenient ajar position and fix it there with a wedge placed between it and the floor. Many doors come with predrilled holes for the latch, dead bolt, and lockset. If the door is not predrilled, measure up from the floor a distance of 36 in. (900 mm) (optional) and mark a horizontal line on both faces and across the edge of the door, which will be on a level with the center of the knob or thumb latch. Now, following the instructions and using the template provided, mark the centers of the holes required on the faces and edge of the door and drill holes of the proper size. Holes in the face of the door should be bored from both sides to prevent any splintering. In place of the template, a *boring jig* may be used to locate holes in the

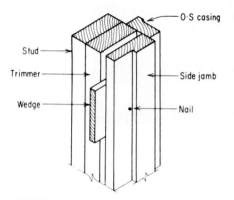

**FIGURE 9-57:** *Nailing side jamb wedge.*

Stud

Trimmer

Wedge

O·S casing

Side jamb

Nail

proper position. Drill holes in the jamb about $1\frac{1}{8}$ in. (29 mm) deep at the location of the mortise for the latch bolt and the dead bolt and square the holes out with a chisel.

Lay out the position of the rebates for the lock anchor plate and the striker plate, one on the edge of the door and the second on the jamb, over the mortise just completed and cut them out with a chisel. A *mortise marker* may be used to mark out the rebates. When drive-in latches are used, the latch is driven in using a block of wood between the latch and the hammer to avoid damaging the latch. (For details on lock installation, see Chapter 10.)

## WALL SHEATHING PAPER

Wall sheathing paper is applied to the exterior of the walls of a frame building to provide an extra barrier for wind and rain that might penetrate the cladding. It must be permeable enough to allow the escape of any water vapor that might enter the wall from the interior. One layer of sheathing paper is usually used over wall sheathing and is usually applied horizontally with 4-in. (100-mm) lap at the joints. The upper sheets will overlap the lower sheets. At door and window frames a good lap should be provided over paper projecting from under the casings [see Fig. 9–48(a)].

When wall sheathing is not used, two layers of paper are used unless a panel-type siding, like plywood, is used. Both layers are applied vertically, with joints stapled and lapped 4 in. (100 mm) along the studs.

## TYPES OF EXTERIOR WALL FINISH

A great many exterior finishes are used today, particularly for a wood frame. They include *stucco, siding, shake and shingle siding, hardboard siding, metal siding, vinyl siding, vertical wood, panel, and masonry finishes.*

**Stucco.** Stucco finish can be applied directly over a masonry wall, but when a sheathed wood frame is to be stuccoed, wire backing must be applied first. The wire should be of a type that has a relatively small mesh—about 2 in. (50 mm) is satisfactory—and is formed as illustrated in Fig. 9–58. When nailed in place, the main body of the wire stands away from the wall surface, allowing plaster to form all around it.

The wire should be stapled, with the curves to the wall, at least every 8 in. (200 mm), and therefore the sheathing must be a solid material that will allow such nailing between studs. Figure 9–59 illustrates typical application of a stucco finish.

**FIGURE 9–58:** *Stucco wire.*

*(a) First coat—wire only filled.*

*(b) Second coat—minimum thickness ¼ in. (6 mm).*

*(c) Finish coat—applied by trowel.*

*(d) Acrylic finish coat—sprayed on.*

**FIGURE 9-59**

**FIGURE 9-60:**  *Bevel siding in place.*

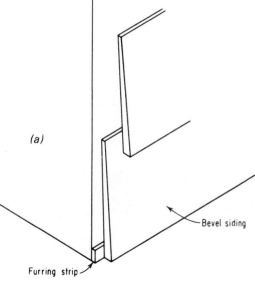

**Lumber siding.** Lumber siding is available in a variety of species with cedar being one of the more common types. The use of pressure-treated lumber for siding is becoming more popular especially in areas prone to decay. In humid areas an air space is often formed behind the siding to prevent water penetration and to vent moisture away from the wall.

**Horizontal application.** A number of styles of horizontal wood siding are manufactured, but probably the most popular is bevel siding, available in widths from 5½ in. (140 mm) to 11¼ in. (286 mm). Each course should overlap the one below approximately 1 in. (25 mm), the exact lap and exposure depending on the width of board being used and the space to be covered.

Under the bottom edge of the first course, nail a furring strip about 1 in. (25 mm) wide and the thickness of the siding at the point of overlap. This furring strip will allow the surface of the first course to have the same slope as that of succeeding courses (see Fig. 9-60).

*(a) Mitered corner.*

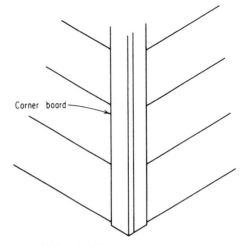

Corner board

*(b) Bevel siding at external corners.*

**FIGURE 9-61**

There are two common methods of fitting bevel siding at external corners. One is to miter the two meeting ends. Another method is to butt the siding ends against corner boards (see Fig. 9-61).

At internal corners, nail a $1 \times 1$ (25 × 25 mm) strip into the corner and butt the siding ends to it from both sides.

Plan to have butt joints between boards in a course fall on a stud. Be very careful that the ends meet in a perfect joint (see Fig. 9-62). Use one $2\frac{1}{2}$-in. (65-mm) siding nail per board at each stud, just above the lap. This system of nailing will allow seasonal contraction and expansion without interference. Do not drive the nails so hard as to crack the siding.

*(a) Angle cut at butt joint.*

**FIGURE 9-62**

*(b) Applying bevel siding.*

**Vertical application.** This type of exterior finish is similar in style to boards and battens. However, the materials have tongue-and-groove or shiplap edges so that battens are not needed to cover the joints (see Fig. 9–63). Horizontal joints in vertical boards should be sloped to the outside to shed water (see Fig. 9–64). A light layer of caulking in these joints will ensure a weathertight joint. On some occasions, to provide variety, this siding is placed at an angle, as illustrated in Fig. 9–65.

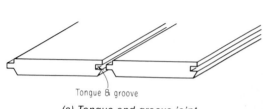

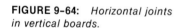

Tongue & groove

*(a) Tongue and groove joint.*

*(b) Vertical wood siding.*

**FIGURE 9–63**

**FIGURE 9–64:** *Horizontal joints in vertical boards.*

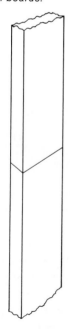

**FIGURE 9–65:** *Angle application of tongue and groove siding.*

Vertical boards may be fastened to $\frac{9}{16}$ in. (14.3 mm) lumber sheathing, $\frac{1}{2}$ in. (12.5 mm) plywood, $\frac{1}{2}$ in. (12.5 mm) waferboard or strandboard. The use of 2 × 2 (38 × 38 mm) blocking fitted between the studs 24 in. (600 mm) or 1 × 3 (19 × 65 mm) strapping can be used for support of the vertical lumber siding.

**Shake and shingle siding.** Shakes and shingles are applied to sidewalls in either single or double course. They may be applied directly to walls with solid sheathing, but in other cases, furring strips must first be nailed to the wall, spaced the required amount of exposure (see Figs. 9-66 and 9-67).

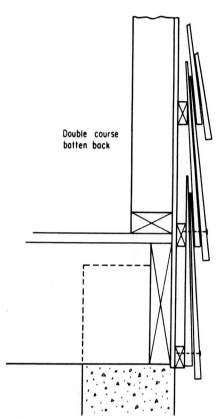

Double course batten back

**FIGURE 9-67:** *Sidewall shingles.*

**FIGURE 9-66:** *Shingle siding.*

**Boards and battens.** This is the name given to a type of finish in which square-edged boards are placed vertically on the wall, and the joints between them are covered with narrow strips about $2\frac{1}{2}$ in. (64 mm) wide called battens. Boards may be all the same width, two different widths placed alternately, or random widths. Cedar is the best material, either dressed or rough-sawn.

For this type of finish, nail in two rows of blocking, evenly spaced, between the top and bottom plates. Boards can then be nailed at four points. Allow approximately $\frac{1}{8}$ in. (3 mm) between boards.

**Hardboard siding.** This type of siding is made from wood fibers pressed into a hard, thin sheet, $\frac{1}{2}$ in. (12 mm) thick and used as a horizontal lap channel siding. They are impregnated with a baked-on colored tempering compound providing a tough facing (see Fig. 9-68). When used as bevel siding, a starter strip is needed under the first row to maintain the bevel. A special strip

**FIGURE 9-68:**   *Hardboard siding.*

is mounted on the back of siding to provide attachment without requiring face nailing (see Fig. 9–69). Special aluminum strips are used for butt joints (see Fig. 9–70), and exterior and interior corner pieces are used to finish ends of siding pieces.

**FIGURE 9-69:**   *Mounting strip.*

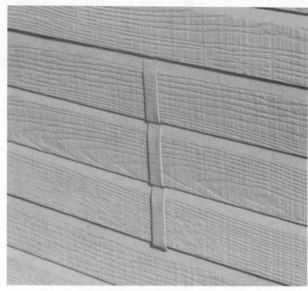

**FIGURE 9-70:**   *Butt-joint attachment.*

**Aluminum siding.** Aluminum siding is available in horizontal and vertical applications (see Fig. 9–71). Metal siding has a baked-on finish that requires little maintenance or care. Textures are applied to some surfaces to simulate wood siding, and insulation-backed siding manufactured by some companies provides greater insulative value to the building (see Fig. 9–72).

Horizontal application starts with a starter strip at the bottom of the wall (see Fig. 9–73). The pieces are interlocking along the bottom edge (see Fig. 9–73) and are nailed in the slots at the top edge with rust-resistant nails. The nail should not be driven

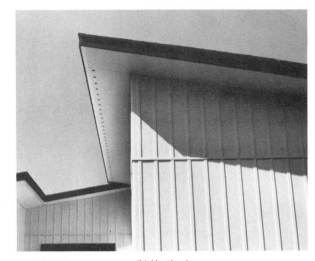

*(a) Horizontal.*                                                                    *(b) Vertical.*

**FIGURE 9–71:** *Aluminum siding.*

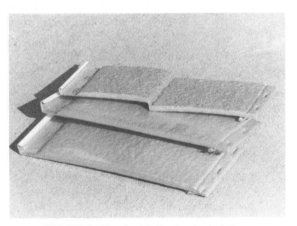

**FIGURE 9–72:** *Insulative-backed siding.*

**FIGURE 9–73:** *Horizontal metal siding application.*

*(a) Starter strip.*                                                        *(b) Interlocking effect.*

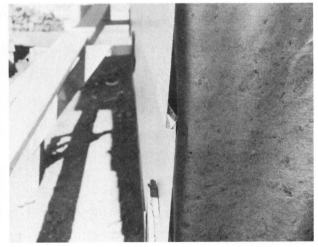

*(c) J mold.*

*(d) Interior corner.*

home so that movement is possible without buckling of the face. Special molding is used at window and door frames (see Fig. 9–73), and either individual or full-length corner pieces are used to finish exterior corners.

Vertical application siding has the interlocking feature on one side, and the strips are nailed or stapled along the other side (see Fig. 9–74). Similar moldings are used to finish edges and corners, though on some occasions the pieces are bent around a corner [(see Fig. 9–71(b)].

**Vinyl siding.** Vinyl siding is a low-maintenance product and is the same color all the way through so it is not affected by scratches as is metal siding. The application is similar to metal siding and is illustrated in (Fig. 9–75). Siding is available in single or double lap or cove patterns. Vinyl, the most economical of all sidings, is used extensively. It is, however, more suscepti-

**FIGURE 9–74:** *Application of vertical metal siding.*

(a) Vinyl siding.

(b) "J" molding next to frame.

(c) Exterior and interior corner moldings.

(d) Siding snapped into place.

**FIGURE 9-75**

ble to movement; so care must be taken during application, leaving space for expansion and contraction. The panels easily snap into the preceding rows, holding the strips in place until nailing is completed (see Fig. 9–75).

**Plywood siding.** Any exterior grade of plywood is suitable for siding purposes. Plywood panels are made with a smooth or decorative surface and are usually applied vertically. The joints are shiplap or butted, sometimes covered with a batten. Plywood is available with a resin-impregnated paper surface, providing a smooth, moisture-resistant surface that resists checking or splitting. The panel can be applied directly to the studs without sheathing (see Fig. 9–76).

## Masonry Finishes

Masonry finishes may be used in walls in a number of ways in light construction. One is to use it as a *veneer* over a wood frame, concrete block, or concrete backup wall. Veneering is

**FIGURE 9-76:** *Plywood siding.*

done in two ways: (1) by facing a wall with a single wythe of brick or stone, nominally 4 in. (100 mm) in thickness, and (2) by facing it with a thin layer of brick or stone material approximately ½ to ¾ in. (12 to 20 mm) in thickness. Another way is to build a wall using the masonry (usually brick) as the structural portion of the wall as well as the finish.

### Brick Veneer

**Over wood frame.** A single wythe of brick, 3⅝ in. (90 mm) thick, is often used to face a sheathed wall providing an exceptionally durable, maintenance-free finish. Both the building frame and the brick wythe must be supported by the building foundation. The brick facing can either rest on the concrete foundation (see Fig. 9–77), or it can be set on an angle iron that has been fastened to the wall (see Fig. 9–78).

**FIGURE 9-77:** *4″ (100 mm) brick veneer.*

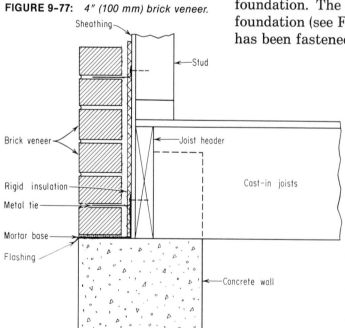

**FIGURE 9-78:** *Angle iron support for veneer.*

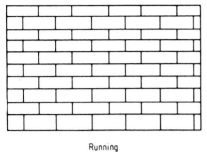

Running

Flemish

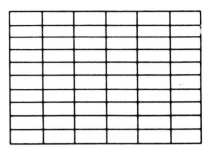

Stack

**FIGURE 9-79:** *Typical patterns.*

A 1-in. (25-mm) space should be left between the brick and the sheathing paper to stop the migration of moisture from the facing to the frames wall. A base flashing should extend from the outside over the top of the supporting ledge and at least 6 in. (150 mm) up the wall behind the sheathing paper.

The brick must be anchored to the frame by noncorrosive metal straps nailed to the studs and embedded in the mortar joints between the masonry. The straps are not less than 22 gauge (0.76 mm) thick and 1 in. (25 mm) wide, and are spaced in accordance with Table 6-4.

The brick pattern used will depend on the desired aesthetic effect. Several patterns are in use, some of the more common ones being running, flemish, and stack (see Fig. 9-79).

Brick veneer and bevel siding may be used together. In this case, one material will be used to finish all or part of one wall from top to bottom. The other material then is used either on the remainder of that wall or on an adjoining one. The two materials should meet at an external corner or at a vertical dividing piece of the same size as the outside casing (see Fig. 9-80).

**FIGURE 9-80**

*(b) Brick veneer.*

*(a) Brick veneer—wood siding finish.*

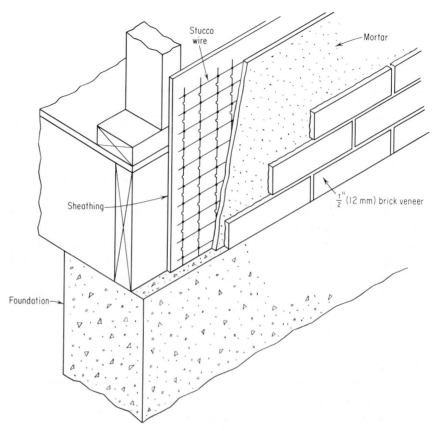

**FIGURE 9-81:**  *Thin brick veneer.*

The second type of brick facing is set into a mortar base. The wall is prepared as if a stucco finish were to be used. A base coat of plaster is applied over stucco wire and allowed to harden. As the second coat is applied, the brick facing pieces are set into it in the same positions as regular brick would be (see Fig. 9–81), and the joints are dressed after the mortar has partially hardened.

**Over concrete block.** Four-, six-, or eight-inch (100-, 150-, or 200-mm) block may be used as a backup wall for a 4-in. (100-mm) brick veneer face, depending on the height of wall. This veneer should be separated from the backup by an unfilled space of at least 1 in. (25 mm) (see Fig. 9–82). When rigid insulation is used on the outside of the block backup, the space must be increased in size so the 1-in. (25-mm) space exists between the insulation and the facing. The facing wythe has to carry its own weight but otherwise is not considered to contribute to the vertical or lateral load resistance of the wall. The backup is designed to resist vertical or lateral loads. The space serves as a drainage gap between the veneer and the backup wall, and any forces on the facing are transmitted across the gap to the backup by ties.

Tying to the backup wall can be accomplished by using corrugated ties embedded in the mortar joints with the tie spacing

**FIGURE 9-82:**  *Brick veneer.*

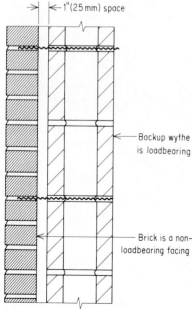

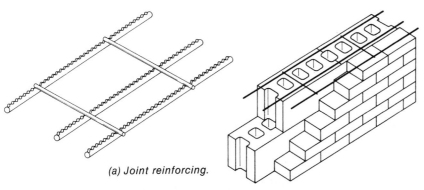

(a) Joint reinforcing.

**FIGURE 9-83:** *Joint reinforcing and ties.*

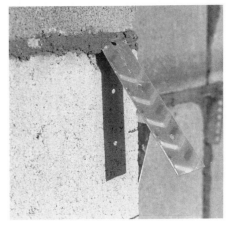

(b) Corrugated ties.

regulated by Table 6-4 or by using continuous joint reinforcing in every second or third row of the block backup (see Fig. 9-83).

*Flashing* is provided at the bottom of the cavity between wythes to direct any moisture that collects within the wall toward the outside wythe (see Fig. 9-84), and *weepholes* in the outside wythe allow that moisture to drain to the outside (see Fig. 9-85).

The brick veneer over openings in walls must be supported by a *lintel*, usually a steel angle with its ends supported on the brick on either side of the opening. The maximum allowable opening span depends on the size of lintel used.

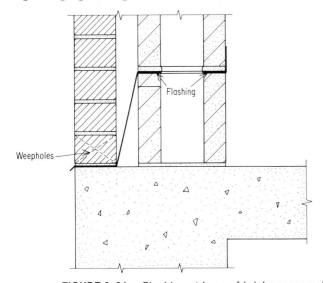

**FIGURE 9-84:** *Flashing at base of brick veneer wall.*

**FIGURE 9-85:** *Weephole in brick veneer wall.*

## Single-Wythe Brick Walls

Solid brick walls in one-story buildings and the top story of two-story buildings may be constructed of $5\frac{1}{2}$-in. (140-mm) solid units, provided that the wall is not over 9 ft, 2 in. (2.80 m) high at the eaves and not more than 15 ft, 1 in. (4.60 m) high at the peaks of the gable ends. Solid units or grouted hollow units are normally used for this type of construction.

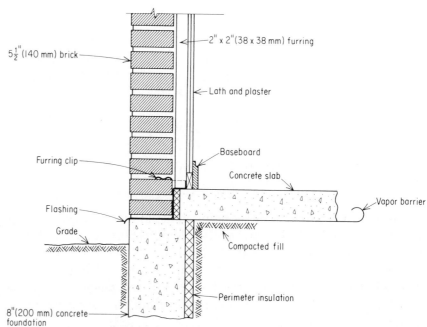

**FIGURE 9-86:** *6-in. (150 mm) brick walls.*

On the inside surface, the wall may be *furred out,* and interior finish is applied to this furring. This furring allows for application of a vapor barrier, makes for easy installation of electrical facilities, and provides space for the introduction of insulation. However, it is possible to plaster directly to the inside face of the brick, or face brick may be used, in which case no other finish is required.

An 8 in. (200-mm) foundation wall is adequate, but the details of construction will depend on the type of floor being used. Figure 9–86 illustrates a typical method of construction using a single-wythe wall.

### Laying Brick

One of the primary requisites for a good brick structure is good mortar. To be able to fulfill its purpose, mortar must possess a number of important qualities, both in the *plastic* stage and after it has hardened.

In the plastic stage, the important qualities are *workability, water retentivity,* and a *consistent rate of hardening.* Hardened mortar must have *good bond, durability, good compressive strength,* and *good appearance.*

Good workability is the result of a combination of factors, including the *quality of aggregate* used, the use of a small quantity of *hydrated lime or lime putty,* the use of *masonry cement,* the *amount of water* used, proper *mixing facilities,* and the ability of the mortar to *retain water.*

Mortar with good workability should *slip readily on the trowel, spread easily* on the masonry unit, *adhere to vertical surfaces,* and *extrude readily* from joints as the unit is being placed, without dropping. The consistency must be such that the unit can be properly bedded but its weight and the weight of following courses will not cause further extrusion of the mortar.

To obtain good masonry construction, it is essential that all mortar joints be completely filled as the bricks are being laid. Failure to do so will result in voids through which water can penetrate. Not only will water pass through the wall to mar the interior finish, but water in the wall may dissolve salts from the brick and then deposit them on the surface as *efflorescence* when it returns to the outside and evaporates. In addition, water in the wall may freeze and cause deterioration in the wall itself.

Mortar for the bed joint should be spread thickly, with a shallow furrow down the center of the bed (see Fig. 9–87). There will then be enough excess mortar in the bed to fill the furrow and allow some mortar to be extruded at the joint when the bricks are bedded to the line. The bed mortar should be spread over only a few bricks at a time so that water will not evaporate before the bricks are laid and thus result in poor adhesion. Figure 9–88 illustrates mortar which has good adhesion qualities.

Care must be taken that all vertical joints in both stretcher and header courses are completely filled with mortar. To obtain a full head joint in a stretcher course, apply plenty of mortar to the end of the brick being placed, so that when it is set, mortar will be extruded at the top of the head joint (see Fig. 9–89).

Closures in stretcher courses need careful attention. Mortar should be spotted in the ends of both bricks already in place, and both ends of the brick to be placed should be well buttered. Then set the closure brick without disturbing those already in place (see Fig. 9–90).

**FIGURE 9–87:** *Furrowed bed joints.*

**FIGURE 9–88:** *Mortar with good adhesion.*

**FIGURE 9–89:** *Full head joint.*

**FIGURE 9–90:** *Setting closure brick.*

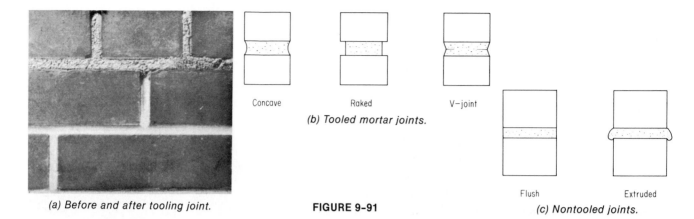

*(a) Before and after tooling joint.*

Concave     Raked     V-joint

*(b) Tooled mortar joints.*

**FIGURE 9-91**

Flush          Extruded

*(c) Nontooled joints.*

*(a) Coursed stone ashlar.*

*(b) Stone set in mortar (random).*

**FIGURE 9-92**

Tooling the mortar joint compacts the mortar, making it more dense, and helps to seal any fine cracks between brick and mortar [see Fig. 9-91(a)]. A number of styles of joint are used providing variety to the aesthetic effect of the brick [see Figs. 9-91(b) and (c)].

## STONE CONSTRUCTION

In modern light construction, stone is used almost entirely as a veneer—an exterior facing over a wood frame or unit masonry structural wall or as an interior decorative material used for fireplaces, mantels, feature walls, and finish floors.

Stone for this purpose is available in two forms. One is a

small stone block, commonly known as *ashlar,* usually 2, 3, or 4 in. (50, 75, or 100 mm) thick, with regular or irregular face dimensions. Stones will usually not exceed 2 ft (600 mm) in length, while the height will vary from 4 to 12 in. (100-300 mm). The other is a thin, flat slab, from ½ to 1 in. (12–25 mm) thick, with either the edge or the face set into mortar on the wall face (see Fig. 9–92(a)).

Ashlar veneer is applied in the same way as brick veneer. The stone must rest on the foundation and is bonded to the wall with metal ties, with one end nailed to a wood frame backup wall or laid in the mortar joints of a unit masonry wall. If the stones are cut to specific dimensions, they can be laid with regular course lines, and the result is known as *coursed ashlar.* But if the face dimensions are irregular, the result will be *random ashlar,* illustrated in Fig. 9–92(b).

## REVIEW QUESTIONS

9–1. List five building operations that may be classed under the general heading of "exterior finishing."

9–2. **(a)** What are *wind blocks?*
**(b)** Under what circumstances are they used?

9–3. Where is each of the following located:
**(a)** Lookouts
**(b)** Soffit
**(c)** Finish fascia

9–4. Name five different types of roofing that may be applied to light construction roofs.

9–5. Why should poly eave protection not be used under wood shingles?

9–6. Fill in the blanks in each statement below:
**(a)** Joints in successive rows of cedar shingles should be not less than _____ mm apart.
**(b)** Each shingle should be fastened with _____ nails only.
**(c)** Standard exposure for 16-in. (400-mm) #1 shingles is _____ in. (mm).
**(d)** Proper spacing of shingles in a course is _____ in. (mm).

9–7. What is the primary advantage of concrete tiles?

9–8. What is meant by *triple-tab* asphalt shingles?

9–9. By means of a diagram, illustrate how concrete tiles are placed on a roof.

9-10. Describe briefly the chief distinguishing characteristic of each of the following window styles:
  (a) Slider
  (b) Casement
  (c) Awning
  (d) Hopper

9-11. List four types of mortar joints that may be used in masonry work.

9-12. (a) What should be the minimum overlap when applying bevel siding?
  (b) What is the purpose of a furring strip under the first course bevel siding?
  (c) List two ways of fitting bevel siding at outside corners.

9-13. Outline two advantages of vinyl siding.

9-14. (a) What is meant by *brick veneer?*
  (b) Name two types of brick veneer used in exterior finish.
  (c) Explain how a brick course is tied to a wood sheathed wall.

# 10

# INTERIOR FINISHING

Upon completion of the exterior of the building, attention may then be given to the interior. This part of the job can be done at any time of the year, and it is wise to plan so that interior finishing can be done when the weather does not permit outside work.

First, arrangements must be made to have the wiring, plumbing, heating, and air conditioning installed. This is necessary for two reasons. One is that a considerable portion of these services will be situated in the walls and partitions and above the ceiling, and the work must be done while the space is open. The other is that heat and power particularly may be required during the finishing operation.

## INSULATION

Once these services have been installed, the next step is the placement of insulation in the outside walls, ceilings, and basement walls if applicable. The effectiveness of a building assembly in resisting the flow of heat is measured as its *thermal resistance* or *R value* (RSI). Most materials have some resistance to the flow of heat, but insulation effectively resists this loss of heat from the building. Insulation is manufactured from a variety of materials and is available in several forms, such as batts, loose-fill, rigid, and foamed-in-place.

*Batts* are commonly used for insulating in framed walls. They are usually friction-fit batts that are stuffed into the stud space and held there by the friction of the batts on the studs. Batts are available in a variety of thicknesses depending on the needs of the client. The application of a polyethylene vapor barrier on the warm side of the insulation is recommended to achieve an effective seal (see Fig. 10–1).

A *loose-fill thermal* or *acoustical insulation* is appropriate for horizontal or moderately sloped attic areas up to a 1 in 3 slope. Insulation is placed by manual or pneumatic methods in

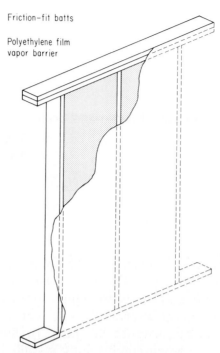

Friction-fit batts

Polyethylene film
vapor barrier

**FIGURE 10-1:** *Vapor barrier over friction-fit batts.*

open horizontal or moderately sloped locations with care taken to ensure full coverage. Minimum coverage will be determined by local code requirements.

*Rigid insulation* is best suited for application against flat surfaces, such as concrete or masonry foundation walls, as a sheathing over wall studs (see Chapter 6), and over a roof deck. It can be cut to fit between studs, but it is not very cost effective or easy to place. Over concrete or masonry walls, rigid insulation can be applied with an adhesive or with mechanical fasteners. Insulation on walls to be backfilled are usually only nailed along the top and held in place by the backfill material. Insulation is nailed to a wood surface or to studs with large-headed galvanized nails.

*Foam insulation* can be either sprayed or injected under pressure, using special applicators to adhere to surfaces or to fill wall cavities. The foam sets into a rigid mass quickly after application as the foaming action is the last stage in the manufacture of the product. The installer must be highly skilled to provide a product of uniform quality and consistency.

## Vapor and Air Barriers

A *vapor barrier* is an essential component of a building wherever there is a considerable difference between inside and outside temperature and where the inside air has a high moisture content. The function of the vapor barrier is to stop or retard the passage of moisture as it diffuses through the wall or ceiling assembly. *Diffusion* is a process by which vapor migrates through materials. The rate at which it diffuses depends on two factors: the difference in vapor pressure between the inside and outside air, and the ability of the wall materials to resist moisture migration. If the temperature in the wall is low, the vapor will condense there to form water or ice. If the insulation in the wall becomes damp as a result of this condensation, its effectiveness is reduced. In addition, trapped moisture may cause the wood frame to deteriorate.

All materials have some resistance to moisture diffusion, but a vapor barrier offers a higher resistance than most other materials. A number of materials would be suitable as vapor barriers—materials such as aluminum foil, metal or glass—but polyethylene film seems to be the most common. The vapor barrier must be placed on the warm side of the insulation for it to effectively control condensation. A vapor barrier need not be perfectly continuous to control moisture migration. Unsealed laps, pinholes or minor cuts do not increase the overall rate of moisture diffusion, but it is worthwhile to keep these imperfections to a minimum.

Vapor barriers are applied in horizontal room height strips, so that the number of joints can be kept to a minimum. Polyethylene joints are lapped and stapled over a framing member, as illustrated in Fig. 10-2. Where openings occur, the vapor barrier must be made to fit tightly around them.

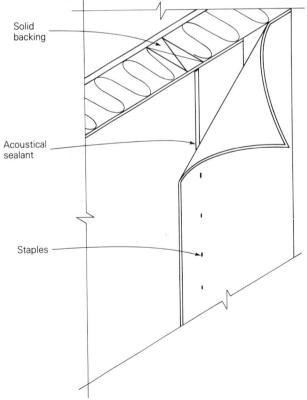

**FIGURE 10-2:** *Installation procedures for vapor barriers.*

Solid backing

Acoustical sealant

Staples

**FIGURE 10-3:**  *Exterior air barrier.*

The *air barrier* must be able to withstand the combined forces of wind, chimney effects, and fan pressures that are imposed on the wall assembly. The pressure it must resist is much greater than vapor diffusion, and failure to do so will result in a much greater volume of moist air in the wall cavity. The resulting condensation can create great amounts of damage to the materials within the wall. The barrier must be able to support the air pressure loads exerted from the inside or outside of the building. The material must be designed to support the pressure without rupturing, tearing, or coming loose from the surface to which it is attached. Materials chosen for air barriers must be as air impermeable as possible. They need not be vapor impermeable as long as a vapor barrier is also incorporated in the wall. Some examples of air barrier materials are gypsum board, plywood, concrete, or reinforced sheet membranes.

The air barrier may be placed at any point on the building envelope, not only on the warm side of the insulation as is the case with a vapor barrier. Polyethylene placed on the inside can serve as a vapor and an air barrier, but more care must be taken to ensure a continuous surface. All joints must be sealed with an acoustical sealant to resist the movement of air through the material. Material used as an air barrier located near the outer surface of a wall assembly must allow the passage of water vapor from the inside of the wall assembly, or deterioration will occur. Several housewraps are available that will perform as an effective outer air barrier, as illustrated in Fig. 10-3. All joints must be taped with a pressure-sensitive polypropylene adhesive tape to ensure a continuous surface.

## INTERIOR WALL AND CEILING FINISHES

Interior finish includes any material that is used to cover the interior wall and ceiling framing. Today, the principal type of interior finish is gypsum board (drywall); however, plywood, hardboard, lumber, tile, masonry finishes, and suspended ceilings are used.

## Gypsum Board Finish

*Drywall* is a term used to describe a finish produced by applying gypsum board to the inside of walls and ceilings. This material is made in sheets 4 ft (1.2 m) wide, from 8 to 16 ft (2.4 to 4.8 m) in length, and in thicknesses of ½ or ⅝ in. (12.7 or 15.9 mm). The ½-in. (12.7 mm) thickness is the most commonly used for interior finishing, but the ⅝-in. (15.9 mm) thickness is used in some applications and does offer some advantages. The board is usually applied in single thickness, but double thickness (*laminated drywall*) is used in some applications.

In single application, the sheets may be applied horizontally or vertically. On ceilings, the board is generally applied with the long dimension at right angles to the joists or trusses. In many cases the horizontal application of long sheets reduces the number of fasteners, and fewer joints need to be filled than with vertical application. Horizontal joints at 4 ft (1.2 m) above the floor are below eye level, making them less conspicuous. The sheets are usually ordered in a variety of lengths as needed in the building, so that vertical joints in some rooms will occur only in the corners.

Gypsum board is first fastened with supplementary nails to hold the sheets in place until final fastening can be completed. The gypsum board can be permanently attached with nails, adhesive and nails, or drywall screws. Nails should be nonrusting ringed nails long enough to penetrate the support ¾ in. (20 mm). They should be spaced 6 to 8 in. (150 to 200 mm) o.c. along the edges of the board, and double nails 2 in. (50 mm) apart are set at 12 in. (300 mm) intervals along intermediate supports. The double nailing system draws the board tighter to the support and helps to prevent *nail popping* (see Fig. 10-4). Use enough force when driving the nails so that a slight depression is made in the surface when the nail is fully driven, but, at the same time, care should be taken not to break the surface of the paper.

When gypsum board is applied with drywall screws, the screws should be spaced not more than 12 in. (300 mm) o.c. along horizontal supports, or 16 in. (400 mm) o.c. along vertical supports no more than 16 in. (400 mm) o.c. The screws should be long enough to penetrate the support at least ⅝ in. (15 mm). Avoid using extra long screws or nails as it will increase the possibility of nail or screw popping due to the shrinkage of framing members.

The adhesive and nail application method is the most common method used to fasten gypsum board. This method can only be used on interior walls since the adhesive will not stick

FIGURE 10-4: *Double nailing system.*

to the vapor barrier. Adhesive is applied with a caulking gun along the intermediate wall studs in short strips 16 in. (400 mm) o.c. or in a continuous bead. The strips of adhesive should be thick enough to ensure effective adhesion of the board to the stud. This method will reduce the number of spots where filling is required, and nail popping is eliminated. Exterior walls are still fastened with drywall screws since adhesive cannot be used where polyethylene is used as a vapor barrier.

The long edges of the board are depressed where two sheets meet so that a recess appears on the surface that must be filled to hide the joint and to produce a flat surface. To do this, gypsum joint filler and paper tape are used. The joint tape is about 2 in. (50 mm) wide and has *feathered* edges. The joint filler is purchased premixed and is applied with a mechanical applicator or with a drywall trowel or broad spatula. The first layer of joint cement is applied in a strip 5 in. (125 mm) wide along the joint. The tape is pressed in the first coat of fresh filler with a wide putty knife or a trowel. Remove excess cement and ensure edges are feathered. After drying, a second coat is applied in a strip 8 in. (200 mm) wide on recessed joints and even wider on butt joints. The final coat is applied 12 in. (300 mm) wide and is thinner than the second coat (see Fig. 10-5). Its purpose is to fill in spots missed with the second coat and to feather the edges of the joint. Nail or screw indentations are filled with several layers of joint cement to ensure a flat surface. After a light sanding, the surface is ready for painting (see Fig. 10-6).

At internal corners, a strip of joint tape is folded at right angles and set into a bed of filler. The second and third coats are added and finished as with flat joints. At external corners metal corners are nailed to the corner prior to filling. The corner is then treated in the same way as other joints. At door or win-

**FIGURE 10-5:**  *Applying joint cement.*

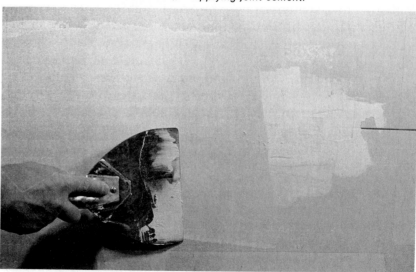

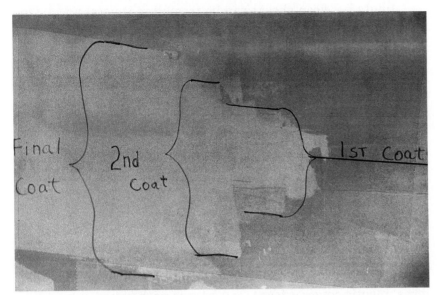

**FIGURE 10-6:** *Finishing gypsum board.*

dow openings, the gypsum board is stopped against the frame and the joint is covered with casing, as illustrated in Fig.10-7.

The board is usually applied to the ceilings first so that the edges of the board at the wall connection are supported by the board on the walls. A small space between sheets is recommended, but a large space will make taping and filling of the drywall joints more difficult. Decorative cove strips are available, made of either gypsum board, wood, or polyurethane to provide an architectural effect at the ceiling wall joint.

## Plywood Finishes

A great variety of plywoods is available for interior finishing, both in hardwood and softwood. They may be obtained in plain sheets, in a number of decorative faces, such as simulated driftwood or pressed patterns, and in sheets which have been scored in imitate plank or tile.

**FIGURE 10-7:** *Opening trimmed with casing.*

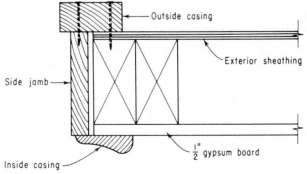

Joints between sheets can be treated in several ways. One is to make the edges meet as tightly as possible in an attempt to hide the joint. This is relatively easy with patterned plywoods, but it is difficult with plain sheets, particularly those in light colors. In such a case it is better to chamfer the meeting edges so as to accentuate the joint. Another method of finishing is to use battens over the joints.

Plywoods are nailed with 1¼- to 1½-in. (30- or 40-mm) finishing nails or glued in place with a panel adhesive. If the gluing process is being used, nailing is used at the top and bottom of the sheet to hold it in position.

## Hardboards

Hardboards are produced in a great variety of face patterns for inside finishing. There are tile and plank effects, wood grain patterns, plastic-covered faces, and boards with baked enamel surface, among others. A very important consideration in applying any of the hardboards, other than those with plastic or enameled face, is that of pre-expansion. Since these are wood fiber products, they will expand and contract with changes in humidity. Therefore, it is desirable that they be applied while at their maximum size. Otherwise, any expansion on the wall would cause buckling between studs. To pre-expand hardboard, wet the sheets on the backside and stack them flat, back to back, for 24 hours. Hardboard can be fastened in place with staples or nails colored to match the panel finish, or an adhesive can be used to support the panel. They can be fastened directly to the studs, provided that ¼-in. (6-mm) thick sheets are used for supports up to 16 in. (400mm) o.c. Panels not meeting this minimum thickness require a gypsum board backing underneath for support.

## Tile

For interior finish, ceramic, plastic, or metal tiles are in common use, particularly in bathrooms and kitchens. The base used for ceramic tile must be suitable for the location; plywood or ordinary gypsum board is suitable in kitchens or laundry rooms. Moisture-resistant drywall or a cement board base is required for shower stalls or walls above bathtubs. The tiles are cemented to the surface and joints are grouted after adhesive has set. A silicone sealer is applied to the surface after grouting has set. A silicone corner bead is put in all corners to ensure a watertight area. Refer to page 324 for additional information on the installation of ceramic tile.

## Lumber

Lumber is sometimes used as a decorative finish for walls and ceilings. Solid wood boards are available in an attractive range of hardwoods and softwoods. Hardwood species include maple, birch, and cherry; softwoods include cedar, pine, and hemlock. In any of these species, the boards are easy to install. Special effects can be obtained by installing the boards horizontally or vertically, or in a combination of both. In some applications the boards are placed on an angle to give special effect. Vertical application of boards requires the placement of horizontal furring strips for backing (see Fig. 10-8). Boards are available in butt or "V" joint tongue and groove, or in an offset shiplap joint producing a grooved pattern (see Fig. 10-9).

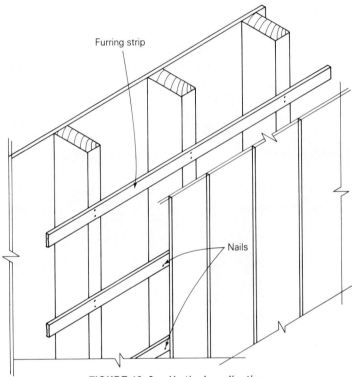

**FIGURE 10-8:** *Vertical application.*

Some of these species are available in plywood form, usually available in random groove pattern, simulated board and batten, and tongue and groove joints. Installation of these panels is similar to standard plywood paneling.

## Masonry Finishes

Masonry products have an important place as interior finishes. In addition to brick, tile, concrete block, and stone of various types, thin veneers of brick, tile and stone, both real and artifi-

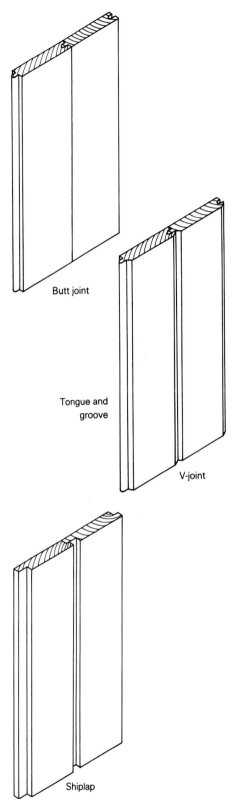

**FIGURE 10-9:** *Joint patterns.*

cial, are available. These may be fixed to a solid backing by adhesives, the joints being filled with grout after the units are in place.

### Suspended Ceilings

Suspended ceiling tile is one of the fastest and least expensive ways to finish a ceiling and is often used to finish a basement ceiling or a dropped ceiling in a kitchen. The 2 × 4-ft (1200 mm) ceiling panels come in a variety of textures, colors and designs. Flexible vinyl-coated acoustical panels are very common since they are light and easy to install. Fluorescent light fixtures are available to fit into the suspended ceiling gridwork. The panels are supported by a gridwork made of wall angles, main and cross tees (see Fig. 10–10).

**FIGURE 10-10:** *Suspended ceiling gridwork.*

The installation procedures are:

1. Plan the layout of your ceiling panels, adjusting the layout to ensure that you do not end up with a narrow panel at either side or end. The edge panel should be more than half the panel width or length.
2. Locate the ceiling level, either by measuring up from the floor or down from the ceiling frame. Be sure to allow 3 in. (75 mm) clearance between the ceiling and the joists. Nail the wall angle around the perimeter of the ceiling at that level, as illustrated in Fig. 10–11.
3. Fasten screw eyes into joists at the appropriate locations

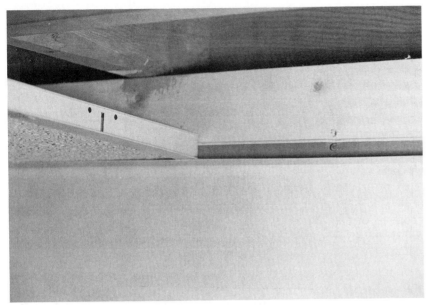

**FIGURE 10-11:** *Wall angle.*

and attach wires to support the main tees. Temporarily attach wires to main tees. If the main tees run at right angles to the joists, locating their position is relatively easy.

4. Insert cross tees into main tees to form the gridwork (see Fig. 10-12). Cut the pieces at the edge to fit into the remaining space. Level the gridwork and place light fixtures.

5. Insert ceiling panels, cutting the ones at the edges to size.

A suspended ceiling allows easy access to the area above the ceiling, making it possible to make future adjustments without major renovations.

**FIGURE 10-12:** *Cross T—Main T connection.*

### FLOORING

Flooring materials include *hardwood* in strip or parquet form, *resilient flooring* in tile or sheet form, *ceramic tile*, and *carpet*. Each has some particular advantages, and many require some special preparation.

### Hardwood Strip Flooring

Hardwood strip floors are a popular choice for many buildings, with *oak, birch, beech,* and *maple* all being used. Flooring is milled in a number of widths and thicknesses with tongue-and-grooved edges and ends. The minimum thickness of wood strip flooring required for most interior applications is $5/16$ in. (7.9 mm) for floor joist spacings of 16 to 24 in. (400 to 600 mm) o.c.

The tongue and groove used to link the strips together is placed below the center of the piece to allow for more wear, and the bottom surface is hollowed for a tighter fit against the sub-floor and for greater resilience (see Fig. 10–13). The top face of the strip is slightly wider than the bottom so that the joint is tight when the strips are driven together. The tongue must fit snugly, since a loose fit can cause squeaks in the floor.

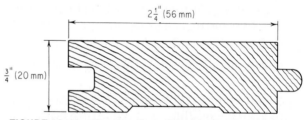

**FIGURE 10–13:**  *Section through hardwood flooring strip.*

Hardwood flooring should be laid only after the humidity caused by the placement of the basement floor and the gypsum board taping has been brought to the normal range. The material should be stored in the warmest and driest place in the building until it is installed.

Following is the procedure for laying strip flooring over a wood subfloor:

1. Plan to lay the floor the long dimension of the room, and if possible lay it at right angles to the floor frame.

2. If lumber subflooring is used, it is usually laid diagonally over the floor frame, so the strips can be laid either parallel or at right angles to the joists.

3. Start the first strip of flooring against the long wall. Place the grooved edge to the wall and leave a $1/4$-in. (6-mm) space between the floor and the wall to allow for

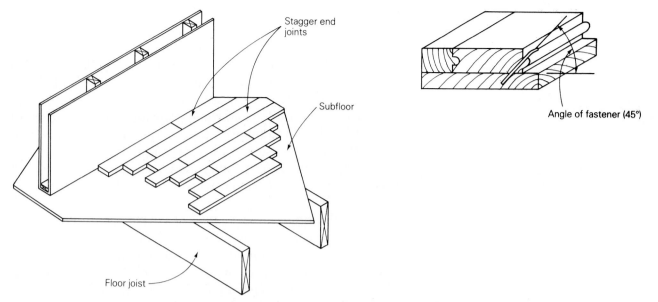

**FIGURE 10-14:** *Hardwood strip application.*

expansion (see Fig. 10–14). The nails or staples driven through the face of the first strip should be driven close enough to the edge so that the base will cover the fasteners.

4. Succeeding strips are blind nailed or stapled (see Fig. 10–14) with flooring nails or staples. The length and the spacing of fasteners depend on the thickness of the flooring, and there should be no fewer than two fasteners per strip. Be sure that the strip is snug against the preceding one and that the end joints are tight. Many applicators use a stapler or a mallet-driven nailing tool to drive the nails in the proper location. Nails should not be driven home with a hammer; a nail set should be used to avoid damage to the flooring. To avoid splitting, it is sometimes necessary to predrill nail holes through the tongue.

5. Use the piece cut off at the end of one strip of flooring to start the next strip wherever possible. Watch that end joints in successive strips are at least 6 in. (150 mm) apart. Arrange the pieces in the floor so that there is as wide a separation of end joints as possible, and that there is a smooth blending of color and grain variation from piece to piece.

Sanding unfinished hardwood floors is usually done by qualified finishers using drum-type power sanders, preparing the surface for the final finish.

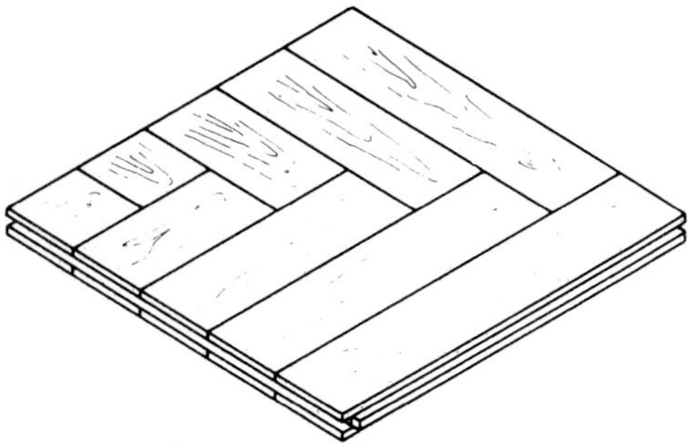

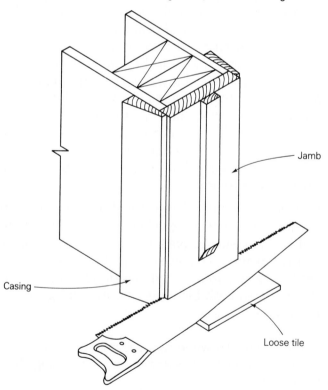

**FIGURE 10-15:** *Parquet flooring.*

## Parquet Flooring

Parquet flooring is an easy way of having hardwood flooring without all the work and cost of hardwood strip flooring. The tiles come in a variety of special patterns and species of wood, and, since the tiles are prefinished, the floor is complete as soon as installation is complete. Parquet flooring consists of small sections of hardwood laminated together, usually in three thin layers in the form of squares or rectangular strips (see Fig. 10-15). Parquet flooring usually has two adjacent tongued edges and two grooved edges, which fit together to make an integral unit.

Parquet flooring is laid much like vinyl tiles; the direction of the strips in squares are alternated to produce a checkerboard effect while the rectangular shapes are all laid in the same direction. An allowance of $\frac{1}{4}$ in. (6 mm) should be left around the edge to allow for expansion. Both types of flooring are laid in adhesive and aren't blind nailed like hardwood strip flooring.

With this method, prime the floor with a primer and after drying, apply the adhesive with a notched adhesive trowel. The tiles are started at the edge from a previously established line and they are set in place and then tapped to ensure a good bond. Trim the bottom end of door casings and jambs to allow the tile to fit underneath, as illustrated in Fig. 10-16.

**FIGURE 10-16:** *Trimming door jamb and casing.*

Jamb

Casing

Loose tile

## Resilient Flooring

Resilient floor tiles of all kinds require a smooth, regular surface in order to give satisfactory service and to maintain a good appearance. In most cases the conventional subfloor does not provide a surface which is smooth and even enough, and some type of *underlayment,* such as plywood, particle board, or hardboard, must be applied over the subfloor.

Large defects in the subfloor, such as knotholes, should be patched before hardboard is used, and the material should be allowed to stand unwrapped in the room for at least 24 hours to adjust to the prevailing humidity conditions. A space of approximately $\frac{1}{16}$ in. (1 mm) should be left between sheets when they are laid to allow for expansion. The end joints in the panels should be staggered, and the continuous joints should be at right angles to those in the subfloor.

Plywood and particle board are dimensionally stable products, and sheets may be butted against one another when they are laid. They are also rigid enough that they will bridge most defects in the subfloor. Joints should be staggered in the same manner as with hardboard.

*Annular grooved* or *spiral* nails or *divergent* staples are used as fasteners for all these underlayment materials, with spacing not over 6 in. (150 mm) around the edges of the panels and 8 in. (200 mm) for the rest of the panel. The joints between panels and any defects in the surface should be filled with a non-shrink filler compound that will bond to the underlay. The filler should be sanded prior to application of the flooring.

Following is the procedure for laying resilient tile:

1. Clean the surface thoroughly and check to see that it is smooth and the joints are level. Remove any rough edges with sandpaper or plane.

2. Snap a chalk line down the center of the room in the direction of the long dimension.

3. Lay out another centerline at right angles to the main one, using a framing square to get the chalk line in its proper alignment.

4. Spread adhesive over one-quarter of the total area, carrying it up to, but not over, the chalk lines. Use the type of spreader recommended by the manufacturer of the adhesive.

5. Allow the adhesive to acquire an initial set. It should be slightly tacky but not sticky, and the length of time required to achieve this condition will depend on the type of adhesive.

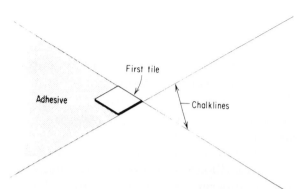

**FIGURE 10-17:**   *First tile laid to center lines.*

6. Lay the first tile at the center of the room, with two edges to the two chalk lines (see Fig. 10-17).

7. Lay a row of tiles to both chalk lines, being careful to keep the butt joints tight and the corners in line. Lay each tile in position—do not slide it into place.

8. Cut the last tile in each row to fit against the wall, with the cut edge to the wall.

9. Complete the installation of the tile over that quadrant of the floor and repeat the procedure for the rest of the floor.

10. Finally roll the floor with a heavy roller to ensure effective bonding of the tiles.

### Sheet Flooring

Resilient sheet flooring is usually installed after most other trades have finished their work. Solid vinyl is the most common type of sheet flooring used; however, rubber flooring is used in many cases. It is produced in rolls from 6 to 12 ft (1.8 to 3.6 m) wide, in various thicknesses and with plain or patterned surfaces.

The following is the procedure for laying sheet flooring:

1. Cut the bottom ends of door casings and jambs shorter to allow room for the flooring to fit underneath. Then clean the surface to be covered to ensure that no particles are left under the flooring. Lay out the sheet and cut the flooring so that it is about 3 in. (75 mm) oversize.

2. Position the entire piece so that the edge curls up each wall. Make sure that patterned pieces line up precisely with the wall and then trim the flooring so it fits the room leaving a ⅛-in. (3-mm) gap at the walls for expansion and contraction.

3. Roll back half of the sheet and apply adhesive to the underlay with a notched trowel and return the flooring

to its original location. Repeat the operation for the other half of the floor.

4. Clean the surface and roll the floor with a heavy roller to remove the air pockets. Start from the middle of the floor and work to the edge.

5. If the floor includes a seam, fasten one of the pieces to the floor leaving the adhesive 10 in. (250 mm) back from the seam. Position the second piece so that it overlaps the seam at least 2 in. (50 mm). If the flooring is patterned, make sure the patterns from both pieces will match. Cement the second piece to the underlay, again leaving the adhesive back from the seam. Overlap the two pieces at the seam and cut through both pieces with a linoleum knife or a sharp utility knife (see Fig. 10-18). Lift up both pieces and apply the adhesive, reset the pieces, and roll the surface of the seam. Clean the seam and use a seam sealer to complete the application.

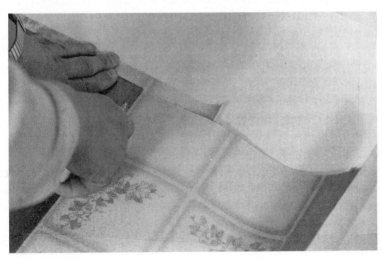

**FIGURE 10-18:**  *Cutting a seam.*

### Ceramic Tile

Ceramic tile is often used as a floor covering for bathrooms, front halls, kitchens, and fireplace hearths. Ceramic tile may be laid over a concrete base or attached with a special adhesive to particle board or plywood underlay. A mortar base adhesive is used when laying ceramic tile on a concrete base. When laying tile over a wood floor, the underlay over the subfloor should be at least ½ in. (13 mm) thick to ensure a good rigid base for the tile. Floors that allow movement will result in the tiles breaking up and coming loose from the floor. The procedure for the installation of the tile is similar to the procedure used on walls; the type of grout, however, is different since it contains sand.

## Carpets

Carpets do not usually require underlayment because normally a rubberized underpad is laid under the carpet as part of the installation. However, the subfloor should be flat and even and cracks and knotholes filled with a reliable crackfiller. Actual carpet installation is normally done by a carpet layer, using specialized equipment for stretching the carpet and holding it in place.

## INSIDE DOOR FRAMES

Interior door frames will include standard hinged doors, either prebuilt at a shop or totally built on the construction site, folding doors, pocket and sliding doors. *Folding doors* are available in either accordion or bifold type in a variety of sizes to meet most situations. *Pocket door* and *sliding door* kits are available to allow for easy installation.

Interior *hinged doors* come in a variety of sizes ranging from 24 to 36 in. (610 to 914 mm) width, 1⅜ and 1¾ in. (35 and 45 mm) in thickness and are usually 80 in. (2032 mm) in height. Prebuilt door frames can be manufactured either with the casing attached to a split door jamb, reducing onsite work, or more commonly without casing, which is installed onsite.

The two most common styles of door jambs used to make inside door frames are indicated in Fig. 10-19. The economical flat jamb, ¾ in. (19 mm) thick cut to a width equal to the thickness of the wall is most often used. A door stop is fastened to the face of the jamb after the door frame is installed in the rough door opening, providing a good fit to the face of the door. Rabbeted jambs are used in better grade finishing and they have one edge ploughed out ½ in. (13 mm) deep by 1⅜ or 1¾ in. (35 or 45 mm) wide, depending on the thickness of the door used.

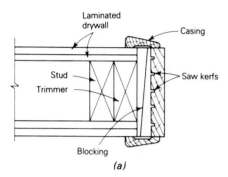

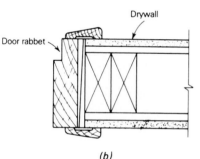

**FIGURE 10-19:** *Inside door frames.*

### Installing Inside Door Frames

Once the door frame has been sanded and assembled and the door hung, it is ready for installation into the rough door opening. Prebuilt door frames are built with a head jamb at either end and the door knob hole in the middle of the door height allowing use with either end up (see Fig. 10-20). The hinges are also set at an equal distance [11 in. (280 mm)] from the top and the bottom of the door to allow this universal use. The jamb at the bottom end is then removed and the frame is ready for installation.

The procedure for the installation of inside door frames is as follows:

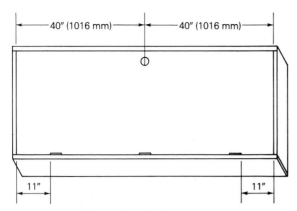

**FIGURE 10-20:**  *Prebuilt door frame.*

1. Check to ensure the rough opening is the correct size for the door frame. An opening width equal to the door frame width plus a clearance of $\frac{1}{2}$ to $\frac{3}{4}$ in. (13 to 19 mm) allows for proper plumbing of the frame. The rough opening height should have a $\frac{3}{8}$ in. (9.5 mm) space above the head jamb, and at least a $\frac{3}{4}$ in. (19 mm) space under the door plus allowance for the thickness of the carpet, undermat, and underlay if applicable—$1\frac{1}{2}$ to $1\frac{3}{4}$ in. (38 to 44 mm), as illustrated in Fig. 10–21. This space under the door will ensure better circulation throughout the building.

**FIGURE 10-21:**  *Rough opening height.*

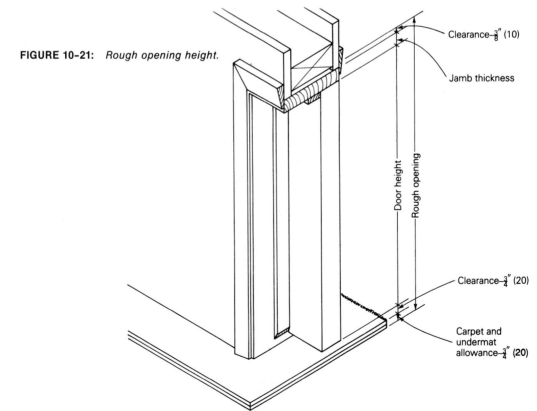

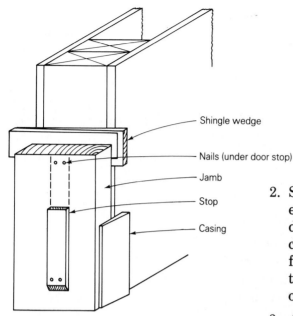

Shingle wedge

Nails (under door stop)

Jamb

Stop

Casing

**FIGURE 10-22:** *Wedging and securing door frame.*

2. Set the frame in the opening and wedge it into position ensuring the door is approximately centered. Plumb the door frame both ways, especially the hinged jamb. Secure the wedges by nailing or stapling through the frame into the trimmer, as shown in Fig. 10-22. Hide the nails or staples behind the door stop in a flat jamb or in the corner of the rabbet.

3. Adjust the wedges until the jambs are straight, using the edge of the door as a straight edge. A space of ⅛ in. (3mm) between the jamb and the door should eliminate binding.

4. Wood screws are used to hold the frames for heavier doors in place. The support is especially important on the hinge side of the frame. The screws are concealed by placing them behind the door stop or by replacing standard length screws in the hinges with ones long enough to fasten the frame firmly to the trimmer. Screws that are visible can be recessed and covered with wooden plugs, and sanded down flush with the jamb surface.

Door frames that are site built will involve additional work prior to the installation of the frame into the opening. Jambs will require dadoing for head jamb, and the hinge gains are cut into the door and the jamb so that the door can be set into the frame prior to installation in the opening. The lock side of the door should have a 5° bevel toward the closing side (see Fig. 10-23). Doors that are not predrilled will require drilling for installation of latch bolt and knob assembly.

**FIGURE 10-23:** *Door edge bevel.*

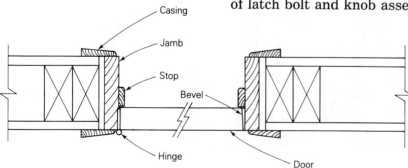

Casing

Jamb

Stop

Bevel

Hinge

Door

A hinge jig can be used with an electric router to cut gains, or a hammer and chisel can be used if a jig is not available. Care should be taken to ensure the gain is not cut too deeply or hinge bind will occur. The proper depth of the gain should be equal to the thickness of the hinges used (see Fig.10–24) and the edge should be set ¼ in. (6mm) back from the face of the door.

The hinges must be set to allow an ⅛-in. (3-mm) space between the door and the top and side jambs of the frame. Hinges are placed 7 in. (175 mm) from the top and 11 in. (275 mm) from the bottom, but these distances may vary slightly—especially in panel doors. Two 3-in. (76-mm) hinges are used on smaller lightweight doors; larger and heavier doors require additional and larger hinges. Some large doors will require as many as four 5- to 6-in. (127- to 152-mm) hinges. Additional hinges have an advantage in that they resist warpage and hold doors straighter. During the operation it is necessary to support the door firmly on edge, and this may be done with the aid of a woodworker's vise clamped to a sawhorse or a jig, as illustrated in Figs. 10–25 and 10–26.

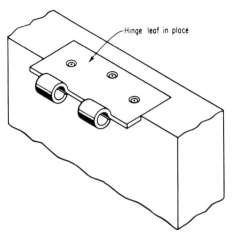

**FIGURE 10-24:** *Proper depth of gain.*

**FIGURE 10-25:** *Sawhorse vise.*

**FIGURE 10-26:** *Door jig.*

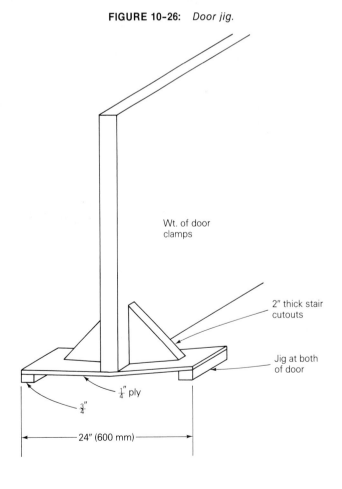

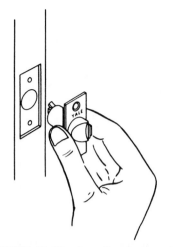

**FIGURE 10-27:**   *Installing latch unit.*

## Installing a Lockset

When the door is hanging properly, it is ready for the lockset. Two types are in common use: *cylinder locks* and *mortise locks*. The first is mounted through the face of the door and the latter through the edge.

### Installing a Cylinder Lock

1. The lockset is mounted in the predrilled holes in the face and the edge of the door.
2. The latch bolt is placed first, fastened with screws through the latch bolt strike and set into a gain in the edge of the door (see Fig. 10–27) or the friction fit type is driven in.
3. The exterior knob is installed into the hole in the face of the door (see Fig. 10–28).
4. Next, install the interior knob as described in Fig. 10–29.
5. Find the location of the strike plate and install it into a gain in the jamb (see Fig. 10–30). Use the template supplied with the lockset to locate and mark the location of the holes for doors that are not predrilled. The standard knob height is 36 in. (914 mm) from the floor, and locks should be installed accordingly.

Place exterior rosette with spindle into latch as shown below. Depress latch, position spindle and rosette stems correctly. Pass spindle and stems through holes in latch.

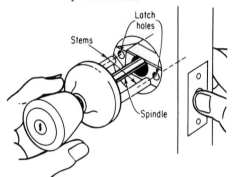

**FIGURE 10-28:**   *Installing exterior knob.*

After exterior knob and rosette is placed, install interior knob and rosette as shown below and push rosettes tight against door. Line up screw holes with stems, insert screws and tighten until lockset is firm.

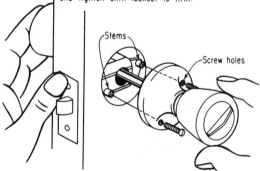

**FIGURE 10-29:**   *Installing interior knob.*

**FIGURE 10-30:**   *Installing a strike plate.*

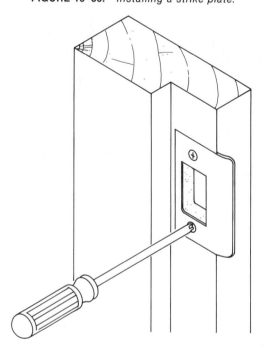

## Installing a Mortise Lock

1. Measure up 36 in. (900 mm) from the floor and mark that height on the face and edge of the door (see Fig. 10-31).

2. Measure the thickness and height of the *lock case* and lay out a mortise on the edge of the door with dimensions slightly larger than the height and thickness. Make sure that the layout is centered on the edge of the door and is located so that the center of the knob will fall on the *height-above-floor* line.

3. Select a wood bit with the same diameter as the thickness of the mortise layout and, from the centerline, drill a series of holes into the edge of the door ¼ in. (6 mm) deeper than the width of the lockcase (see Fig. 10-32).

4. With a sharp chisel, remove the remaining wood around the holes to form a rectangular mortise. Check to see that the lock will fit in the space.

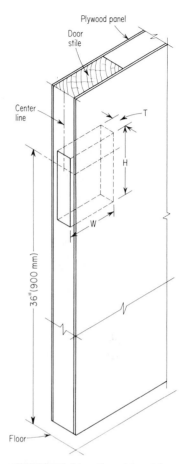

**FIGURE 10-31:** *Door layout for mortice lock.*

**FIGURE 10-32:** *Holes drilled for lock mortice.*

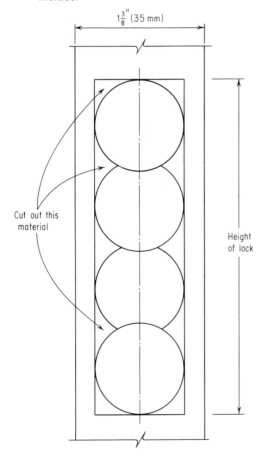

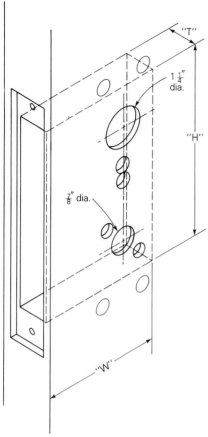

**FIGURE 10-33:** *Lock mortice complete.*

5. Slip the lock into the mortise, and with a marking knife, lay out the outline of the lock-mounting plate on the door edge. Cut a gain for the plate as shown in Fig. 10-33.

6. Measure the distance from the face of the mounting plate to the center of the knob shank hole and the keyhole. Lay out these points on the face of the door and drill holes of the size required.

7. Fit the lock into the mortise, drill pilot holes from the lock-mounting screws, and fasten the lock in place.

8. Install knob shank and knobs according to instructions included with the lockset.

9. Mark the location of the center of the latch bolt pocket on the jamb and fit the strike plate accordingly. A gain must be cut into which the strike plate fits and pockets for the latch bolt and dead bolt drilled and squared out (see Fig. 10-34). The strike plate must be positioned laterally so that the latch bolt will just engage when the door is closed and hold the door snugly in the closed position.

**FIGURE 10-34:** *Strike plate in place.*

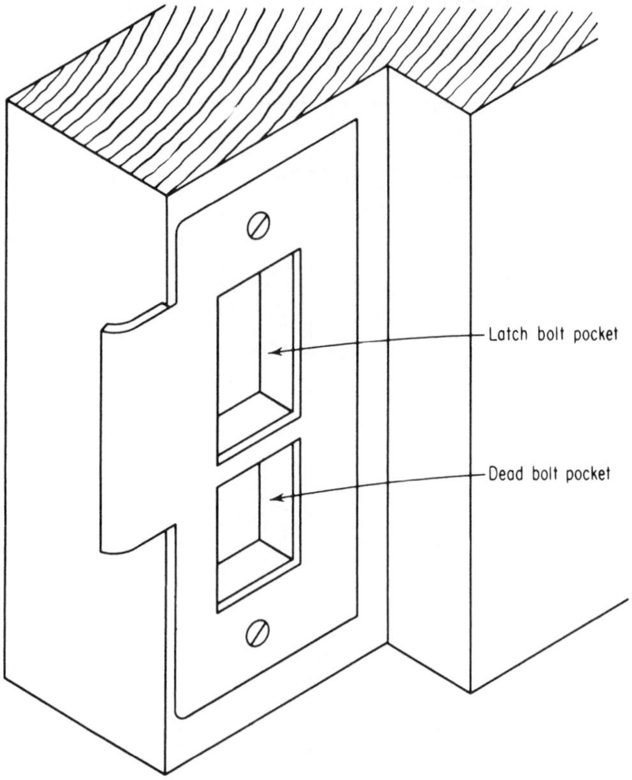

Latch bolt pocket

Dead bolt pocket

## The Hand of Doors

The term to describe the direction in which a door is to swing and the side from which it is to be hung is the *hand* of the door. The hand is determined from the outside.

The outside is the street side for entrance doors; it is the corridor side for doors leading from corridors to rooms; it is the room side for doors from rooms to closets; and it is the stop side—the side from which the butts cannot be seen—for doors between rooms.

Stand outside the door. If the hinges are on your right, it is a right-hand door, and if they are on your left, a left-hand door. If the door swings away from you, it is a regular, and if toward you, a reverse (see Fig. 10–35).

**FIGURE 10-35:** *Left-hand reverse door.*

## Sliding and Folding Doors

In addition to conventional hinged doors, a number of other types are commonly used in modern construction. They include *pocket-type sliding* doors, *bypass sliding* doors, and *folding* doors.

**Pocket-type sliding door.** This type of door is considered to be a space saver, since it opens by sliding into an opening in the partition. During the framing stage an opening is framed twice the door width with allowance for jamb plus clearance—1½ in. (38 mm). The height of the opening will be equal to the door height plus room for the track at the top—2 in. (50 mm) and finish floor plus underlay and clearance at the bottom—1½ in. (38 mm). The size of the opening can vary depending on the type of hardware used (see Fig. 6–30).

The door frame consists of one solid and one split side jamb and a split head jamb. The track is an extruded aluminum product, and the rollers are usually nylon for longer wear and silent operation (see Fig. 10–36).

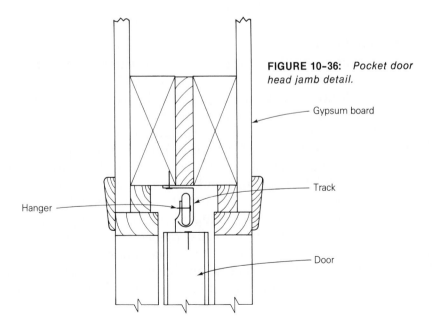

**FIGURE 10-36:** *Pocket door head jamb detail.*

Gypsum board

Track

Hanger

Door

**Bypass-type sliding doors.** Two doors sliding past one another in an opening are used in this case, so that only half the width of the opening can be utilized at a time. A standard type of door frame may be used, with a head jamb long enough to accommodate two doors. The track may be mounted on the underside of the head jamb (see Fig. 10–37), or a split head jamb may be used to recess the track to permit the door to ride flush with the underside of the jamb (see Fig. 10–38).

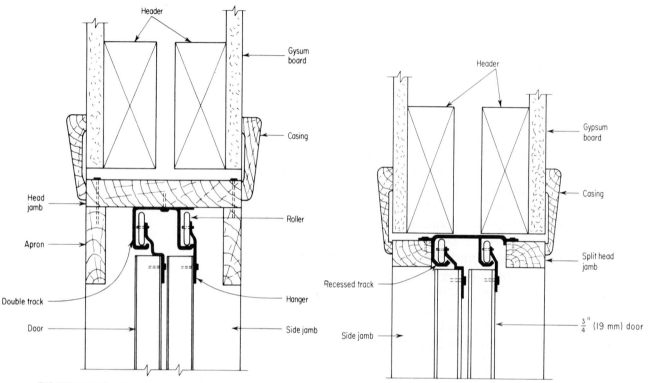

**FIGURE 10–37:** *Track mounted on underside of jamb.*

**FIGURE 10–38:** *Recessed track for sliding doors.*

**FIGURE 10–39:** *Folding door pivot bracket.*

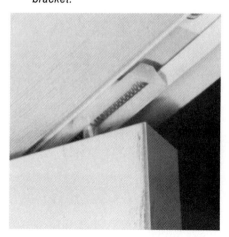

**Folding doors.** A folding door unit (*bifold doors*) consists of one or a pair of doors hinged together at the center and pivoted top and bottom at the outer edges. The pivots fit into *pivot brackets*, which are adjustable to provide the proper clearance between the edge of the door and the finish opening. The pivot is also adjustable to raise or lower the door to set clearance at the top. The doors are manufactured to provide the required clearance, such as a 48-in. (1220-mm) wide door will fit into a 48-in. (1220-mm) finished opening, and the doors will fit in a standard finished opening height of 80 in. (2032 mm). The folding action is provided by the hinges joining pairs of doors together and is guided by a horizontal nylon roller pinned to the traveling edge of the door and enclosed in an overhead track (see Fig. 10–39).

Accordion-type folding doors consisting of metal, vinyl, or wooden slats joined with vinyl hinges finished to simulate various wood or fabric finishes are also used and are available in a variety of door widths.

## INTERIOR TRIM

Most windows and exterior doors used in construction come to the job as a complete unit—frames with outside casing attached and sash, glass or doors already installed. All that is normally required is that the frames be *trimmed* on the inside. Interior finish between walls and floors, and the joints between walls and ceilings are placed as required.

### Window Trim

Windows are usually cased on all four sides with natural wood or prefinished moldings made of wood or plastic. *Casing* is the edging trim used around window and door openings. Many standard patterns in various widths and thicknesses are obtainable. When casing is used, apply the bottom casing first, mitered on both ends, then proceed with the side casings and the top. The casing should be set back from the inside edge of the frame a distance of ⅛ in. (3 mm), and all mitered connections should be glued because a glued joint is less likely to open when slight shrinkage occurs. Wood casings are stapled or nailed to both the framing studs and the jambs with staples or finishing nails. Fasteners should be spaced about 16 in. (400 mm) apart and should be countersunk and filled. A good job of fastening plastic moldings is not possible unless they are glued. Some windows are trimmed without the use of casing. This is commonly done by using a paper-backed metal angle set into the saw kerf in the jamb (see Fig. 10-40) when a drywall finish is applied.

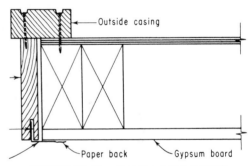

**FIGURE 10-40:** *Opening trimmed with metal angle.*

### Door Trim

Casings are applied to both sides of interior doors to cover the space between the frame and the wall, to secure the frames to the wall, and to hold the jambs in a rigid position. They must therefore be nailed, stapled, or glued to both the jambs and the wall frame. The procedure is as follows:

1. Set the side casings in place, with its inner edge set ⅛ in. (3 mm) back from the inside edge of the jamb. Raise the casing up enough to allow the finish floor to fit under the end of the casing [⅛ in. (3 mm)]. Mark the top and then cut to the desired length using a miter saw.

**FIGURE 10-41:** *Trim blocks.*

2. Nail, staple, or glue the side casings into the proper location.

3. Fit the head piece into place, using a small block plane to ensure a tight fit. Glue the corner miter joint prior to fastening the casing into place. Wood trim blocks are sometimes used at the corners to provide an alternate finish (see Fig. 10-41).

4. Sand the exterior corners where side and head casings meet, and set and fill fastener holes.

### Base Trim

When the vinyl and wood floors have been laid and the doors trimmed, the base trim can be installed. To get a coping line, cut the base at a 45° interior corner mitre and then cut the base along the corner of the cut as shown in Fig. 10-42. The base is raised ½ in. (13 mm) above the floor in areas where carpet is to be placed. This allows the edge of the carpet to be pushed under the base and makes it much easier to remove the carpet when it must be replaced.

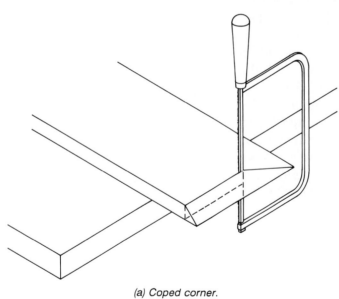

(a) Coped corner.

(b) Coped corner.

**FIGURE 10-42**

## CABINETWORK

Kitchen and bathroom cabinets, desks, shelving, mantels, and other millwork items are installed at the same time as the interior trim (see Fig. 10-43). Such items may be *custom-built* in a cabinet shop for specific installation, *mass-produced* in components in a millwork factory, or *built on the job.*

FIGURE 10-43: *Kitchen cabinets.*

## Installing Mill or Factory-Built Cabinets

Most kitchen cabinets are built in a mill cabinet shop or in kitchen-cabinet manufacturing plants, and then installed by a skilled tradesperson following plans supplied by an architect or a kitchen planning specialist. Most cupboards are built in modules varying from 12 to 36 in. (300 to 900 mm) in a variety of units. Base units vary from door to drawer units or a combination of both. Corner units are available with rotating lazy susans, providing a good solution to the corner problem. Upper wall cabinets come in standard, overappliance, and corner units. When modular cupboard units are installed, there are several basic procedures to be followed:

1. The base for all of the lower units is built first 3½ to 4 in. (89 to 100 mm) high, usually out of ¾-in. (19-mm) material (see Fig. 10–44). Make sure the base is level so as to eliminate future problems.

FIGURE 10-44: *Base for cupboards.*

2. To install base cabinets, first place the cabinets in their approximate locations as close as possible to the wall on the leveled base.

3. Start with the corner units fitting the units properly in place, finishing with the filler piece that fits against the wall or against the other corner unit in "U" shaped cupboards (see Fig. 10–45).

**FIGURE 10–45:** *Installing base cabinets. (Courtesy Merit Kitchens Ltd.)*

**FIGURE 10–46:** *Installing countertop. (Courtesy Merit Kitchens Ltd.)*

4. Once the base cabinets are properly fitted, they are bolted together and fastened to the wall with screws through the nailing strips into the studs. Shims are placed between the cupboard and the stud wherever spaces occur.

5. Some cupboards come with countertops already covered with plastic laminate, but this is not usually part of the cabinetry. The usual procedure is to fit a ¾-in. (19-mm) particle board or plywood top on the base cabinets (see Fig. 10–46).

6. Prior to starting the installation of upper cabinets, first build supports on which cabinets can rest while being installed (see Fig. 10–47).

7. Place the cabinets in position, starting with the corner ones and fitting the units in place. Check to ensure that units are level and plumb. If the wall is uneven or out of plumb, put wood shims behind the cabinets and then fasten the units together and to the wall studs.

8. Finally finish the upper units with a filler piece cut and fitted against the other wall or other corner unit (see Fig. 10–48).

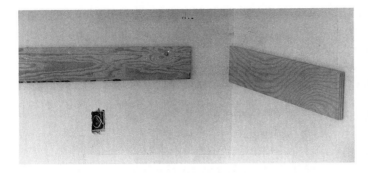

FIGURE 10-47: *Supporting upper cabinets. (Courtesy Merit Kitchens Ltd.)*

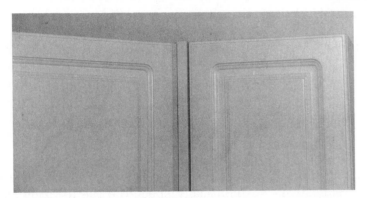

FIGURE 10-48: *Filler piece.*

Plastic laminate can be cut in many ways, either with a table saw or a handsaw. A small scoring tool, as illustrated in Fig. 10-49, is very useful since the surface need only be scored and then it is snapped upward with the face up. This method is especially good for irregular cuts, but the scoring must be deeper to ensure proper breakage. Special support of the laminate is not necessary since scoring works very effectively on a flat surface like the floor.

FIGURE 10-49: *Cutting plastic laminate.*

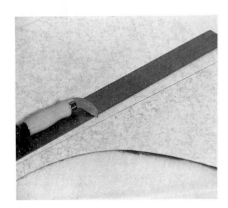

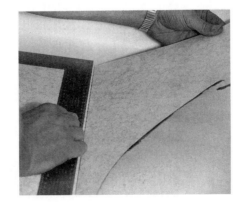

**FIGURE 10-50:** *Laminate trimmer.*

Contact should be ensured by using a rubber roller on the surface or tapping a wood block on the surface with a hammer. The overhang can be removed with a laminate trimmer, or a router with a special cutter can be used (see Fig. 10–50). A flat file can also be used to trim the edge, always filing with a downward stroke at an angle to avoid damaging the edge. Bevel edge wood or plastic laminate moldings are sometimes used on the edge of the top to provide a more decorative finish to the countertop edge.

The vertical wall surface between the base and upper cupboards can be finished in a variety of ways. The surface can be covered with the same plastic laminate as is used on the countertop, cementing the laminate directly to the wallboard. Care must be taken to ensure a tight joint at the connection with the countertop; a small bead of silicone is an effective way of sealing this joint. Ceramic tile is often used on this surface and is set in the following way:

1. Lay out the tile on the surface to be covered, marking vertical and horizontal lines so that the tile may be aligned precisely. If the end tiles should work out to less than a half-tile width, move the vertical or horizontal working lines one way or the other by half the width of the tile. This will eliminate ending up with an unattractive narrow tile.

2. Most ceramic tile has tiny lug spacers along the four edges that automatically space the tile for grout lines. If the tile you use does not have this feature, you should use the small plastic spacers to establish the grout lines (see Fig. 10–51).

3. Spread the tile mastic over the surface with a V-notched adhesive trowel. Usually for standard wall tile the notches are $3/16$ in. deep. Work in small areas at a time, so you don't lose track of your guidelines on the wall.

**FIGURE 10-51:** *Tile spacers.*

4. Starting at the countertop, set the tiles in place, avoiding sliding because that will cause the mastic to come up in the spaces to be grouted. Every few tiles, tap the tiles with a hammer and a block of plywood to ensure tiles are well set. As you work, add spacers (if the tiles are not prespaced as previously mentioned). The partial tiles in corners or at the edge are cut with a tile cutter prior to placement. Clean off any adhesive from the tile surface.

5. Once the mastic has set, the surface is ready for grouting. The grout is spread with a rubber float or grout spreader over the tiles in a diagonal direction, preventing the grout from being drawn out of the joints. Once the joints are full, smooth the joints with a grout smoothing tool. When the grout has hardened, clean the haze from the surface with an adhesive cleaner.

6. Apply a grout sealer to the grout once it is fully set and apply a bead of silicone along the joint with the countertop.

## Sinks

One important item in cabinet building is the installation of a sink, and it is common practice to wait until the plastic laminate top is on before installing it. Kitchen sinks are available in several materials, ranging from stainless and porcelainized steel to cultured marble and to the new popular acrylic sinks.

The first step in the installation is to trace the shape of the sink from the template supplied with most sinks and cut the appropriate hole for the sink. Most sinks sit on top of the countertop; so the hole must be at least $\frac{1}{4}$ in. (6 mm) smaller on all sides than the sink to provide adequate support. A bead of caulking compound should run all around the edge of the hole under the lip of the sink to ensure a watertight fit. The sink is then placed in the opening and secured to the countertop from the underside, as illustrated in Fig. 10-52.

**FIGURE 10-52:** *Sink in place.*

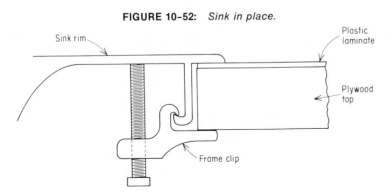

## REVIEW QUESTIONS

**10-1.** (a) Where in a frame wall is an *air barrier* located?

      (b) What are three materials that can be used as an air barrier?

**10-2.** (a) What are three ways to fasten gypsum board to a frame wall?

      (b) Why is drywall applied to the ceiling before the walls?

**10-3.** List four types of insulation used to prevent heat loss.

**10-4.** What material is suitable for a backer board in a shower stall?

**10-5.** What is the difference between an air barrier and a vapor barrier?

**10-6.** What is the main advantage of *parquet flooring?*

**10-7.** Explain what is meant by a *laminated drywall finish.*

**10-8.** Illustrate four methods of treating joints between sheets of plywood used as interior finish.

**10-9.** Explain how the pre-expanding of hardboards is carried out.

**10-10.** (a) List four types of hardwood flooring in common use.

      (b) Why is the bottom surface of hardwood flooring strips concave?

      (c) Why is a $\frac{1}{4}$-in. (6-mm) space left between hardwood flooring and the wall?

      (d) What is meant by "blind" nailing?

**10-11.** What is the basic difference between a mortice lock and a cylindrical lock?

**10-12.** (a) Where is the strike plate located?

      (b) What is the normal height of a door knob from the floor?

      (c) What is a hinge *gain?*

**10-13.** (a) How is the hand of a door determined?

      (b) If a door from the outside swings toward you, with the hinges on the left hand, it is a _____ door.

**10-14.** What size of rough opening is needed for a 30 × 80-in. (762 × 2032-mm) pocket door?

**10-15.** What is meant by *coping* a joint in base trim?

**10-16.** Give the usual dimensions for:

      (a) Height of toe space under kitchen counter section.

      (b) Height of counter section above the floor.

      (c) Distance between upper and lower sections of kitchen cabinets.

# 11

# ENERGY-EFFICIENT HOUSING

Housing in cooler regions has taken a significant change due to the ever-increasing concern with saving energy. The cost of fuel has risen dramatically in the past few years, resulting in additional cost to homeowners to keep dwellings comfortable. Clearly the construction of houses that are as energy-efficient as possible makes good long-term common sense. These houses are likely to be here for many years, and as costs will likely rise in the future, efficient construction is going to be continually more important.

Initially *typical construction* was upgraded by increasing the thickness of the insulation and being more careful with the placement of the vapor barrier. Insulation of the foundation and the outside of the wall frame followed, resulting in more efficient housing. Recently better design and construction technology has brought forth a new breed of highly efficient houses. These houses are described by such terms as "super-energy-efficient" or "super-insulated." Energy-efficient housing does not dwell exclusively on cutting heat losses. Heat gains are augmented where possible through an effort to increase *passive solar gain.*

The increase of methods used to reduce heat loss should not take place without an understanding of the possible problems associated with moisture in buildings. In a typical house the moisture generated escapes to the outside through flues and chimneys and by seeping out through cracks and holes, carrying water vapor with it. Water vapor also escapes by diffusing through building materials. Moisture escaping through cracks and holes and by diffusing through materials does not disappear without a trace. As air and moisture pass through the structure from the heated interior, air is cooled, thus reducing its ability to hold moisture. This cooling may result in condensation within the walls or the attic of the house (see Fig. 11-1). Water condensation in the wall can cause a loss in insulation effectiveness and increase degradation of materials.

**FIGURE 11-1.** *Condensation in walls.*

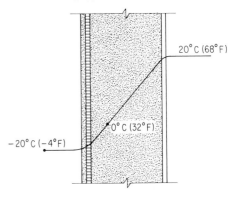

Water condenses and freezes at some point in the wall.

20°C (68°F)

0°C (32°F)

−20°C (−4°F)

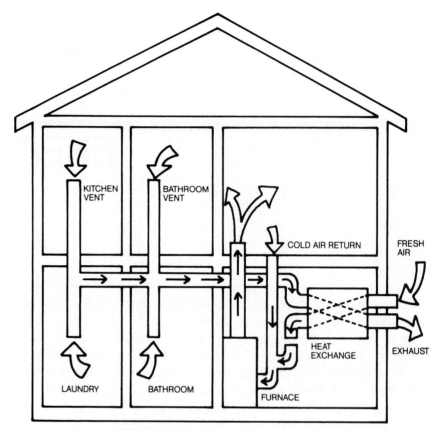

**FIGURE 11-2:**   *Air-to-air heat exchanger.*

In older houses, a vapor barrier was normally installed to prevent moisture damage. Vapor barriers do reduce the moisture loss through materials but do very little to control condensation associated with air leakage. Conventional houses are so leaky that the inside air tends to be dry, and less condensation will take place. Energy-efficient housing is more vulnerable to condensation problems as it does not benefit from this air movement. Careful control is necessary to effectively seal moisture inside the house. The installation of an air barrier will prevent air leakage into the shell.

Since energy-efficient houses are built to be airtight, the indoor air supply must be regulated. A fresh air supply is needed to maintain good-quality air. The provision of controlled ventilation is needed to replace stale air. Stale air is exhausted through one vent, and fresh air is drawn through another vent. Heat loss is minimized by maintaining the minimum acceptable rate and by incorporating a heat exchanger to recover heat from the exhaust air (see Fig. 11–2).

## FOUNDATIONS

Foundations to be considered in this section will include *slabs-on-grade, crawl spaces,* and *basements.* These foundation types can be insulated from the interior of the building or the exterior, each requiring special considerations.

## Slabs-on-Grade

In this type of foundation, the concrete slab can be the combined foundation and finish floor (see Fig. 11–3), or the slab can be isolated from the load-bearing foundation wall (see Fig. 11–4).

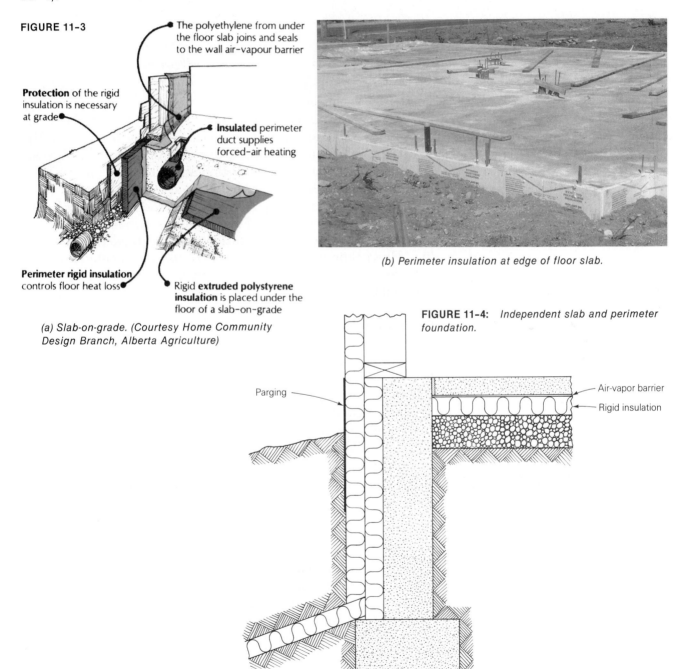

FIGURE 11-3

The polyethylene from under the floor slab joins and seals to the wall air-vapour barrier

**Protection** of the rigid insulation is necessary at grade

**Insulated** perimeter duct supplies forced-air heating

**Perimeter rigid insulation** controls floor heat loss

Rigid **extruded polystyrene insulation** is placed under the floor of a slab-on-grade

(a) Slab-on-grade. (Courtesy Home Community Design Branch, Alberta Agriculture)

(b) Perimeter insulation at edge of floor slab.

FIGURE 11-4: Independent slab and perimeter foundation.

Parging

Air-vapor barrier

Rigid insulation

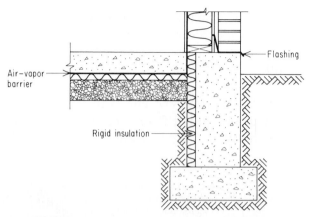

**FIGURE 11-5:**  *Slab-on-grade (interior insulation).*

Rigid polystyrene insulation is used below the slab to lower floor heat loss. Perimeter insulation is also used at the edge of the floor slab to reduce heat loss. Polyethylene is placed under the floor slab and seals to the wall air-vapor barrier (see Fig. 11–3). Protection in the form of parging or preserved plywood should be placed over the insulation around the perimeter. Even foundation walls that are separated from the slab on grade allow for extra load-bearing capacity because the load is carried by the footing under the wall. This system is also less susceptible to frost action since the foundation can be extended to the frost line. Even though slabs-on-grade are usually insulated on the outside of the foundation, insulation is placed on the inside in some cases (see Fig. 11–5).

**Crawl Spaces**

In a crawl space foundation, the main concerns are to provide insulation in the right places and to protect the crawl space from moisture build–up. This space is often used for mechanical services; so insulation is needed to keep the temperature above freezing. If this space is heated, insulation is needed on the exterior walls and under the floor slab. The walls may be insulated on the inside or the outside. A moisture barrier is placed between the floor slab and the underslab insulation. Unheated crawl spaces must be ventilated by openings with a cumulative area of at least 1 ft² for every 500 ft² (0.1 m² for every 50 m²) of floor area with the main insulation provided between the floor joists. R (RSI) values should equal or exceed those indicated in Table 11–1. When batt insulation is used, it should be supported from underneath with particle board or with wire mesh of small enough size to prevent the entry of rodents. All ductwork and plumbing in an unheated space is wrapped with insulation of the same R (RSI) value as used between the floor joists. A moisture barrier, usually covered by a layer of sand, is placed over the ground surface to keep the space dry (see Fig. 11–6).

**TABLE 11-1:** *Appropriate energy—efficient insulation levels*

|                                            | R value | R SI (metric) |
| ------------------------------------------ | ------- | ------------- |
| Ceilings                                   | 40–60   | 7–11          |
| Walls                                      | 20–40   | 3.5–7         |
| Foundation walls (50% or more below grade) | 12–20   | 2–3.5         |
| Floors over crawl spaces                   | 30–40   | 5–7           |
| Slabs-on-grade                             | 10      | 1.8           |
| Basement floors                            | 10      | 1.8           |

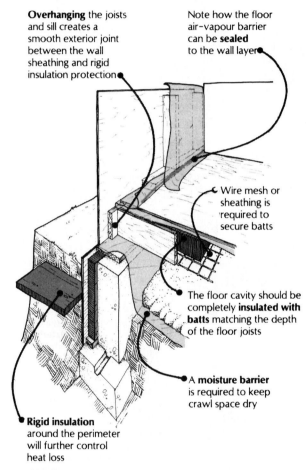

**Overhanging** the joists and sill creates a smooth exterior joint between the wall sheathing and rigid insulation protection

Note how the floor air-vapour barrier can be **sealed** to the wall layer

Wire mesh or sheathing is required to secure batts

The floor cavity should be completely **insulated with batts** matching the depth of the floor joists

A **moisture barrier** is required to keep crawl space dry

**Rigid insulation** around the perimeter will further control heat loss

**FIGURE 11-6:** *Crawl space construction. (Courtesy Alberta Agriculture)*

## Basements

Preserved wood and concrete are the two main types of basements, though concrete block is popular in some areas. Wood foundation walls can be economical and easy to insulate. The spaces between the studs provide an ideal place for friction-fit batt insulation. An air-vapor barrier covers the insulation on the inside. (see Fig. 11-7). The polyethylene from under the floor

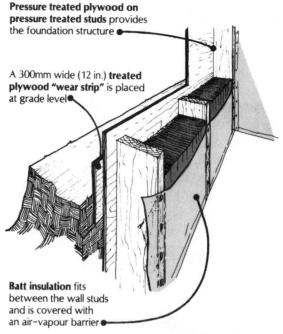

**Pressure treated plywood on pressure treated studs** provides the foundation structure ●

A 300mm wide (12 in.) **treated plywood "wear strip"** is placed at grade level●

**Batt insulation** fits between the wall studs and is covered with an air-vapour barrier ●

**FIGURE 11-7:**  *Insulating a wood foundation. (Courtesy Alberta Agriculture)*

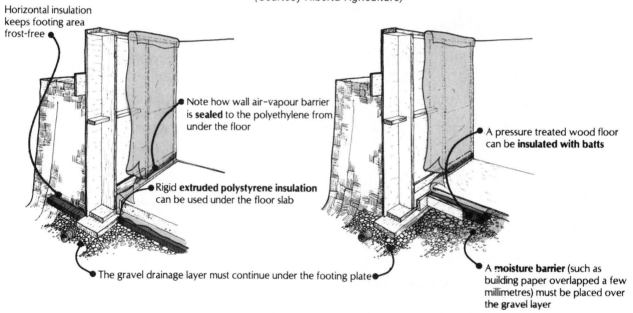

Horizontal insulation keeps footing area frost-free ●

● Note how wall air-vapour barrier is **sealed** to the polyethylene from under the floor

● Rigid **extruded polystyrene insulation** can be used under the floor slab

● **A** pressure treated wood floor can be **insulated with batts**

● The gravel drainage layer must continue under the footing plate●

● **A** **moisture barrier** (such as building paper overlapped a few millimetres) must be placed over the gravel layer

**FIGURE 11-8:**  *Wood foundation floors. (Courtesy Alberta Agriculture)*

is sealed to the wall vapor barrier (see Fig. 11–8).Two types of basement floors used in wood basements are illustrated in Fig. 11–8.

The best place for insulation in a concrete basement is on the outside. The foundation is then less susceptible to frost damage and leaking. The foundation wall is inside the insulation, and so its large thermal mass acts as a vehicle for heat storage. The exterior insulation can be continued up the wall,

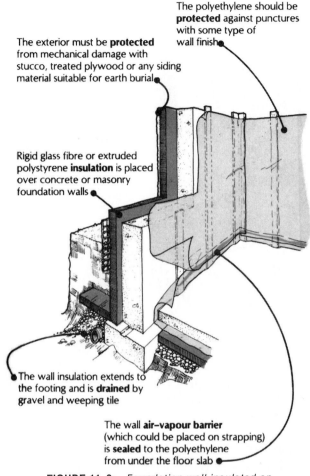

The exterior must be **protected** from mechanical damage with stucco, treated plywood or any siding material suitable for earth burial

The polyethylene should be **protected** against punctures with some type of wall finish

Rigid glass fibre or extruded polystyrene **insulation** is placed over concrete or masonry foundation walls

The wall insulation extends to the footing and is **drained** by gravel and weeping tile

The wall **air–vapour barrier** (which could be placed on strapping) is **sealed** to the polyethylene from under the floor slab

**FIGURE 11-9:** *Foundation wall insulated on outside. (Courtesy Alberta Agriculture)*

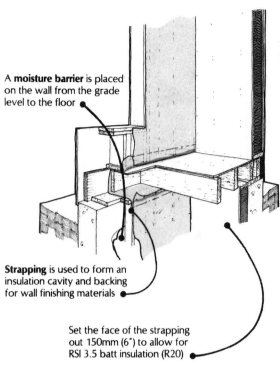

A **moisture barrier** is placed on the wall from the grade level to the floor

**Strapping** is used to form an insulation cavity and backing for wall finishing materials

Set the face of the strapping out 150mm (6˝) to allow for RSI 3.5 batt insulation (R20)

**FIGURE 11-10:** *Foundation wall insulated on inside.*

making an effective blanket. The polyethylene is placed on the inside of the concrete wall and sealed at the bottom to the poly from under the floor and at the top to the polyethylene around the header. Insulation and a vapor barrier are placed under the floor to provide a warm dry floor (see Fig. 11-9).

Most masonry and many concrete walls will continue to be insulated from the inside, as illustrated in Fig. 11-10. A moisture barrier must be placed against the concrete wall from floor level up to the grade (see Fig. 11-10). This will protect the building materials from moisture migration.

## FLOOR FRAME

The floor frame is a major point of heat loss as it is more difficult to insulate and still have a continuous air-vapor barrier at this point (see Fig. 11-11). A strip of polyethylene must be installed around the joist header during framing. The polyethylene must be under the floor frame and over the foundation wall

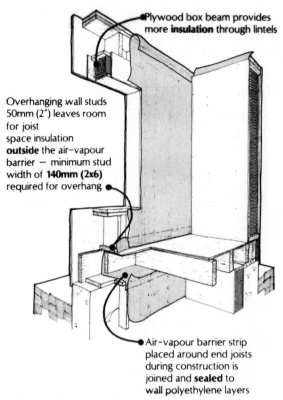

Plywood box beam provides more **insulation** through lintels

Overhanging wall studs 50mm (2˝) leaves room for joist space insulation **outside** the air-vapour barrier — minimum stud width of **140mm (2x6)** required for overhang

Air-vapour barrier strip placed around end joists during construction is joined and **sealed** to wall polyethylene layers

**FIGURE 11-11:**   *Placement of vapor barrier around header. (Courtesy Alberta Agriculture)*

sealed to the basement wall polyethylene. The upper edge will extend under the wall plate and be sealed to the wall vapor barrier. Two layers of insulation are placed outside the header to give it sufficient *"R" value.* To make a better connection, the bottom wall plate should be narrower to allow room for the insulation to cover the outside (see Fig. 11–12).

**FIGURE 11-12**

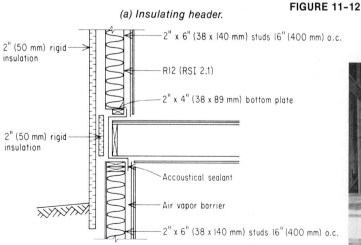

*(a) Insulating header.*

2" (50 mm) rigid insulation

2" (50 mm) rigid insulation

2" x 6" (38 x 140 mm) studs 16" (400 mm) o.c.

RI2 (RSI 2.1)

2" x 4" (38 x 89 mm) bottom plate

Accoustical sealant

Air vapor barrier

2" x 6" (38 x 140 mm) studs 16" (400 mm) o.c.

*(b) Insulated floor frame header.*

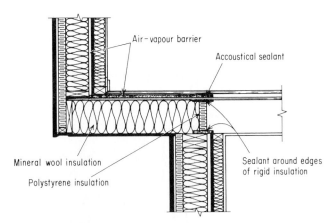

**FIGURE 11-13:** *Cantilevered floor.*

Cantilevered floor projections create a special problem. They do provide for additional floor space but create problems in providing a continuous vapor barrier. Figure 11-13 illustrates a method using polystyrene insulation between the floor joists as a vapor barrier. Even with sealing around these pieces, the floor joists still do pierce the vapor barrier.

*(a) Rigid insulation over plywood sheathing.*

*(b) Single stud wall with exterior application of rigid insulation.*

**FIGURE 11-14**

## WALL FRAME

Traditional wall construction seriously restricts the level of energy efficiency that can be achieved. A number of variations in design have been developed to increase the efficiency of walls. The typical single-stud walls have been increased in thickness to accommodate additional insulation by using larger studs and more effectively by strapping the inside of the studs. This strapping allows a place for the installation of electrical wires without

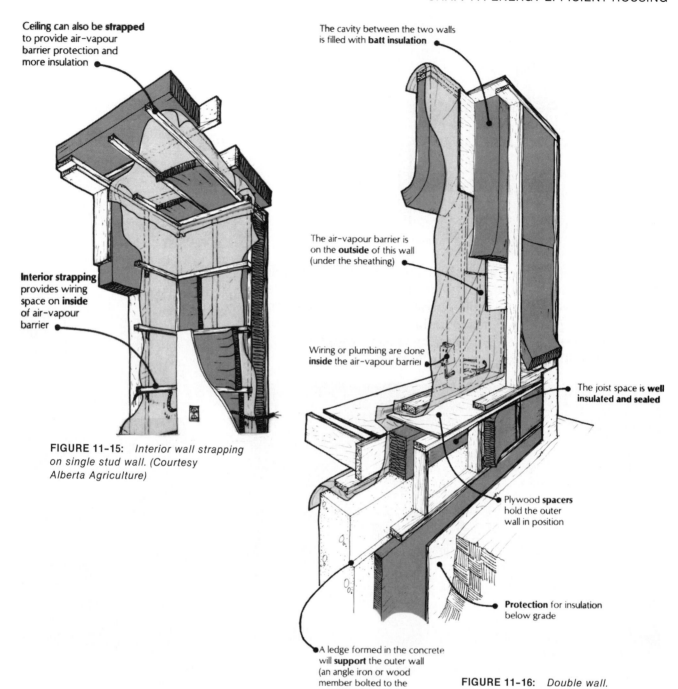

Ceiling can also be **strapped** to provide air-vapour barrier protection and more insulation

**Interior strapping** provides wiring space on **inside** of air-vapour barrier

**FIGURE 11–15:** *Interior wall strapping on single stud wall. (Courtesy Alberta Agriculture)*

The cavity between the two walls is filled with **batt insulation**

The air-vapour barrier is on the **outside** of this wall (under the sheathing)

Wiring or plumbing are done **inside** the air-vapour barrier

The joist space is **well insulated and sealed**

Plywood **spacers** hold the outer wall in position

**Protection** for insulation below grade

A ledge formed in the concrete will **support** the outer wall (an angle iron or wood member bolted to the wall can be used)

**FIGURE 11–16:** *Double wall. (Courtesy Alberta Agriculture)*

interfering with the vapor barrier, as the barrier is placed between the strapping and the studs (see Fig. 11–15). Double-stud walls are very effective in increasing the energy efficiency of walls (see Fig. 11–16).

### Single-Stud Walls

The use of single-stud walls is the most common form of construction. The size of the stud has been commonly increased to a 2 × 6 (38 × 140 mm) to be able to increase "R" values (RSI values) in the cavity (see Fig. 11-11). The walls are often offset over the edge of the floor frame to allow for a layer of insulation on the outside of the joist header. In an effort to provide additional insulation and to cut down on the thermal bridges (studs) in the wall, a rigid insulation is added to the outside of the sheathing (see Fig. 11-14). Probably the most effective way of increasing the efficiency of this wall is to strap the inside of the wall with 2 × 3's (38 × 64 mm) at right angles to the wall studs after the insulation and air-vapor barrier have been applied to the exterior wall (see Fig. 11-15). This provides a convenient space for electrical wires and some plumbing vents so the barrier is not punctured. Two-thirds of the insulation value should be outside the vapor barrier.

## Double-Stud Walls

Double-stud walls include two frame walls with a space between them. These walls can be built to almost any thickness to achieve very high insulative values. The air-vapor barrier can be easily isolated in a protected position in the wall assembly (see Fig. 11-16). The inside wall is the structural wall and includes lintels, double plates, and sheathing. The vapor barrier is placed under the outside sheathing on the outside of this wall. The outside wall is placed out from the structural wall, and it provides support for the exterior finishing material. Plywood spacers [½ in. (12.5 mm) thick] can be used to position the exterior wall (see Fig. 11-16). The vapor barrier flaps at the top and bottom of the structural wall are stapled to the inside of the plates to limit damage and to provide for easy sealing with polyethylene from the floor frame and the attic. This air-vapor barrier is usually 6 mil (150 µm) and is sealed with an acoustical sealant.

## Modular Wall System

Some manufacturers produce modular energy-efficient systems. One available on the market is a system using solid polystyrene panels. Chemically bonded within the panel are wood studs or structural steel tubing (see Fig. 11-17). The panels are lightweight and easy to handle, allowing for speedy assembly. Special lintels are provided over window and door openings (see Fig. 11-17). Figure 11-18 illustrates the use of polystyrene panels in residential construction.

## Air-Vapor Barrier

The air-vapor barrier in an energy-efficient house must be installed in such a way as to provide a nearly completely sealed

FIGURE 11-17: *Polystyrene lintels and panels.*

(a) Panels in place.

(b) Sealing edge of panels.

(c) Completed modular system.

**FIGURE 11-18**

building envelope. It must be sealed with an acoustical sealant to provide a long-lasting seal. An acoustical sealant does not harden or form a skin and is used for sealing polyethylene. The air-vapor barrier controls air leakage and prevents vapor movement. To ensure an effective seal, all joints between polyethylene must be made on a wood backing. The first layer is stapled to the framing member, a continuous bead of sealant is placed, and the second sheet is placed over the first and stapled (see Fig.11-19).

Special consideration is needed to seal the air-vapor barrier

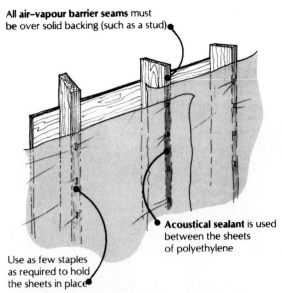

**FIGURE 11-19:** *Joining air-vapor barrier layers.*

at obstructions. To achieve a continuous envelope at partition walls in single-stud walls, a piece of polyethylene is placed behind the end stud and then sealed to the vapor barrier (see Fig. 11-20). At plumbing pipe openings a plywood backing is installed and sealed to the vapor barrier (see Fig. 11-21). Around electrical outlets a *vapor barrier pan* can be used to achieve a seal (see Fig. 11-22). Placing a piece of polyethylene around the box before installation and then sealing to the vapor barrier can be quite effective (see Fig. 11-23).

**FIGURE 11-20:** *Sealing air-vapor barrier at partition.*

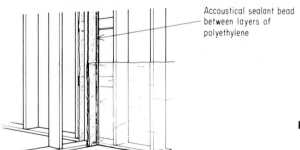

**FIGURE 11-21:** *Sealing plumbing pipe.*

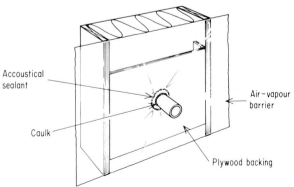

FIGURE 11-22

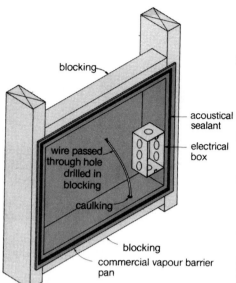

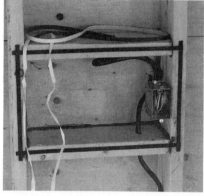

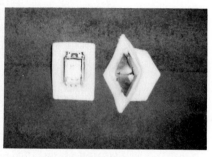

(a) Vapor barrier around electrical box.    (b) Sealing around an electrical box.    (c) Commercial vapor-barrier pan.

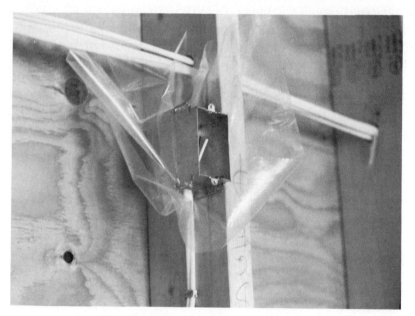

FIGURE 11-23:   Vapor barrier behind box.

Windows and doors also need special consideration. To achieve an energy-efficient building, energy-efficient windows and doors must be used. Casement, awning, and hopper windows are good performers. Metal insulated doors are good as they do not warp easily, and so a good seal is maintained. Figure 11–24 illustrates an effective method of achieving a good vapor barrier seal around openings. Double or triple glazing provides some resistance to heat loss, increasing R (RSI) values from 0.85 to 2.16 (0.15 to 0.38). Increasing the spacing between panes can also have a positive effect. The use of low-emissivity coatings to the glass will reduce radiant heat loss. Thermal shades are added to the outside to cut heat loss (see Fig. 11–25).

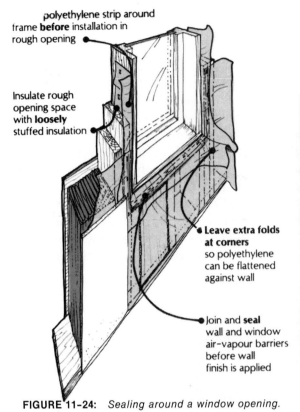

polyethylene strip around frame **before** installation in rough opening

Insulate rough opening space with **loosely** stuffed insulation

• **Leave extra folds at corners** so polyethylene can be flattened against wall

• Join and **seal** wall and window air-vapour barriers before wall finish is applied

**FIGURE 11-24:** *Sealing around a window opening.*

**FIGURE 11-25:** *Window shades.*

## CEILINGS AND ROOFS

Most houses have sloped roofs with interior ceilings either flat or sloped. A complete, well sealed air/vapor barrier is essential but, because of light fixtures, chimneys, plumbing vents, and attic access, is difficult to install. Strapping the ceiling in a manner similar to walls, allowing room for wires, as illustrated in Fig. 11-26, can help. Light fixtures such as pot lights need special boxes built over the fixture so that an effective seal can

**FIGURE 11-26:** *Sealing vapor barrier and strapping ceiling. (Courtesy Alberta Agriculture)*

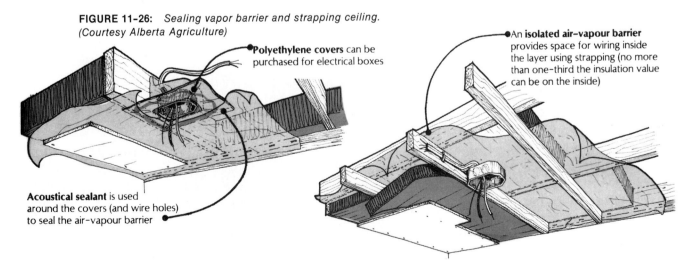

• **Polyethylene covers** can be purchased for electrical boxes

• An **isolated air-vapour barrier** provides space for wiring inside the layer using strapping (no more than one-third the insulation value can be on the inside)

**Acoustical sealant** is used around the covers (and wire holes) to seal the air-vapour barrier

**FIGURE 11-27:** *Sealing around an electrical light.*

be attained (see Fig. 11-27). Polyethylene can be placed above electrical boxes and sealed to the vapor barrier to provide a continuous membrane. Metal firestops around chimneys should be sealed at the ceiling level to impede the passage of sparks (see Fig. 11-28). Vent stacks can be sealed around the opening they pass through at the wall plate line (see Fig. 11-29). Attic access probably provides the greatest loss of heat and vapor leakage. If the access cannot be eliminated from the ceiling, seal and insulate the hatch as illustrated in Figure 11-30. To provide a continuous seal over partitions, a piece of polyethylene is placed between the top plates and then sealed to the ceiling vapor barrier (see Fig. 11-31). Attic ventilation can be maintained by installing insulation stops between the trusses above the plate line (see Fig. 11-32). Ventilation can be provided in a sloped ceiling by using a wide truss with openings for ventilation (see Fig.11-33).

**FIGURE 11-28:** *Firestop around chimney.*

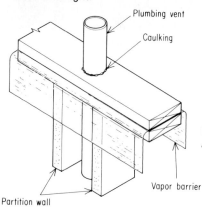

**FIGURE 11-29:** *Sealing around vent stack.*

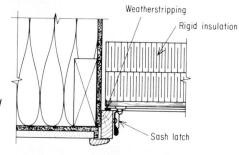

**FIGURE 11-30:** *Sealing and insulating attic access.*

**FIGURE 11-32:** *Insulation stops.*

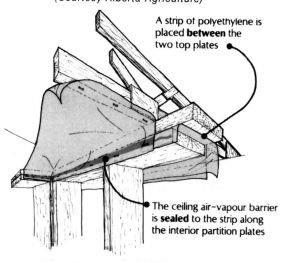

**FIGURE 11-31:** *Seal over partition. (Courtesy Alberta Agriculture)*

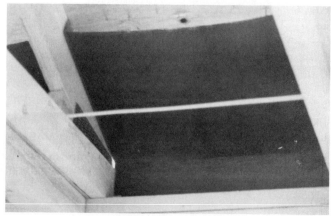

**FIGURE 11-33:** *Sloped truss ceiling.*

## PASSIVE SOLAR GAIN

A building designed for passive solar gain catches heat from the sun, stores it, and then releases it slowly to reduce energy costs. Passive systems are designed as part of the building; as such they have little cost and operate by themselves. Active systems, on the other hand, utilize collectors to collect energy and can be expensive to operate (see Fig. 11-34). Passive systems utilize south-facing windows and patio doors to collect energy. Windows on the north side lose heat in the winter due to cold north winds. Windows on the north side should be as small as possible, and large windows should face south.

On sunny days, rooms with southern exposure may become overheated while other areas are still cold. To maintain a more uniform temperature, the heat gained must be stored and released when the temperature drops. This heat gain can be stored

**FIGURE 11-34:** *Solar collector panels.*

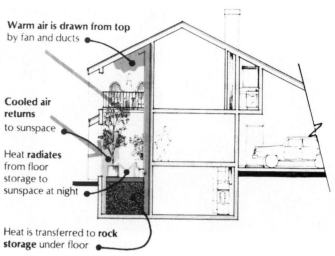

Warm air is drawn from top
by fan and ducts

Cooled air
returns
to sunspace

Heat radiates
from floor
storage to
sunspace at night

Heat is transferred to rock
storage under floor

**FIGURE 11-35:** *Passive heat storage. (Courtesy Alberta Agriculture)*

in a large thermal mass such as concrete or masonry walls and floors or a rock bin or water storage (see Fig. 11–35). Care must be taken that windows do not take up too much wall area, making temperature difficult to manage. Sun spaces can be effective, as they are directly heated and will provide indirect heating (see Fig. 11–36). Ventilation must be provided for these spaces so excess heat can be released in hot seasons.

The overhang of the building should be designed to allow full sun into the house during the cold season and provide shade during the hot season (see Fig.11–37). An adjustable overhang is ideal. A large awning or movable overhang will do this quite effectively. Window shutters or shades can be used to prevent overheating during warmer weather (see Fig.11–25).

**FIGURE 11-36:** *Sun space.*

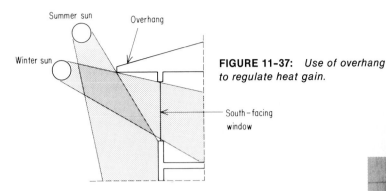

**FIGURE 11-37:** *Use of overhang to regulate heat gain.*

**FIGURE 11-38:** *Infrared scanning equipment.*

## BUILDING EVALUATION

The special demand of cold climates, coupled with the growing requirement for energy efficiency, provides an opportunity to develop building enclosures appropriate to our environment. To do this we must assess the actual performance of existing buildings and develop a greater ability to predict the performance of new buildings.

All objects radiate energy to their surroundings. This infrared energy is a function of the objects' surface temperature and emissivity. The process of utilizing an infrared scanning system to produce a thermal image is called *thermography*. The technique of utilizing infrared scanning procedures on both new and existing buildings is a primary diagnostic tool for determining the thermal performance of a building envelope.

**FIGURE 11-39:** *Thermal image.*

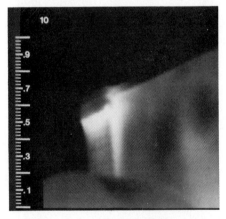

Thermography can identify surface temperature variations of the building that relate to problems in the structure. The surface temperature is also influenced by air flow within or through the building envelope. Surface temperature irregularities can indicate defects in the structure such as insulation defects, thermal bridging, moisture content, or air leakage. Thermography can play an important role in identifying design, construction, and material problems as well as deterioration of components within the envelope. These defects can be detected throughout the structure, including roof, walls, and foundations.

The two primary mechanisms for heat loss in buildings are *conduction* and *air leakage*. Both can be detected from the surface of a building with an infrared scanning device, as illustrated in Fig. 11-38. Figure 11-39 illustrates an example of a picture of the scan showing the differences in temperature that are evident. Bright white color on the scan indicates higher temperature and level of heat loss. The flaring effect of the image usually indicates an area of air leakage.

**FIGURE 11-40:** *Fan depressurizing door.*

Another method to determine air leakage is to have an air leakage test performed on the house to determine the integrity of the air barrier. The fan depressurization door illustrated in Fig. 11-40 can be used to determine the air leakage rate of houses. The target for some energy-efficient houses is 1.5 air changes per hour at a pressure difference of 0.00725 PSI (50 Pascals). This means that at a pressure of 0.00725 PSI (50 Pascals), a volume of air equivalent to 1.5 times the house volume will be drawn into the house every hour through leaks in the building envelope.

## REVIEW QUESTIONS

11-1. Why is it difficult to achieve an effective air-vapor barrier in typical single-stud wall construction?

11-2. Explain how an air-to-air heat exchanger works.

11-3. What should be done with spaces in walls and ceilings that are too small to insulate or to eliminate condensation associated with air leakage?

11-4. What problems can occur with buildings that are sealed so tight that air exchanges are minimal?

11-5. Why is it better to insulate concrete foundations on the outside as opposed to the inside?

11-6. What properties do acoustical sealants have that make them suitable for sealing air-vapor barriers?

11-7. How can the thermal bridges in a single-stud wall be eliminated?

11-8. What percentage of the insulation thickness must be outside the air-vapor barrier to achieve an effective barrier against moisture condensation?

11-9. Explain the principle of passive solar systems.

11-10. What building defects can an infrared scanning device detect?

11-11. What are the two primary mechanisms for heat loss in buildings?

# INDEX